Practical Lakehouse Architecture
Designing and Implementing Modern
Data Platforms at Scale

Gaurav Ashok Thalpati

Beijing · Boston · Farnham · Sebastopol · Tokyo

Practical Lakehouse Architecture

by Gaurav Ashok Thalpati

Published by O'Reilly Media, Inc., 1005 Gravenstein Highway North, Sebastopol, CA 95472.

O'Reilly books may be purchased for educational, business, or sales promotional use. Online editions are also available for most titles (*http://oreilly.com*). For more information, contact our corporate/institutional sales department: 800-998-9938 or *corporate@oreilly.com*.

Acquisitions Editor: Andy Kwan	**Indexer:** Ellen Troutman-Zaig
Development Editor: Jeff Bleiel	**Interior Designer:** David Futato
Production Editor: Christopher Faucher	**Cover Designer:** Karen Montgomery
Copyeditor: Nicole Taché	**Illustrator:** Kate Dullea
Proofreader: Tove Innis	

August 2024:   First Edition

Revision History for the First Edition

2024-07-24:   First Release

See *http://oreilly.com/catalog/errata.csp?isbn=9781098153014* for release details.

978-1-098-15301-4

[LSI]

Table of Contents

Preface

It's 2024—the year of AI!

Just like 2023 and 2022, and a few years before that.

In today's world, AI is everywhere. But AI needs data. Data that is of good quality. Data that is discoverable. Data that humans and machines can easily consume.

But how do we ensure that we make such data available?

By implementing robust data platforms that ingest, store, and maintain this data to democratize it with all its users.

Today's best-in-class, data-driven organizations leverage AI and heavily depend on data. They have invested in modern data platforms that support their current and future demands. Modern data platforms need modern data architectures, like lakehouses, to support their BI to AI needs.

Lakehouse architecture—the main topic of this book—leverages technology advancements to simplify data platform design and enables organizations to build scalable and open platforms. Lakehouse has gained popularity in the last few years, with several organizations, product vendors, and data practitioners implementing their platforms using this architecture. There won't be a better time to explore, understand, and evaluate the lakehouse for your use cases, and this book can help you get started on your journey.

Who Should Read This Book?

This book is for all data practitioners who handle large volumes of data and are responsible for designing and implementing modern data platforms.

This book is a comprehensive guide for data architects and can help them understand key considerations, establish design principles, and make critical decisions when implementing a data platform. For data engineers, this book will help them understand key concepts like open table formats, schema evolution, and time travel, which they can leverage when implementing data pipelines. Other data personas, like data analysts and data scientists, will learn about crucial topics like lakehouse data management, data discovery, access control, and sensitive data handling.

Data practitioners new to lakehouse architecture can read this book to learn the core concepts. Experienced data architects and senior data engineers can use this guide to make key design decisions during the design phase. And data leaders can refer to this book when planning their lakehouse initiatives.

Why I Wrote This Book

When I started working on a lakehouse project a few years back, the open table formats were still evolving, and not all cloud services supported lakehouse technologies like open table formats. Not many data practitioners knew the benefits of lakehouse architecture, either, or understood how it could help simplify their data landscape. There was not much material available for end-to-end guidance to design and implement a lakehouse using different technologies across cloud platforms. That's when I started blogging about these topics to share what I had learned and explored. When I got the opportunity to write this book on the same subject, I thought it was the right time to share my knowledge and observations with a larger audience.

This book is my attempt to explain in simple words how to design and implement a lakehouse. I've provided several examples across AWS, Azure, GCP, Databricks, Snowflake, and other platforms to explain various data management and governance processes. I hope you will find this book helpful for implementing your data platforms.

Navigating This Book

This book has nine chapters, each covering a different aspect of designing and implementing a lakehouse data platform.

Chapter 1 introduces you to lakehouse architecture and the key concepts, features, and benefits of implementing a data platform using lakehouse architecture. This chapter will also help you understand the fundamental concepts for building data platforms.

Chapter 2 discusses traditional architectures like data warehouses and data lakes and covers how lakehouse architecture stands out compared to these patterns. If you are new to data warehouses or data lakes, this chapter will be a good primer for understanding these architectures.

Chapter 3 explores the storage layer—the heart of the lakehouse. This chapter explains open table formats like Apache Iceberg, Apache Hudi, and Delta Lake. It also describes the key considerations for evaluating different file and table formats in order to select the right one for your use case.

Chapter 4 focuses on data catalogs and will help you understand the overall metadata management process within a lakehouse. It provides an overview of data catalog services across AWS, Azure, and GCP platforms, along with some popular third-party products.

Chapter 5 explores the different compute engine options for data engineering and consumption activities. It describes factors that will impact your decision making process when selecting the right compute engine.

Chapter 6 discusses the governance and security aspects of data and AI assets within a lakehouse. It also lists the activities you should perform, based on your role, to maintain the governance and security of data within the lakehouse.

Chapter 7 gives the big picture view of designing your lakehouse by combining storage, compute, and data catalogs. This chapter is critical for data architects who have to make choices during the design process. At the end of this chapter, you will find a questionnaire you can refer to during talks with different stakeholders.

While all the previous chapters discuss an ideal lakehouse implementation, Chapter 8 provides a reality check by highlighting the challenges you can face while implementing a lakehouse. This chapter gives you ideal versus real-world scenarios and explains how to tackle these to build a lakehouse in the real world.

The final chapter, Chapter 9, explores the future of lakehouses. It introduces some of the new file and table formats, innovative products, and new approaches to implementing a lakehouse platform.

O'Reilly Online Learning

 For more than 40 years, *O'Reilly Media* has provided technology and business training, knowledge, and insight to help companies succeed.

Our unique network of experts and innovators share their knowledge and expertise through books, articles, and our online learning platform. O'Reilly's online learning platform gives you on-demand access to live training courses, in-depth learning paths, interactive coding environments, and a vast collection of text and video from O'Reilly and 200+ other publishers. For more information, visit *https://oreilly.com*.

Conventions Used in This Book

The following typographical conventions are used in this book:

Italic
> Indicates new terms, URLs, email addresses, filenames, and file extensions.

`Constant width`
> Used for program listings, as well as within paragraphs to refer to program elements such as variable or function names, databases, data types, environment variables, statements, and keywords.

> This element signifies a tip or suggestion.

> This element signifies a general note.

> This element indicates a warning or caution.

How to Contact Us

Please address comments and questions concerning this book to the publisher:

> O'Reilly Media, Inc.
> 1005 Gravenstein Highway North
> Sebastopol, CA 95472
> 800-889-8969 (in the United States or Canada)
> 707-827-7019 (international or local)
> 707-829-0104 (fax)
> *support@oreilly.com*
> *https://oreilly.com/about/contact.html*

We have a web page for this book, where we list errata, examples, and any additional information. You can access this page at *https://oreil.ly/lakehouse-architecture*.

For news and information about our books and courses, visit *https://oreilly.com*.

Find us on LinkedIn: *https://linkedin.com/company/oreilly-media*

Watch us on YouTube: *https://youtube.com/oreillymedia*

Acknowledgments

I accidentally started my data journey a couple of decades ago. While interested in becoming an animator, I landed a job as a trainee ETL developer. These past 20 years have been about learning, understanding, and exploring data in various forms. Many people have helped, supported, and encouraged me during this journey and this book is the result of their efforts.

I'm deeply grateful to all my colleagues, mentors, and customers for providing me with opportunities to work on some of the most exciting data and analytics projects. A big shout-out to the various data communities, user groups, content creators, and book authors around the globe for sharing their knowledge. You all have inspired me to write this book.

My heartfelt thanks to Shivam Panicker, Sivakumar Ponnusamy, and Ankush Gautam, the tech reviewers of this book, for their insights and suggestions, which have improved the book and genuinely added more value for readers.

Writing a book on my favorite topic is a dream come true. Thanks to the entire O'Reilly team for this once-in-a-lifetime opportunity. I'd like to thank:

- Andy Kwan, my acquisition editor, for trusting me to write this book and helping me through the initial proposal and approval process.
- Jeff Bleiel, my development editor, for supporting me throughout my book-writing journey. This book would not have been possible without his edits, suggestions, and encouragement.
- Nicole Taché, for copyediting and bringing this book to a better shape and form.
- Christopher Faucher, my production editor, for coordinating and managing the production process and providing the final touches to this book.

Finally, I'd like to thank my family—my parents, Ashok and Archana, and my elder sister Kirti—for their sacrifices to help me reach this stage in my life. Vishakha, my wife, has been my pillar of strength, and Soham, my son, has been my biggest supporter. This book would not have been possible without their continuous encouragement.

Last but not least, a big thanks to you, the reader of this book, for investing your time in reading it.

CHAPTER 1

Introduction to Lakehouse Architecture

All data practitioners, irrespective of their job profiles, perform two common and foundational activities—asking questions and finding answers! Any data person, whether they're a data engineer, data architect, data analyst, data scientist, or even a data leader like a chief information officer (CIO) or chief data officer (CDO), must be curious and ask questions.

Finding answers to complex questions is difficult. But the more challenging task is to ask the *right* questions. The "art of the possible" can only be explored by: (1) asking the right questions and (2) uncovering answers by leveraging the data. However simple this might sound, an organization needs an entire data platform to enable users to perform these tasks. This platform must support data ingestion and storage, provide tools for users to ask and discover new questions, perform advanced analysis, predict and forecast results, and generate insights. The data platform is the infrastructure that enables users to leverage data for business benefits.

To implement such data platforms, you need a robust data architecture—one that can help you define the core components of the data platform and establish the design principles for putting it into practice. Traditionally, organizations have used data warehouse or data lake architectures to implement their data platforms. Both of these architectural approaches have been widely adopted across industries. These architectures have also evolved to leverage continuously improving modern technologies and patterns. *Lakehouse* architecture is one such modern architectural pattern that has developed in the last few years, and it has become a popular choice for data architects who are designing data platforms.

In this chapter, I'll introduce you to the fundamental concepts related to data architecture, data platforms and their core components, and how data architecture helps build a data platform. Then, I'll explain why there is a need for new architectural patterns like the lakehouse. You'll learn lakehouse architecture fundamentals, characteristics, and the benefits of implementing a data platform using lakehouse architecture. I'll conclude the chapter with important takeaways, which will summarize everything we've discussed and help you remember the key points while reading the subsequent chapters in this book.

Let's start with the fundamentals of data architecture.

Understanding Data Architecture

The data platform is the end result of implementing a data architecture using the chosen technology stack. Data architecture is the blueprint that defines the system that you aim to build. It helps you visualize the end state of your target system and how you plan to achieve it. Data architecture defines the core components, the interdependencies between these components, fundamental design principles, and processes required to implement your data platform.

What Is Data Architecture?

To understand data architecture, consider this real-world analogy of a commercial construction site, such as a shopping mall or large residential development.

Building a commercial property requires robust architecture, innovative design, an experienced architect, and an army of construction workers. Architecture plays the most crucial role in development—it ensures that the construction survives all weather conditions, helps people easily access and navigate through various floors, and enables quick evacuation for people in an emergency. Such architectures are based on certain guiding principles that define the core design and layout of the building blocks. Whether you are constructing a residential property, a commercial complex, or a sports arena, the foundational pillars and the core design principles for the architecture remain the same. However, the design patterns—interiors, aesthetics, and other features catering to the users—differ.

Similar to building a commercial property, data architecture plays the most crucial role when developing robust data platforms that will support various users and various data and analytics use cases. To build a platform that is resilient, scalable, and accessible to all users, the data architecture should be based on core guiding principles. Regardless of the industry or domain, the data architecture fundamentals remain the same.

Data architecture, like the design architecture for a construction site, plays a significant role in determining how users adapt to the platform. The section will cover the importance of data architecture in the overall process of implementing a data platform.

How Does Data Architecture Help Build a Data Platform?

Architecting the data platform is probably the most critical phase of a data project and often impacts key outcomes like the platform's user adoption, scalability, compliance, and security. Data architecture helps you define the following foundational activities that you need to do to start building your platform.

Defining core components

The core components of your data platform help perform daily activities like data ingestion, storage, transformation, consumption, and other common services related to management, operations, governance, and security. Data architecture helps you define these core components of your data platform. These core components are discussed in detail in the next section.

Defining component interdependencies and data flow

After defining the core components of your platform, you need to determine how they will interact. Data architecture defines these dependencies and helps you to visualize how the data would flow between producers and consumers. Architecture also helps you determine and address any specific limitations or integration challenges you may face while moving data across these components.

Defining guiding principles

As part of the data architecture design process, you'll also define the guiding principles for implementing your data platform. These principles help build a shared understanding between the various data teams that are using the platform. They ensure everyone follows the same design approach, common standards, and reusable frameworks. Defining shared guiding principles allows you to implement an optimized, efficient, and reliable data platform solution. Guiding principles can be applied across various components and are defined based on the data architecture capabilities and limitations. For example, if your platform has multiple business intelligence (BI) tools provisioned, a guiding principle should specify which BI tool to use based on the data consumption pattern or use case.

Defining the technology stack

The architecture blueprint also informs the tech stack of the core components in the platform. When architecting the platform, it might be challenging to *finalize* all the underlying technologies—a detailed study of limitations and benefits, along with proof of concept (PoC), would be required to finalize them. Data architecture helps to define key considerations for making these technology choices and the desired success factors when carrying out any PoC activities and finalizing the tech stack.

Aligning with overall vision and data strategy

Finally, and most critically, data architecture helps you implement a data platform that is aligned with your overall vision and your organization's data strategy for achieving its business goals. For example, *data governance* is integral to any organization's data strategy. Data architecture defines the components that ensure data governance is at the core of each process. These are components like metadata repositories, data catalogues, access controls, and data sharing principles.

Data governance is an umbrella term that comprises various standards, rules, and policies that ensure all data processes follow the same formal guidelines. These guidelines help to assure compliance with geographic or industry regulations, as well as to ensure the data is trustworthy, high quality, and delivers value. Organizations should follow data governance policies across all data management processes to maintain consumers' trust in data and to remain compliant. Data governance helps organizations maintain better control over their data, to easily discover data, and to securely share data with consumers.

Now that you better understand data architecture and its significance in implementing data platforms, let's discuss the core components of a data platform.

Core Components of a Data Platform

In this section, we'll look at the core components of a data platform and how their features contribute to a robust data ecosystem. Figure 1-1 shows the core components for implementing a data platform based on a data architecture blueprint.

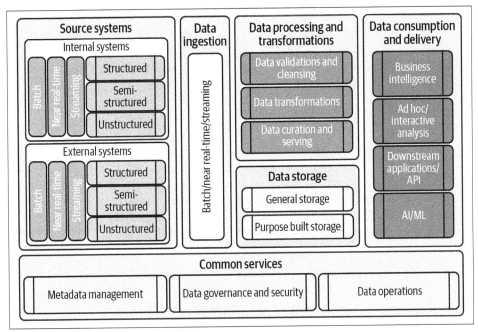

Figure 1-1. Core components of a data platform

Let's explore these core components and their associated processes.

Source systems

Source systems provide data to the data platform that can be used for analytics, business intelligence (BI), and machine learning (ML) use cases. These sources include legacy systems, backend online transaction processing (OLTP) systems, IoT devices, clickstreams, and social media. Sources can be categorized based on multiple factors.

Internal and external source systems.   Internal sources are the internal applications within an organization that produce data. These include in-house customer relationship management (CRM) systems, transactional databases, and machine-generated logs. Internal sources can be owned by internal domain-specific teams that are responsible for generating the data.

Data platforms often need data from external systems to enhance their internal data and gain competitive insights. Examples of data that come from external source systems are exchange rates, weather information, and market research data.

Batch, near real-time, and streaming systems.   Until a couple of decades ago, most source systems could send only batch data, meaning that they would generally send the data at the end of the day as a daily batch process. With the increasing demand for more near real-time insights and analytics, source systems started sending data on a near real-time basis. These systems can now share data as multiple, smaller micro-batches at a fixed interval that can be as low as a few minutes. Sources like IoT devices, social media feeds, and clickstreams send data as a continuous stream that should be ingested and processed in real time to get the maximum value.

Structured, semi-structured, and unstructured data.   Source systems traditionally produced only structured data in tables or fixed structured files. With advances in data interchange formats, there was increased production of semi-structured data in the form of XML and JSON files. And as organizations started implementing big data solutions, they started generating large volumes of unstructured data in the form of images, videos, and machine logs. Your data platform should support all types of source systems, sending different types of data at various time intervals.

Data ingestion

Data ingestion is the process of extracting data from source systems and loading it into your data platform. As seen in the earlier section, based on the source system's capability to produce and send data, the ingestion framework must be implemented to build a batch, near real-time, or streaming system.

Batch ingestion.   Data that is sent once a day (either as the end-of-day or the start-of-day process) can be ingested as a batch process into the data platform. This is the most common ingestion pattern used in traditional data warehouse architectures for generating daily management information systems (MIS) or regulatory reports.

Near real-time.   For more time-sensitive data, ingestion can be done as micro-batches or in near real-time. The ingestion intervals for micro-batches can be between a few hours to a few minutes, while near real-time data can be ingested in a gap of a few minutes to seconds. The data ingestion tools should meet the required service level agreements (SLAs) as per the business demands.

Streaming.   Streaming analytics use cases are extremely sensitive to time and need an architecture that supports data ingestion in real time—as in, within a few milliseconds from the time data is generated. Because this data is time critical, it can rapidly lose value if not ingested and processed immediately. Your data platform's ingestion components should be able to support low-latency requirements to make the data available as soon as the source systems generate it.

A good practice for designing the ingestion process is to design reusable, configurable frameworks that can ingest data from multiple source feeds or entities. This helps to quickly onboard new entities on the data platform. While designing the data architecture, you can consider building reusable solutions across these core components to reduce implementation efforts.

Data storage

Once the data is ingested, it must be stored for durability, easy discovery, and further analysis. Data storage components enable the effective storing of various data types. These components persist data that can be retrieved as and when required and should provide high availability and high durability.

Depending on the use cases, you can categorize data storage into two broad categories: general storage and purpose-built storage.

General storage. All data type in object storage like Hadoop Distributed File System (HDFS), Amazon Simple Storage Service (S3), Azure Data Lake Storage (ADLS), or Google Cloud Storage (GCS). These object stores support persisting the structured, semi-structured, or unstructured data. They provide high availability and durability and are also cost efficient, making them one of the best choices for storing data for a longer durations can be stored

ADLS Gen 2 is a cloud object storage service provided by Azure that is built on Azure Blob Storage. It provides high availability, features for disaster recovery, different storage tiers to save cost and other big data capabilities. It is widely used to implement data lakes within the Azure ecosystem. Previously, Azure also offered ADLS Gen 1 (based on HDFS), which has now been retired. Throughout this book, when we refer to ADLS, we mean the ADLS Gen 2 service.

Purpose-built storage. While object storages are good for cost-effective, long-term storage, you might need a purpose-built storage system that can exhibit features like quick access, faster retrieval, key-based searches, columnar storage, and high concurrency.

There are different technologies and architectural patterns to implement these purpose-built storage systems:

Data warehouses
Provide support for Online Analytical Processing (OLAP) workloads

Relational database management systems (RDBMS)
    Support Online Transaction Processing (OLTP) systems for application backends

In-memory databases
    Provide faster data retrieval

Graph databases
    Store connections and relations

The data storage components are the most widely used components within a data platform. From storing long-term data to serving it quickly, all major activities happen through these components with the help of a compute engine.

Data processing and transformations

Raw data collected from source systems must be validated, cleansed, integrated, and transformed per business requirements. As part of data processing, the following steps are carried out to transform the raw data into a more consumable end product.

Data validation and cleansing. When data is ingested from source systems, it is in raw form and needs validations and cleansing before it can be made available to end users. Both of these steps are important to ensure that data accuracy does not get compromised during its movement to the higher storage zones of the lakehouse ecosystem. The hierarchy of data storage zones—raw, cleansed, curated, and semantic—will be discussed in detail in Chapter 7.

Input data is validated as the first step post-ingestion. These validations apply to structured data and, to some extent, semi-structured data that is used for reports and insight generation. During this step, data flows through various validation lenses, including the following technical and business validations:

Technical validations
    Mainly related to the data types, data formats, and other checks that are technical in nature and can be applied across any domain or industry

Business validations
    Domain- or function-specific and related to particular values in attributes, and their accuracy or completeness

Schema validations
    What the input data feeds should follow, as per the agreed schema defined in the specifications or *data contracts*

Data contract is a relatively new term that describes the agreement between the data producer and its consumers. It defines various parameters associated with the data produced, like its owner, frequency, data type, and format. Data contracts ensure there is a common understanding between producers and consumers of data.

Data transformation. The process of transforming raw data into useful information is known as data transformation. It can consist of a series of transformations that first integrates the data received from multiple source systems and then transforms it into a consumable form that downstream applications, business users, and other data consumers can use per their requirements.

There are multiple data transformations that you can apply based on your use case and requirements. The common data transformations are:

Data integration

As data is ingested from multiple source systems, you must combine it to get an integrated view. An example is integrating customer profile data from external source systems, internal systems, or marketing applications. Different source systems can supply data in different formats and so we need to bring it into a common, standard format for consumption by downstream applications. For example, consider the "date of birth" attribute that can have different formats (like MM/DD/YYYY or DD-MM-YY) in different source systems. It is important to transform all records across source systems into a standard format (like DD/MM/YYYY) before storing them in your central data platform. As part of the transformation process, this integration is done before storing data in the higher storage zones.

Data enhancement

To make data more meaningful, it must be enhanced, or augmented with external data. Examples of data enhancement are:

- Augmenting your internal data with external exchange rates from third-party applications to calculate global daily sales

- Augmenting your internal data with external data from credit rating agencies to calculate credit scores of your customers

Data aggregation

Data needs to be summarized according to business needs for faster querying and retrieval. An example would be aggregating data based on date, product, and location to get summarized views of sales.

Data curation and serving. In the final data processing step, data is curated and served per the business processes and requirements. Data gets loaded in the curated storage zone, based on an industry-standard data model using modeling approaches like dimension modeling. This arrangement of data using industry-specific data models facilitates faster and easier insight generation and reporting. Curated data can then be used to create *data products* that consumers can use directly to fulfill their business needs.

> Data product is a new term used to define a consumable end product specifically curated for its consumers. Data products are generally created by domain teams responsible for the data. These products can be shared with other domain teams and downstream applications. A data product can be a table, view, report, dashboard, or even a machine learning (ML) model that can be easily discovered and consumed by end users.

Data consumption and delivery

The data consumption components in your platform enable users to access, analyze, query, and consume the data. These can be your BI reporting tools or even ML models that are used for making predictions and forecasting. The various workloads supported by these components include:

BI workloads. BI tools help create reports and dashboards for use cases like MIS, regulatory reports, and sales analytics or daily trends. BI has been one of the earliest use cases supported by traditional technologies like RDBMS and architectures built using the data warehouse approach.

Ad hoc/Interactive analysis.   Business users, data analysts, and data leaders often need to perform analysis to support ad hoc requirements or to find answers to impromptu questions that pop up during meetings. The components that enable such interactive, ad hoc analysis provide a simple SQL interface.

Downstream applications and APIs.   Downstream applications need a universal way to interact with your data platform. APIs provide flexibility and can be used by downstream systems to fetch the data easily.

AI and ML workloads.   AI and ML can help support multiple use cases like predictions, forecasting, and recommendations. If these types of use cases exist in your organization, then your data platform should be able to provide tools for the ML lifecycle, including training, deployment, and inferencing the models.

All of these components—BI reporting tools and ML models—enable data consumption and delivery to consumers and play a significant role in increasing user adoption of the platform. These components also provide an interface for users to interact with the data that resides within the platform, and so user experience should be considered when designing the platform.

Common services

There are common services that provide functionality across a data platform and play a significant role in making data easily discoverable, available, and securely accessible for its consumers. These common services are summarized as follows.

Metadata management.   These consist of tools and technologies to help you ingest, manage, and maintain metadata within your ecosystem. Metadata helps ease data discoverability and access for users. You can create data catalogs to organize the metadata with details of various tables, attributes, data types, lengths, keys, and other information. Data catalogs help users to more quickly and effectively discover and leverage data.

Data governance and data security.   Implementing strong data governance and data security policies is essential in order to:

- Ensure good data quality to build consumers' trust in data
- Meet all relevant regulatory compliance requirements
- View data lineage to track the flow of data across systems
- Implement the right levels of access controls for all platform users

- Share data with internal and external data consumers
- Manage sensitive data by abstracting it from non-permissioned users
- Protect data when it is stored or moves within or outside the data platform

These topics will be discussed in detail in Chapter 6.

Data operations. These services help to manage various operations across various stages in the data lifecycle. Data operations enable the following activities:

- Orchestrating data pipelines and defining schedules to run processes
- Automating testing, integration, and deployment of data pipelines
- Managing and observing the health of the entire data ecosystem

Modern data platforms employ *data observability* features for monitoring the health of data overall.

 Data observability is a new term used for understanding the health of data within the ecosystem. It is a process for identifying the issues related to quality, accuracy, freshness, and completeness of data proactively to avoid any data downtimes. Modern data platforms should provide features for data observability, mainly considering the large volumes and rapid data ingestion and processing, wherein any downtime can impact the system severely.

All of these core components form the data platform and enable its users to perform various activities. Data architectures provide the blueprint and guiding principles to build these data platforms. With this basic understanding of data architectures and data platforms and their significance, let's now discuss a new architectural pattern— the lakehouse—which is the main topic of this book.

Why Do We Need a New Data Architecture?

Data warehouses and data lakes have remained the most popular architectures for implementing data platforms. However, in the last few years, some organizations have strived to implement data platforms by leveraging different architectural approaches.

Their motivations to look for new approaches instead of implementing the well-known traditional data architectures, is mainly twofold:

- Traditional architectures have several limitations when implemented as standalone systems. I'll discuss these traditional architectures and their restrictions in Chapter 2.

- There have been multiple technological advancements in the last few years. Innovations within the cloud space and the maturity of open-source technologies have been the main drivers of these advancements.

Organizations have constantly sought to overcome the limitations of traditional architectures and leverage new technologies to build scalable, secure, and reliable platforms. Organizations, independent service vendors (ISVs), and system integrators (SIs) have tried different and innovative approaches to implement more modern data platforms. Some of these approaches include:

- A two-tiered architecture combining a data lake and data warehouse to support BI, data analytics, and ML use cases
- Leveraging hybrid transactional/analytical processing (HTAP) technologies, which use a single storage layer, to unify transactional (OLTP) and analytical (OLAP) workloads
- Building modern cloud data warehouses that can process unstructured data along with structured and semi-structured data
- Implementing proprietary storage formats on cloud object storage that can provide warehouse-like performance
- Building compute engines for performing BI directly on data lakes

All of these efforts indicate a need for a new architectural pattern that can:

- Support implementation of a simple, unified platform that can handle all data formats and a diverse set of use cases to help users easily consume data
- Provide the ACID support, excellent BI performance, and access control mechanisms of a data warehouse
- Provide the scalability, cost efficiency, and flexibility of a data lake

This is how a new pattern—lakehouse architecture—has emerged over the last few years. We'll talk more about it in the next section.

Lakehouse Architecture: A New Pattern

New tools, products, and open-source technologies have changed how organizations are implementing data ecosystems. These new technologies have helped to simplify complex data architectures, resulting in data platforms that are more reliable, open, and flexible to support a variety of data and analytics workloads.

The data lakehouse (referred to as the lakehouse, or lakehouse architecture throughout this book) is a new architectural pattern that leverages new technology for building simple and open data platforms. As shown in Figure 1-2, a lakehouse is, at the core, a data lake with an additional transactional layer and a performant compute layer. The additional transactional layer gives it data warehouse-like ACID properties and other features.

 The additional transactional layer is sometimes referred to as the "metadata layer," as it provides metadata related to the transaction. To maintain consistency, we will refer to it as a transactional layer throughout the book.

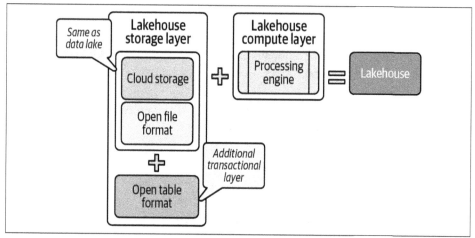

Figure 1-2. Lakehouse architecture layers

We will discuss these layers in more detail soon. But first, let's spend more time understanding the lakehouse concept and how it combines data warehouse and data lake features.

The Lakehouse: Best of Both Worlds

Data platforms built using lakehouse architecture exhibit features of a data warehouse *and* a data lake, hence the name lakehouse. Figure 1-3 shows the key lakehouse architecture features, which are a combination of the best features of a data lake and a warehouse. The features of a data lake and a data warehouse will be discussed in more detail in Chapter 2, where I will explain these traditional architectures, their characteristics, and their benefits.

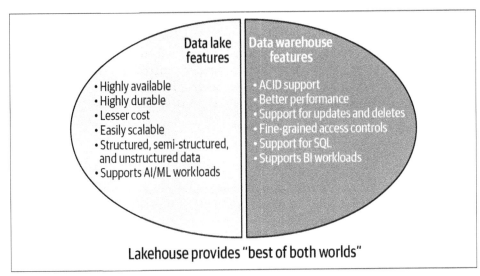

Figure 1-3. Lakehouse features

But how do lakehouses get the best features of both data warehouses and data lakes within a single storage tier? What technologies enable these features?

How does a lakehouse get data lake features?

Like a data lake, a lakehouse uses cloud object storage like Amazon S3, ADLS, or GCS and stores the data in open file formats like Apache Parquet, Apache Avro, or Apache ORC. This cloud storage enables lakehouses to have all the best features of data lakes, like high availability, high durability, cost efficiency, scalability, support for all data types (structured, semi-structured, unstructured), and support for AI and ML use cases.

How does a lakehouse get data warehouse features?

Compared to a data lake, a lakehouse has one additional component: the transactional layer, which is an additional layer on top of the file formats. This extra layer separates a lakehouse from a data lake. It enables lakehouses to get data warehouse capabilities like ACID compliance, support for updates and deletes, better BI performance, and fine-grained access control. The technology used to implement this transactional layer is known as "open table formats," which we will discuss in detail in the next section.

Lakehouse architecture has attracted interest within the data community, and various organizations have started adopting it to build platforms to support multiple use cases, such as ETL processing, BI, ML, data science, and streaming analytics. Apart from the leading cloud service providers, multiple commercial product vendors provide SaaS or PaaS offerings to support implementing data platforms-based lakehouse architecture. These include products from Databricks, Snowflake, Dremio, and Onehouse.

A Bit of History About the Lakehouse Approach

When Hadoop was on the rise, organizations implemented data platforms using a similar concept to lakehouse. They used HDFS as the storage and Hive as the open table format. The platforms used Hive's metastore as the metadata layer, and they used its engine for processing the data stored on HDFS. However, Hive initially lacked the much-required ACID features for file formats like Parquet. Only later did it begin providing ACID support for ORC files.

In 2021, Databricks founders published a paper at the Conference on Innovative Data Systems Research (CIDR) titled "Lakehouse: A New Generation of Open Platforms that Unify Data Warehousing and Advanced Analytics" (*https://oreil.ly/MqVkA*). The paper argued that a new architectural pattern called lakehouse could replace the data warehouse in the coming years. Since then, lakehouse architecture has gained momentum and data practitioners across the globe have started exploring it.

Let's dive deeper into lakehouse architecture and the underlying technologies that it uses.

Understanding Lakehouse Architecture

Figure 1-4 shows a simple view of lakehouse architecture, comprised of the storage and compute layers along with the underlying technology options. This is a granular view of Figure 1-2, seen earlier in this chapter.

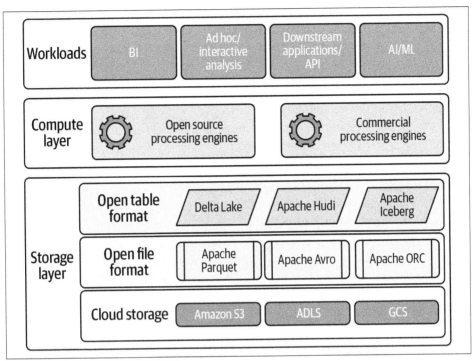

Figure 1-4. More granular view of lakehouse architecture

As we've discussed, lakehouse architecture consists of a storage layer and compute layer. Data platforms built using lakehouse architecture enable data and analytics workloads to consume data from the storage layer while using the compute engine.

Storage layer

Let's first understand the technology options in the storage layer. This layer is comprised of three components: cloud storage, open file format, and open table format.

Cloud storage. Cloud storage is a service that offers the high availability, durability, and scalability required for implementing data lake and lakehouse platforms. Leading cloud service providers offer the following services for implementing lakehouse platforms:

- Amazon S3 by Amazon Web Services (AWS)
- ADLS by Microsoft Azure
- GCS by Google Cloud Platform (GCP)

Organizations can also implement a lakehouse using on-premises HDFS storage. Using only cloud object storage for implementing a lakehouse is not necessary. However, considering features like low cost, separation of compute and storage, and easy scalability, it is advisable to use cloud object storage as the underlying infrastructure for implementing a lakehouse.

This book will only discuss modern platforms that organizations implement using cloud technologies. We will learn more about modern platforms in Chapter 2.

Open file formats. Data platforms can store data in different file formats in cloud storage. File formats like CSV, JSON, and XML are the most popular. For analytics platforms, the three most widely adopted file formats used are Parquet, ORC, and Avro.

All of these are open file formats, that is they are part of an open-source ecosystem. These are not proprietary; anyone can easily use them for storing data. Any compatible processing engine can interact with such open file formats. Many other features make these three formats suitable for analytical workloads. We will discuss these file formats in more detail in Chapter 3.

Open table formats. As discussed earlier, open table formats bring transactional capabilities to a data lake to make them a lakehouse. These open table formats are the heart of the lakehouse. There are three such formats gaining popularity among the data community: Apache Iceberg, Apache Hudi, and Linux Foundation's Delta Lake.

Let's have a quick look at these three open table formats:

Apache Iceberg
Apache Iceberg is an open table format that can be used with cloud object stores and open file formats like Parquet, Avro, and ORC for implementing lakehouse architecture. It supports features like time travel, schema evolution, and SQL support, making lakehouse implementation faster and easier.

Apache Hudi
Apache Hudi helps to implement a transactional data lake and can be used to bring data warehouse-like capabilities to the data lake. It provides ACID transactional guarantees, incremental processing, time travel capabilities, schema evolution, and enforcement features.

Linux Foundation's Delta Lake
Started by Databricks as an internal project, the Linux Foundation's Delta Lake is commonly known as an open-source storage framework for building lakehouse architecture. Delta Lake provides the metadata layer and ACID capabilities to data lakes. It also provides features like time travel, schema enforcements and evolution, and audit trail logging.

There are now two different distributions of Delta Lake. The commercial version comes along with the Databricks platform. The open-source version is available on the Linux Foundation's website, and you can use it with other non-Databricks environments. Though Databricks has made all of its Delta Lake features open source, the latest open-source version might not be available immediately with managed Apache Spark services like Amazon EMR or Azure Synapse Analytics. You will have to wait till these managed cloud services offer the latest Spark and Delta Lake versions to leverage all of the latest Delta Lake features.

All these open table formats will be discussed in more detail in Chapter 3.

Compute layer

One of the main advantages of lakehouse architecture is its open nature and ability to be directly accessed or queried by any compatible processing engine. It does not need a specific, proprietary engine for running BI workloads or interactive analysis. These compute engines can be open-source or purpose-built commercial query engines designed explicitly for lakehouse architectures.

Open-source engines. You can use open-source engines to access data from a lakehouse. These are not vendor specific and you don't need to purchase a license to use them. Examples of open-source compute engines are Spark, Presto, Trino and Hive.

Commercial engines. These are query engines specifically built for getting better performance for running workloads on lakehouses. Commercial engines are generally built from the ground up, taking into consideration the underlying open data formats and how effectively they can get the best performance. Examples of commercial compute engine vendors are Databricks, Dremio, Snowflake, and Starburst.

Both the storage and compute layers work together to power lakehouse architectures with the best features of data lakes and data warehouses. As a result, lakehouse architecture addresses the limitations of traditional data architectures and support different workloads, from BI to AI, and different downstream applications to leverage data from a data platform.

A data platform based on lakehouse architecture exhibits key characteristics that help solve the limitations of traditional architectures. The following section details these characteristics.

Lakehouse Architecture Characteristics

The following characteristics set lakehouse architecture apart from other traditional data architectures.

Single storage tier with no dedicated warehouse

As seen in earlier sections, a lakehouse, at its core, is a data lake built using cloud object storage with an additional transactional layer. There is no separate storage like a dedicated data warehouse to support BI workloads. All consumers read, access, or query data directly from the data lake. The same cloud object storage supports all use cases, including BI and AI/ML workloads.

Warehouse-like performance on the data lake

Cloud storage is not suitable for BI workloads and lacks the performance provided by purpose-built proprietary storage of cloud data warehouses. Data platforms built using lakehouse architecture provide excellent performance for BI use cases by offering optimization levers at storage and compute layers. You can get excellent performance using the right combination of open data (file and table) formats and compute engines built explicitly for lakehouse architecture.

Decoupled architecture with separate storage and compute scaling

Lakehouse architecture is based on a decoupled approach with separate storage and compute engines. The previous generations of data platforms used architectures with integrated storage and processing layers. Examples are databases, traditional on-premises warehouses, and Hadoop ecosystems. Scaling of storage or compute power was not possible with such integrated architectures.

The decoupled lakehouse architecture helps scale storage and compute capacities individually. You can easily add more storage without increasing the compute capacity and vice versa. Figure 1-5 shows platforms implementing lakehouse architecture with decoupled storage and compute.

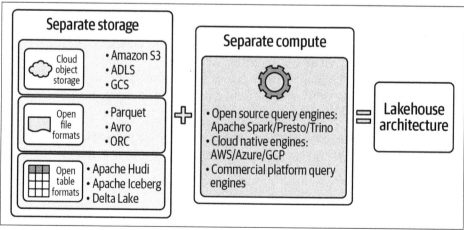

Figure 1-5. Decoupled storage and compute in lakehouse architecture

Open architecture

The lakehouse architecture uses an "open" approach for implementing data platforms. This means you have the freedom to employ open-source data formats and open-source compute engines for your data platforms. Unlike proprietary warehouses, where you have to use the native processing engine bundled within the warehouse software, lakehouses allow you to use any distributed processing engine that is compatible with the underlying storage formats. Such open architecture enables data consumers to access the data directly from cloud storage, without needing vendor-specific software.

Support for different data types

Traditionally, on-premises warehouse architectures only supported structured data. They could not store, manage, or maintain semi-structured and unstructured data. Some modern cloud warehouses can now support semi-structured data like JSON and XML files.

Data platforms built using the lakehouse approach support *all* data formats—structured, semi-structured, and unstructured images; audio; and video data—within a single storage tier.

Support for diverse workloads

As lakehouse can handle all data formats, it can support all types of workloads, including BI, AI/ML, ETL, and streaming. You do not need to implement separate storage tiers or purpose-built storage to support these workloads. Lakehouse architecture can support all of these within a single storage tier.

Next, let's discuss the key benefits of lakehouse architecture and how it can help build a simple, unified, and open data platform.

Lakehouse Architecture Benefits

A data platform implemented using the lakehouse approach provides many significant benefits, especially in a world that demands building data platforms that are not just scalable and flexible but also secure and reliable.

The following is a list of benefits that you would get by implementing a data platform based on lakehouse architecture.

Simplified architecture

In lakehouse architecture, all the data resides in a single storage tier. The data architecture is simplified because there is no separate warehouse and the additional ETL pipeline required to move data from data lakes to data warehouses is reduced.

Lakehouse architecture also avoids delays, failures, or data quality issues associated with integrating lakes and warehouses.

This architecture with a single storage tier has several benefits:

- No additional efforts are required to sync data between the data lake and the warehouse. Syncing data between two different storage types is always a challenge.

- You don't need to worry about changing data types between data lakes and warehouses. The schema in these two often does not match, as data types can differ.

- Data governance becomes much easier in the lakehouse as you only need to implement access controls in one place. In a two-tier storage system, you have to maintain separate access control mechanisms to access data from the data lake and warehouse, and ensure these are always in sync.

- ML workloads can read data from the lakehouse, directly accessing underlying Parquet, Avro, or ORC storage files. This removes the need to copy any aggregated data from the warehouse to the lake if required by ML workloads.

Support for unstructured data and ML use cases

A large volume of data produced in today's world is unstructured. A lakehouse supports unstructured data along with structured and semi-structured data. This opens up endless possibilities for implementing AI and ML use cases to leverage massive volumes of unstructured data for predictions, forecasting, recommendations, and new insights from data.

No vendor lock-ins

As we've discussed, lakehouses use open formats for implementing data platforms. Open formats enable consumers to query and process data using any compatible processing engine that integrates well with the underlying storage formats. Lakehouses use no proprietary storage format that needs a specific vendor's processing engine. This enables downstream applications to have direct access to data for consumption.

For example, If you implement a two-tier data platform with a data lake and a dedicated warehouse, you must first load the data into the warehouse in order to perform any BI workloads. To query or access this data, you will have to use the proprietary compute engine of the same warehouse vendor. You must use the vendor-provided processing capacities and pay for the same. This leads to vendor lock-in and migrating to other engines takes considerable efforts.

Not all open table formats are compatible with all open-source or commercial query engines. This is a growing space, and multiple independent software vendors (ISVs) are working on building connectors for interacting with various data formats. While deciding your tech stack, you should consider the engine compatibility with underlying open table formats.

Data sharing

As the lakehouse uses open data formats, sharing data with downstream consumers becomes much more manageable. You don't have to onboard consumers on your platforms or share file extracts with them. They can directly access data from the cloud storage based on the data sharing access permissions.

An example of data sharing is the Delta Sharing protocol, an open standard for secure data sharing introduced by Delta Lake. Figure 1-6 shows a simplified version of the Delta Sharing protocol. Please note that the actual implementations would have additional components to manage the permissions and optimize the performance to serve only the required data.

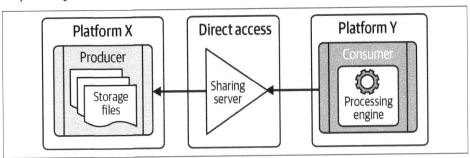

Figure 1-6. Delta sharing in Delta Lake

The key benefit of open data sharing is the freedom for data consumers to use any open-source processing engine or commercial products to query and analyze data. They are not required to use the same product as the data producer to access the shared data. On the other hand, the data producer only needs to share the data and does not have to worry about which processing engines the consumers would use for accessing the data. This feature opens up multiple possibilities for sharing data securely and implementing a marketplace for collaboratively sharing and exchanging data.

This is a growing space and, in the future, multiple vendors and communities might introduce new connectors to access data directly stored in a lakehouse.

Scalable and cost efficient

Lakehouses use cloud storage, which is scalable and much cheaper than traditional data warehouses. Storage cost for lakehouses is the cost set by the cloud storage providers. You can also leverage the lifecycle management policies and cold, or archival, tiers that cloud vendors offer to optimize long-term storage costs.

No data swamps

Many organizations have large volumes of data in their data lakes. However, most of the time, they do not leverage this data effectively due to a lack of data visibility.

Discovering these large volumes of data is difficult without proper metadata management, governance, lineage tracking, and access controls. Without these things, data lakes become *data swamps* and leveraging this data becomes challenging. Lakehouses help make data easily discoverable for the platform's consumers by offering features like unified metadata management (across data and AI assets), lineage tracking, and more.

> Data swamps are data lakes with large volumes of data without proper organization or structure. The data stored within such data lakes are not well-governed and do not have well-organized metadata in the form of catalogs, making data discovery extremely challenging and reducing the overall visibility of the data for consumers. In short, data swamps are data lakes with data that is not leveraged for business needs due to the absence of robust metadata and governance processes.

Schema enforcement and evolution

Technologies used in lakehouse architecture support enforcing schema validations to avoid schema mismatches while storing data. These technologies also support schema evolution, using different approaches to help accept source schema changes. These features enable a flexible system with better data quality and integrity. Let's briefly discuss the benefits of these two features.

Schema enforcement. Schema enforcement ensures that the data stored in the lakehouse follows the schema defined by the metadata of that table. The ETL process rejects any additional attributes or mismatching data types. These validations help in storing correct data, thus improving the overall data quality. For example, if a string value arrives in an attribute defined as an integer in the schema, it will get rejected.

Schema evolution. While schema enforcement improves data quality by implementing strict validations, schema evolution supports relaxing these validations by offering more flexibility while storing the data in a lakehouse. Any additional attribute not defined in the table metadata can be stored using schema evolution. Depending on the open table format, various approaches exist to store the extra attribute. This feature helps keep new attributes or data type mismatches without rejecting them. The key benefit of this approach is that you never lose any data and can accommodate changes on the fly.

While schema enforcement helps improve data quality by enforcing strict rules on specific attributes, schema evolution provides flexibility to accommodate metadata changes in the source systems. You can use both while implementing your lakehouse to maintain data quality as well as accommodate any source metadata changes.

Unified platform for ETL/ELT, BI, AI/ML, and real-time workloads

As we've mentioned, the lakehouse architecture enables you to implement a unified data platform to support diverse workloads. Let's discuss these workloads and the benefits of using a lakehouse to implement them in more detail.

ETL/ELT workloads.   To implement ETL workloads, you can use popular processing engines like Spark to perform transformations *before* storing data in the higher zones of the lakehouse storage hierarchy. You can also implement an ELT workload to perform transformations using SQL queries using any compute engine. Data practitioners who are more conversant with SQL prefer to perform SQL-based ELT operations for transforming data.

BI workloads.   With performance at par with data warehouses, you can implement your BI workloads using a lakehouse. Since a lakehouse provides a transactional layer to the data lake, operations like updates and deletes are possible and quicker than when performed in data lakes.

AI/ML workloads.   Since a lakehouse supports unstructured data along with structured and semi-structured data, you can perform AI/ML use cases by directly accessing data in the lakehouse.

Real-time workloads.   A unified lakehouse architecture supports diverse workloads, including real-time processing. In the past few years, due to the rise of real-time data generated from IoT devices, wearables, and clickstreams, organizations have tried to implement platforms that can support real-time workloads. Earlier data architectures, such as the Lambda architecture, supported real-time workloads using different processing streams. Lakehouses support real-time workloads using a unified architecture that supports executing batch *or* real-time jobs using the same code base.

Lambda architecture is a traditional approach to processing large volumes of data ingested at varied frequencies. Lambda architecture has two different layers for processing batch data and streaming data. The batch and streaming data components for these layers are also separate, based on factors like latency and associated SLAs. This results in a complex data architecture with additional efforts to maintain different code bases for different layers.

Time travel

The transactional layer in a lakehouse enables it to maintain various versions of data. This helps it perform time travel to query and fetch older data that has been updated or deleted. Let's look at one example to understand the time travel feature. Table 1-1 shows a product table with three columns.

Table 1-1. A lakehouse table with sample records

product_id	product_name	product_category
22	keyboard	computer accessory
12	mouse	computer accessory
71	headphone	computer accessory
11	mobile case	mobile accessory

Consider a case where the third row, with product_id 71, gets updated to change the category from "computer accessory" to "mobile accessory." Table 1-2 shows the updated table.

Table 1-2. A lakehouse table with updated records

product_id	product_name	product_category
22	keyboard	computer accessory
12	mouse	computer accessory
71	headphone	mobile accessory
11	mobile case	mobile accessory

Now, if you query the product table, you will be able to see the updated data, but the older value of product_category for the updated record won't be visible.

If you use open table formats like Iceberg, Hudi, or Delta Lake, you would be able to see the previous records also by just querying the table using an earlier version number or older timestamp as shown next.

Retrieve older data based on version.   You can retrieve the older status of records by using the version number:

```
select * from product as of version <older version number>
```

Retrieve older data based on timestamp. You can retrieve the older status of records by using the earlier timestamp:

```
select * from product as of <older timestamp>
```

 The exact SQL commands will differ based on the open table format and compute engines used for implementing the lakehouse.

This time travel operation is not possible in the traditional data warehouses or data lakes. Some NoSQL databases (like HBase) and modern cloud warehouses store all versions of data, but traditional warehouses lacked this feature.

These benefits enable all data personas to access, manage, control, analyze, and leverage data quickly and efficiently compared to earlier data architectures.

Considering the benefits, lakehouse architecture can soon become the default choice for implementing data platforms and could see a widespread adoption similar to data warehouses and data lakes. Advanced technologies, growing communities, and multiple ISVs working on lakehouse-based products indicate a growing demand and popularity of lakehouse architecture.

Key Takeaways

If you are learning about lakehouse architecture for the first time, I understand this is a lot of information to digest on the first go. I'll summarize the key points I discussed in this chapter to help you remember the most important concepts as you read the following chapters in this book.

Understanding data architecture
- Data architecture is the foundation of any data platform. It defines the core components and their interdependencies. It provides the blueprint for building the data platform and helps establish the guiding principles for designing the system.
- The core components of the data platform are source systems, data ingestion, data storage, data processing and transformations, data consumption and delivery, and common services like metadata management, data governance and data security, and data operations.
- Designing the data architecture is one of the most critical steps in setting up the data infrastructure. You should make every effort to architect a scalable, flexible, reliable, and above all, simple platform. This will enable quicker user adoption.

Lakehouse architecture characteristics

- Lakehouse architecture is a new architectural pattern that has emerged in the last few years. It provides the best features from data warehouses and data lakes.

- Lakehouse architecture stores the data in a cloud store with an additional transactional layer, enabling warehouse-like capabilities.

- You get the scalability, flexibility, and cost efficiencies of a data lake, as well as the performance, ACID compliance, and better governance of data warehouses.

- Lakehouse architecture has only a single storage tier and no separate warehouse storage. It employs decoupled architecture where compute and storage layers are separate and scale independently.

- It supports storing and managing all data types, including structured, semi-structured, and unstructured. It also supports diverse workloads like ETL, streaming, BI, and AI/ML.

Lakehouse architecture benefits

- Lakehouse architecture helps you implement a simple, unified data platform to implement a diverse set of data and analytics use cases.

- Lakehouses use open technologies for storage; you don't have to worry about vendor lock-in issues. You can use any compatible compute engine to query the data by directly accessing the data stored on cloud object storage.

- Data sharing with data consumers, irrespective of the technology or product they use, becomes easier without the need to replicate the data or send file extracts.

- Lakehouses can help you manage and control your data more efficiently with features like schema enforcement, schema evolution, time travel, and more.

As you read this book further, you will dive deep into more advanced topics to understand how to design and implement practical lakehouse architectures and to see their benefits over traditional architectures like data warehouses and data lakes, or the combined two-tier systems. But for readers new to the data world, we first need to better understand these traditional architectures, their advantages, and their limitations to appreciate the benefits of lakehouse architecture. I'll discuss this in the next chapter.

References

- Apache Parquet (*https://parquet.apache.org*)
- Apache Avro (*https://avro.apache.org*)
- Apache ORC (*https://orc.apache.org*)
- Delta Lake (*https://delta.io*)
- Apache Iceberg (*https://iceberg.apache.org*)
- Apache Hudi (*https://hudi.apache.org*)
- Databricks (*https://www.databricks.com*)
- Snowflake (*https://www.snowflake.com*)
- Ahana (*https://docs.ahana.cloud/docs*)
- Starburst (*https://www.starburst.io*)
- Onehouse (*https://www.onehouse.ai*)
- Amazon Web Services (*https://aws.amazon.com*)
- Microsoft Azure (*https://azure.microsoft.com*)
- Google Cloud (*https://cloud.google.com*)
- Monte Carlo Data (*https://www.montecarlodata.com*)
- Acceldata (*https://www.acceldata.io*)
- Guidelines and patterns for migrating Azure Data Lake Storage from Gen1 to Gen2 (*https://oreil.ly/k2P7G*)

CHAPTER 2

Traditional Architectures and Modern Data Platforms

In Chapter 1, we discussed lakehouse architecture—a new approach for implementing data platforms. To truly appreciate any new technology, you first need to understand the capabilities and limitations of its previous generations. Thus, to appreciate the value of lakehouse architecture, it's essential to understand the current and previous generations of data architectures. We will discuss these previous generations, also known as the "traditional architectures" in detail in this chapter.

We'll first discuss how the traditional architectures like data warehouses and data lakes are implemented using the on-premises infrastructure. I'll walk you through the key characteristics, benefits, and limitations of data platforms built using these architectures.

Next, we'll explore the modern data platforms built using cloud technologies and what today's data-driven organizations expect from them. Organizations implement their modern data platforms using either a standalone or combined approach:

The standalone approach
    Comprises a system built using a data warehouse or a data lake

The combined approach
    Uses both the data warehouse and the data lake, making it a two-tier architecture

As seen in Chapter 1, lakehouse architecture also helps build modern data platforms and is gaining industry attention. In the last section of this chapter, we'll compare the standalone and combined approaches with the lakehouse architecture to understand how lakehouses are different and offer more benefits compared to these approaches.

Some of you may have already implemented data warehouses and data lakes and would like to skip the early sections of this chapter. I encourage you to read them, though, to relive your data journey. I'll share some of my experiences working with these technologies during my formative years.

While I won't discuss the evolution of these data architectures and related chronological events, I will focus on their practical benefits and limitations. You have likely faced similar challenges and may relate to my experiences.

Let's start by discussing the most widely adopted architectural patterns—data warehouses and data lakes.

Traditional Architectures: Data Lakes and Data Warehouses

In this section, I'll discuss the two widely adopted architectural approaches for implementing data platforms. We'll cover their capabilities and benefits, as well as the limitations that triggered the evolution of modern data architectures.

Data Warehouse Fundamentals

I started my data journey in 2004 as an ETL (extract, transform, load) developer. Back then, only a few large enterprises were executing multi-year data programs to implement BI use cases. While smaller organizations were not focused on building central data repositories, everyone knew the benefits of having a central data platform to support their BI and analytics workloads. The most popular, widely accepted, and probably the only architectural pattern everyone followed was implementing a data warehouse. Organizations that invested in building a warehouse had access to a central data repository that helped in quick decision making. Data warehouse was the most adopted architectural pattern until data producers started generating large volumes of unstructured data—also known as "big data." This is when organizations realized the limitations of data warehouse architectures.

Flat files and databases have been the most widely used storage technologies to persist data. Within organizations, various departments set up their applications with back-end transactional databases. These siloed databases limit cross-department analysis. That's why organizations started implementing data warehouses, an architecture based on database technology—to implement a central repository in which to store their data.

Implementing a data platform using data warehouse architecture requires you to follow a three-step process:

1. Extract data from various disparate source systems.
2. Validate, cleanse, and transform the data in a well-organized data model.
3. Load the data in the data warehouse.

This process is better known as the ETL process, which extracts, transforms, and loads data in the target tables of the data warehouse.

Figure 2-1 shows how a data warehouse helps to implement central storage to persist data from multiple source systems and support BI workloads.

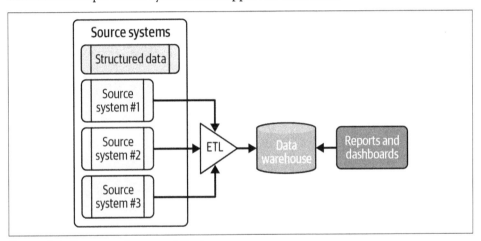

Figure 2-1. Data warehouse architecture

Bill Inmon, often referred to as the father of data warehouses, defined a data warehouse as a subject-oriented, integrated, time-variant, and non-volatile collection of data that can help to make management decisions. Let's look at the fundamental characteristics of a platform built using a data warehouse architecture:

Structured data
A data warehouse persists and processes structured data. Structured data is extracted from multiple source systems and loaded into a warehouse for decision making and insight generation.

Subject-oriented, integrated, and clean data
The data warehouse integrates data from various source systems. The data extracted from source systems goes through multiple validations before it is loaded into subject-specific tables (for example, by products or customers). The

data is validated based on the agreed specifications provided by source systems. Any exceptions are rejected and sent back to the source system for corrections.

Time-variant, non-volatile, and historical data
Data warehouses are built to store large volumes of data. As data changes with time, the data warehouse persists all these changes along with its timestamp. It retains the previous versions of the data without physically deleting the older values.

Some of the most popular data warehouse products are Teradata (*https://www.tera data.com*), IBM Netezza, (*https://oreil.ly/OYqXC*) and Oracle Exadata (*https://oreil.ly/iAokH*)—all of which are widely adopted by several organizations.

When organizations implement a data warehouse, these characteristics enable several benefits.

Benefits and advantages

Let's look at the benefits that have made data warehouses so popular for the last few decades:

Business decision making
The primary use case for a data warehouse is to help organizations implement a system for insight generation and business decision making by leveraging data across their various businesses and departments. A data warehouse helps to implement a decision support system. It enables organizations to look at data holistically across business dimensions and then take data-driven actions based on the generated insights.

Best-in-class BI performance
Data warehouses provide best-in-class performance for BI workloads like creating reports, dashboards, insight generation, or ad-hoc analysis. For enhanced performance, they support features like table partitioning, indexing, materialized views, and temporary tables. The excellent performance makes data warehouses a popular choice for supporting an organization's BI requirements.

Support for ACID, updates, and deletes
The data warehouse supports updating or deleting records stored within the warehouse. Applying updates and performing deletes, even on a single record, is just a matter of executing a simple SQL query. Data warehouses offer strong *ACID* (atomicity, consistency, isolation, durability) support for transactions— you don't have to worry about messy data from transaction failures or incomplete commits or rollbacks in a data warehouse system.

What Is ACID Compliance?

As discussed in earlier chapters, the lakehouse supports ACID properties. ACID is an acronym that represents four fundamental properties of a transaction: atomicity, consistency, isolation, and durability. Let's explore these properties using a simple example.

Consider a customer who has a $500 balance in their bank account. A transaction is executed to deduct $100 from their account:

Atomicity
> Any transaction is either fully committed or not executed at all. If any transaction fails, the balance reverts to its original state (before the transaction started). If the customer's transaction succeeds, the balance will be $400. But if it fails, the balance will be $500.

Consistency
> The customer's transaction should not leave any inconsistent or corrupt data. Data should always be in a consistent state—before and after transactions. After the customer's transaction, the balance of $400 should be stored and displayed whenever queried.

Isolation
> Concurrent transactions do not interfere with each other. They are carried out as isolated transactions, executed in sequence. If there is another joint account holder who performs a transaction (at same time) to deduct $200, it will be executed after the customer's initial transaction. It will not impact the customer's transaction while it is already running.

Durability
> A successful transaction is always durable and stays permanently in the data store, even in the case of system failures. When the customer's transaction completes, the balance will be stored as $400 in the system.

Any system that has these properties is an ACID-compliant system. Relational databases are ACID compliant, but data lakes are not. The emergence of open table formats like Iceberg, Hudi, and Delta Lake have enabled data lakes with ACID features to adopt data warehouse-like transaction management capabilities.

Modeled and organized data
> A data warehouse architecture lets you organize your data in a better way by using different modeling techniques like:
>
> - Entity relationship (ER) modeling to create normalized tables
> - Dimensional modeling to create a star schema that consists of denormalized dimensions and fact tables

Such modeling approaches can help you organize data, reduce data redundancy (ER modeling), and enhance the performance of your BI workloads (dimensional modeling)

A data mart is a subset of the enterprise data. You can create data marts for specific departments within the organizations. Users from a particular department can access only the data present in their data marts. For example, the marketing department will only have access to its data mart to analyze marketing data; sales teams can access only the sales data mart.

There are two approaches to creating your data warehouse: Ralph Kimball's "bottom-up" approach and Bill Inmon's "top-down" approach. In the bottom-up approach, you create multiple data marts that together form the data warehouse. In the top-down approach, you first create an enterprise-level data warehouse and then create separate department-specific data marts from this warehouse.

Better access control

Like a database, the data warehouse also stores data in tables as rows and columns. You can implement fine-grained access control at the table, column, or row level to restrict access permissions to its users. You can also create views to restrict users from accessing data based on specific filter conditions.

Single source of truth

Finally, the data warehouse helps you create a single source of truth for your data. Consumers can query the required tables in the central warehouse without the need to search data in any other places.

Limitations and challenges

While data warehouses provide significant advantages over department-specific siloed databases, they have some fundamental limitations. And these limitations have only grown further with the rise of big data, social media, IoT devices, and the need for streaming workloads:

Tightly coupled storage and compute

Traditional on-premises data warehousing products take the form of appliances bundled with high-end hardware and software. They have a tight coupling between storage and compute. You cannot purchase them individually, so scaling the storage or compute separately is not possible.

Vendor lock-ins

Data warehouses use *proprietary* formats for storing data. Data stored in the warehouse can only be accessed using its native processing engine. This results in vendor lock-ins and restricts you from implementing an open data platform that can support external data consumers with direct access to data.

 Data stored using a proprietary format means only the product encapsulating the storage can access and read data. You cannot query this data from outside, using other compute engines. Proprietary formats are often used in data warehouse products to enhance the overall performance and improve storage management.

No support for unstructured data and AI/ML workloads
Traditional data warehouses only support structured data. There is no direct method for storing unstructured data like text in social media comments, audio, video, or image files. AI/ML use cases mainly need unstructured data for predictions, recommendations, and forecasting.

No streaming support
Data warehouses are built for batch workloads that run once a day or microbatches that run a few times a day. However, they do not offer the throughput and latency required for real time or streaming use cases.

Higher cost
Finally, one of the most critical challenges associated with traditional data warehouses is the high cost of running and maintaining them. There is no provision to stop or pause, release unused capacity, use cheaper storage, or implement lifecycle policies. The high-end hardware requirements also add to the cost significantly.

As technologies have advanced, cloud platforms (which we will discuss later in this chapter) have helped to address some of these limitations. However, overcoming some fundamental limitations (like missing native support for handling unstructured data for AI/ML use cases), requires a fresh architectural approach. That's where data lakes have gained popularity. A data lake is not just an alternative architectural approach for implementing data platforms for insight generation and decision making. Rather, a data lake is an opportunity for organizations to predict and forecast what can happen!

In the next section, we will dive deep into data lakes and how they help to address most of the limitations with data warehouses.

Data Lake Fundamentals

Organizations gradually realized the value of their unstructured data and the limitations of warehouses to handle it. Sources like social media, machine logs, IoT devices, and website clickstreams rapidly generate large volumes of unstructured data. The platforms that are built using data warehouse architecture are significantly limited in persisting and processing such unstructured data for ML use cases. With the rise of Hadoop technologies, organizations saw an opportunity to build data platforms with an architecture that could overcome the limitations of data warehouses. Hadoop introduced a technology called Hadoop Distributed File System (HDFS) that could store structured, semi-structured, or unstructured data. That's when organizations started building data lakes based on HDFS technology.

> Many organizations have used HDFS to implement their first data lakes. HDFS supports storing all types of data, including structured, semi-structured, and large volumes of unstructured data. Along with batch workloads, it also supports real-time use cases.
>
> HDFS uses commodity hardware for storing data, making it a cost-effective solution for implementing data lakes. In the past, organizations have implemented data lakes using HDFS bundled as part of Hadoop distributions or commercial products like Cloudera Data Platform.

A data lake is a central data store that can persist structured, semi-structured, and unstructured data. It stores data from sources including CSV, JSON, XML, databases, images, audio, and videos. Like a data warehouse uses database technology, the on-premises data lake uses HDFS for storing large volumes of data.

Figure 2-2 shows how data lakes help to implement central storage to persist data from multiple source systems for supporting advanced analytics and AI/ML (experiments, predictions, and recommendations) use cases.

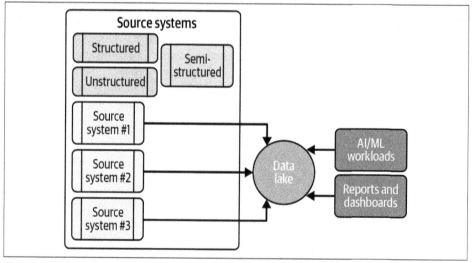

Figure 2-2. Data lake architecture

A standard data lake has the following key characteristics:

Support for all data formats

In a data lake, you can store structured, semi-structured (like JSON, XML), and unstructured data like text, images, audio, and video files. Support for unstructured data is the most significant feature, compared to a data warehouse, and has led to the massive adoption of data lakes across industries.

Schema on read approach

There are no schema restrictions for the data stored in a data lake. Raw data from source systems is written "as-is" in data lakes and further transformed or modeled as needed. There is no data loss due to strict data or schema validation rules. Schema is applied when reading the data for further analysis, also known as the schema on read approach.

Immutable storage

HDFS is an immutable storage system. You cannot change the data stored in a data lake that has been built using HDFS technology; you can only append *new* objects. Modern data lakes, built using cloud technologies like Amazon S3, exhibit similar characteristics to HDFS and store data as immutable objects.

Commodity hardware

Traditional on-premises data lakes use HDFS on Hadoop clusters built using commodity hardware. This helps to reduce the overall cost of the platform, compared to data warehouse systems that use high-end hardware.

Many organizations started implementing data lakes beginning in 2010. The most popular products used were Cloudera (*https://www.cloudera.com*), Hortonworks (now merged with Cloudera), and MapR (later acquired by HPE). Some also leveraged vanilla Hadoop and HDFS.

Benefits and advantages

Data lakes offer multiple benefits compared to data warehouse architecture. Let's discuss these in detail:

Support for AI/ML and data science use cases

Due to its ability to store and manage unstructured data, a data lake is an ideal platform for performing AI/ML and data science workloads. These workloads can directly access the raw data stored using file formats like Parquet, CSV, and JSON.

BI on Hadoop

Though there is no dedicated warehouse, data lakes implemented using HDFS can support BI workloads with the help of Apache Hive—a service within the Hadoop ecosystem that provides structure to data stored in HDFS. It also offers a querying engine based on MapReduce to run SQL queries. You can consider Hive as an early generation open table format that provides a metadata layer on top of the HDFS storage.

Support for real-time workloads

Data lakes can support real-time workloads along with batch workloads. Real-time data is ingested from source systems and made available within the data lake for further analytics. Though data lakes might not be best suited for low-latency (milliseconds) streaming analytics, they can support real-time data with reduced latency (a few seconds).

Cheaper cost

As data lakes use commodity hardware and open-source technologies like HDFS within the Hadoop framework, running these systems costs much less than data warehouse appliances that use high-end hardware and proprietary software.

Limitations and challenges

Along with several benefits, data lakes also have a few limitations. Here are some practical challenges I've faced during my Hadoop days. Those who have implemented data lakes in the past would most likely have also experienced similar challenges and looked for alternative options:

Lackluster BI performance

Moderate BI performance is one of the most common concerns when working with Hadoop-based data lakes. One of the reasons for this limited performance is that the underlying HDFS storage can't efficiently store data for faster BI performance. Also, query engines like Hive (based on the MapReduce processing framework) are not best suited for analytical workloads.

No support for ACID, updates, and deletes

Since HDFS is immutable storage, users running workloads in Hive cannot perform direct updates. You have to handle any updates or deletes programmatically. The missing transactional support and absence of ACID properties are the main reasons data lakes need new technologies like open table formats, which enable developers to perform easy updates and deletes along with providing ACID support.

Reduced data quality

A data lake stores data in its raw form. It does not have strict quality controls like a warehouse. The data does not go through schema, technical, or business validations. These missing validations often lead to inaccurate and incomplete data.

Limited access control

In a data lake, there is limited scope for controlling data access permissions. Unlike data warehouses, there is no granular-level control over the data within a data lake. The access permission can only be set and managed at the object or file level.

Risk of becoming data swamps
    A data lake can quickly become a data swamp where data is dumped and persisted for years, but not leveraged. Reduced quality, limited access controls, and the absence of metadata can reduce data discoverability. This, in turn, affects users' ability to leverage the data for business benefits.

These challenges and limitations with data lakes and data warehouses imply a need to shift to a new architectural notion. In the next section, I'll discuss how modern data platforms leverage cloud technologies to overcome some of these challenges.

Modern Data Platforms

As cloud technology matured over the years, organizations realized that they could benefit by migrating their data workloads to the cloud. With this approach, there was a paradigm shift in implementing the data platforms in the cloud. Cloud not only offered a scalable infrastructure but also enabled organizations to implement data platforms much faster and much easier! Data platforms built using a *cloud-first* approach are popularly known as modern data platforms that offer all the benefits of cloud technologies. In this section, we will discuss these modern data platforms, their advantages, and their limitations.

A cloud-first approach means designing and implementing your platform by using cloud technologies exclusively, instead of being dependent on on-premises infrastructure. You can use IaaS (infrastructure as a service), PaaS (platform as a service), or SaaS (software as a service) cloud services to implement a scalable, durable, and reliable solution.

Finding Answers in the Cloud

Cloud technologies have offered various advantages and helped to overcome some of the limitations of traditional on-premises systems. Many data practitioners have upskilled on cloud technologies and tried to leverage their services to build modern data platforms.

Here are some of the key benefits the cloud offers for implementing modern data platforms:

On-demand provisioning and scalability
    Traditional, on-premises data warehouses and data lakes have always had a limited, fixed capacity. Adding new servers or nodes to existing clusters takes a lot of work. Any capacity extension request goes through long cycles of approval and

procurement process. Cloud helps you overcome these limitations with on-demand capacity extension, enabling you to scale your data platform easily and quickly. Most cloud service providers (CSPs) also offer auto-scaling features to extend the capacity dynamically, based on server loads.

Managed and serverless offerings

CSPs also offer managed or serverless services for processing big data workloads. You don't have to maintain and manage the clusters. Considering the time and effort needed from database administrators (DBAs) and Hadoop administrators in traditional architectures, cloud-managed services make managing the platform more straightforward.

Optimized cost and performance

The fact that traditional data warehouses and data lakes had to be provisioned on-premises and would be up and running 24/7 contributed to their cost significantly. Cloud enables infrastructure to run on demand, only when needed, and provides various levers for cost optimization, including hot and cold storage tiers, *spot* instances/machines, lifecycle management policies, and auto-scaling. Cloud helps to control costs based on required performance. You can provision infrastructure with a smaller configuration for low-priority workloads, thus reducing cost. You can provide larger clusters and memory-optimized compute resources for high-priority analytics workloads and quicker results. Such balanced control over performance and cost is impossible in traditional on-premises systems.

Spot instances/machines use the spare compute capacity provided by the CSPs. These are available at significantly lesser price than on-demand capacity. Since they are based on spare capacity, they can be interrupted at any point of time. If you are running any interruptible workloads (like dev/test), you should consider spot instances to reduce cost significantly.

Rapid innovations and faster time to market

Cloud helps to provision the necessary infrastructure quickly and provides features to scale it dynamically. Developers can focus on implementation activities and innovate faster instead of spending time managing the underlying infrastructure. Cloud also offers services for common data management activities like migration, replication, security, governance, continuous integration, and deployment—all of which helps reduce the time to market for products.

These factors have driven the modernization of traditional data platforms through use of cloud technologies.

Let's now discuss how organizations implement modern data platforms to support their data and analytics use cases. There are mainly two approaches that organizations have settled on to implement their modern data platforms:

- Standalone approach to implement either a cloud data warehouse or a cloud data lake
- A combined strategy to implement a two-tier storage system comprising of a cloud data lake and a cloud data warehouse

Standalone Approach

In this approach, organizations use cloud technologies to implement a data platform based on either a data warehouse architecture or a data lake architecture. These platforms are better known as cloud data warehouses or cloud data lakes based on their architecture.

Examples of some products that help to build these platforms are:

- Amazon S3, ADLS, and GCS (for cloud data lakes)
- Amazon Redshift, Azure Synapse Analytics, and Google BigQuery (for cloud data warehouses)

Benefits

The cloud implementations of a data warehouse or a data lake inherit all the individual benefits of these architectures and the previously mentioned cloud advantages. Cloud technologies help organizations to build a modern, scalable platform and also provide services to seamlessly transition from on-premises to cloud.

Limitations

On the other hand, these standalone platforms bring their own architectural limitations:

- Cloud data warehouses have limited capabilities for persisting and processing unstructured data, supporting AI/ML use cases, and implementing open platforms for cross-vendor data sharing.
- Cloud data lakes have moderate BI performance, missing ACID capabilities, and limited data governance.

Combined Approach

Organizations have started implementing a new architectural pattern combining a cloud data lake and a cloud data warehouse, to overcome the challenges mentioned in the previous section. This combined approach has two storage tiers:

- Cloud data lake to store the unstructured data for supporting AI/ML use cases
- Cloud data warehouse to store structured (and semi-structured) data for supporting BI use cases

This combined approach is not the same as the lakehouse approach, which has a single storage tier. Rather, the combined approach is based on a two-tier storage architecture, which has ultimately led to the evolution of the lakehouses. To simplify things, we will refer to this combined approach as combined architecture throughout this book.

Figure 2-3 shows the combined architecture that uses a cloud data lake (like Amazon S3) and a cloud data warehouse (like Amazon Redshift) for implementing a data platform. It is the architecture that most of today's organizations have adopted to implement their data platforms.

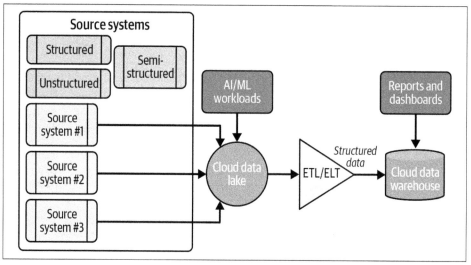

Figure 2-3. Data platform based on a combined architecture (cloud data lake + cloud data warehouse)

Benefits

This combined architecture powered by cloud technologies offers multiple benefits:

Cloud advantages
> On-demand, easy, and quick provisioning of resources helps to overcome the challenges faced by on-premises platforms. You also get the flexibility to use cheaper cloud object storage for data lakes and purpose-built data warehouse services for critical analytics workloads. Cloud object storage like Amazon S3, ADLS, or GCS offers unlimited capacity and can scale on demand. The cloud native warehouse services like Amazon Redshift, Azure Synapse Analytics, or Google BigQuery can also scale quickly based on the capacity required.

Data formats
> A combined architecture can support structured, semi-structured, and unstructured data. You can persist all raw data in the data lake and curated, well-organized, and structured data in the cloud warehouses.

Workloads
> With a two-tier storage approach, you can support diverse workloads like BI, AI/ML, ETL, and real-time use cases. As data lakes support AI/ML workloads and data warehouses help implement BI workloads, a combined architecture allows you to overcome the limitations these architectures face when implemented individually.

A complete platform
> As this architecture supports all data formats and diverse use cases, organizations can build a complete data platform for all data personas—including data engineers, data analysts, ML engineers, and visualization engineers—to implement various data and analytics use cases.

With these benefits, this combined two-tier architecture is one of the best approaches to implementing a modern data platform and supporting diverse use cases. But along with these benefits, it also has some significant limitations, as discussed in the next section.

Limitations

When I first implemented a data platform based on this combined architecture, I thought it was the best possible solution to all problems inherited from the individual architectures. It offered the best features from data lakes and data warehouses and seemed to have the potential to overcome most of the challenges of standalone systems. However, I soon realized that it is complex to implement, maintain, and manage such platforms.

Here are some key challenges I observed when dealing with such architectures:

Data duplication

The combined architecture persists large volumes of data in both storage tiers. While the data lake stores all the data extracted from source systems, a substantial data set is copied to a data warehouse for BI analytics. As the data grows, the amount of data duplicated in the warehouse keeps increasing. Since there are two storage tiers, constant data copying from the data lake to the data warehouse is required. This continuous copying of data means more effort is needed to sync the data between the two tiers. Similarly, copying data from the data warehouse back to the data lake is often required for some ML use cases that need processed or aggregated data.

Metadata mismatches

Metadata (schema) of data lakes and data warehouses are different, and it is not easy to sync the metadata between these systems. The data types used by data lake technologies can differ from those available in a data warehouse. Additional efforts are required to convert the data types when moving data between the two storage tiers.

Difficult access control

Managing access-control policies between two systems is challenging. Data warehouses can have fine-grained controls at the column and row levels. Data lakes govern access at the file or object level. Having similar access control across the two systems often requires bespoke (customized) implementations.

Mediocre user experience

Users need to know where data resides before querying, as there is no unified storage layer to access data from both tiers. Also, it is not easy to join the raw data from the lake and aggregate data from the warehouse for interactive analysis.

The drawbacks of the combined approach have led to the evolution of lakehouse architecture that combines the features of data warehouses and data lakes to form a unified modern platform. Organizations have many expectations from such modern platforms built using these architectural patterns. In the next section, I'll discuss these expectations in more detail.

Expectations of Modern Data Platforms

When organizations invest in a program to implement a data platform, they expect it to do more than just overcome the limitations of their existing platforms. They expect it to be robust, scalable, and future-proof.

Figure 2-4 shows the features that are commonly expected from a modern data platform.

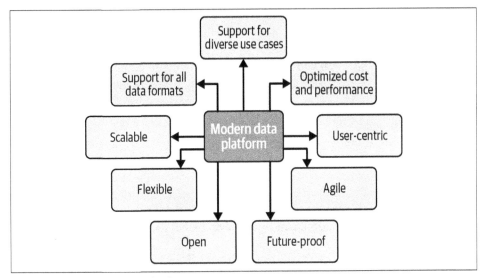

Figure 2-4. Modern data platform expectations

Let's examine these expectations in detail:

Support for all data formats and diverse use cases
Relatively new systems like wearables, smartphones, and IoT-enabled machines generate unstructured data, including images, audio, video, and logs. Modern data platforms should support storing and effectively processing large volumes of structured data as well as unstructured data from external systems to leverage it for diverse use cases. These include BI reporting, advanced analytics, streaming, self-serve analytics, ML, and AI use cases.

Scalable, flexible, and open
As technologies advance rapidly, the modern data platform should leverage and benefit from them to implement scalable and flexible solutions. Modern data platforms should use cloud technologies and should be flexible in order to quickly adjust to changing business demands. Modern platforms should also use open technologies to easily interact with other systems and offer the freedom to integrate with products from different vendors or CSPs.

Optimized cost and performance
Organizations are always striving to strike the right balance between performance and cost. Modern platforms should provide the right levers for optimizing costs with satisfactory performance depending on the workloads. They should give the required flexibility to choose between cost and performance depending on a given workload's priority, urgency, and complexity.

User-centric (easy to adopt)

As data architectures evolved, data platforms used architectures that combined different design approaches to support various analytics use cases. This resulted in complex systems that end users found challenging to adopt. Modern data platforms should be user-centric and simple enough for different data personas to use them effectively.

Agile and future-proof

Agility is one of the most sought-after expectations from modern data platforms. Whether it is a business need for faster time to market or a technology requirement for faster streaming analytics, agility drives design and architecture decisions. Modern data platforms should be agile, enabling organizations to reduce time to market for their products. At the same time, they should be flexible to accommodate future use cases, meet user demands, and leverage technology advancements.

You can now relate these expectations for a modern data platform with the key characteristics of lakehouse architecture you learned in Chapter 1. Lakehouse architecture is a natural progression of the two-tier combined architecture that many organizations are using to implement modern data platforms. Lakehouse architecture overcomes the limitations of standalone systems and, at the same time, also helps to build a simple, unified, and open platform—which are the basic expectations of a modern data platform.

In the next section, we will compare modern data platforms built using the different architectural patterns that we have discussed so far.

Comparison: Data Warehouse, Data Lake, Lakehouse

Now that you understand the traditional architectures, the expectations of modern data platforms, and the fundamental lakehouse concepts discussed in Chapter 1, let's compare platforms built using these architectural patterns.

Based on my observations and analysis, I've listed key points to help data architects and leaders make practical decisions. I've compared the architectures across the following four categories:

- Capabilities and limitations
- Implementation activities
- Administration and management
- Business outcomes

Please note that we will be discussing the modern data platforms built using cloud technologies rather than the traditional on-premises systems. Since today's data-driven organizations are rapidly adopting cloud technologies, it would make sense to compare the modern platforms, categorized as follows:

- The modern versions of the traditional architectures
  — Standalone cloud data warehouse
  — Standalone cloud data lake
- The widely adopted architecture pattern in recent times—a combined approach comprised of a cloud data lake and a cloud data warehouse
- The relatively new lakehouse architecture

Capabilities and Limitations

Here, I compare the capabilities and limitations that data architects should consider when choosing an architecture.

Standalone cloud data warehouse

- Simplified architecture, well-proven, and widely adopted for decades across industries
- Supports storing and processing structured and semi-structured data
- Best-in-class performance for BI workloads; ideal for implementing BI use cases, decision support systems (DSS), and management information systems (MIS)
- Proprietary storage and native processing engines are highly optimized to work together to perform better than data lakes
- Needs to be complemented with a data lake to support unstructured data for enabling AI/ML workloads that need direct access to data
- Suitable for batch processing; can face latency-related challenges for streaming use cases
- Not best suited for sharing data with external data consumers, as the data in the warehouse cannot be shared across vendor platforms

Standalone cloud data lake

- Simple, single-tier storage architecture that supports all data formats; widely adopted since the advent of Hadoop and cloud technologies
- Can easily handle large volumes of unstructured data
- Best suited for AI/ML workloads requiring large volumes of unstructured data
- Can support BI workloads with limited performance; needs to be complemented with a data warehouse to support enhanced BI performance
- Supports real-time processing along with batch processing

- Uses open file formats for storing data in lakes, making sharing data with external consumers easier

Combined architecture

- Complex, two-tier storage architecture needs to constantly sync data between the lake and the warehouse
- Supports large volumes of structured, semi-structured, and unstructured data
- Data lake storage enables implementing AI/ML, streaming, and other use cases; the dedicated data warehouse supports BI workloads
- Excellent BI performance for data residing in the data warehouse; queries executed on the data lake are not performant
- Supports real-time processing along with batch processing
- Data in the warehouse cannot be shared across vendor platforms, limiting the data-sharing capabilities

Lakehouse architecture

- Simple, unified, open architecture that supports all data formats and diverse workloads using single-tier storage
- Supports large volumes of structured, semi-structured, and unstructured data
- Can exhibit excellent BI performance when used with a compatible query engine; underlying open table formats provide better performance compared to data lakes
- Capabilities to implement unified solution for batch and stream processing using the same code with minimum latency and better throughput
- Leverages new, open technologies that can open up multiple possibilities for future use cases like data sharing and exchange with the outside world

Lakehouse architecture enables the building of a simple and open platform that offers all the features of combined architectures and the simplicity of standalone systems. It supports different data formats and diverse sets of data and analytics use cases, making it one of the best architectures for implementing modern data platforms.

Implementation Activities

For each of the four architectures, here are the implementation-related factors that data engineers should consider when implementing data pipelines.

Standalone cloud data warehouse

- Supports various low-code and no-code ETL tools and SQL; Python and Spark support is limited and still evolving
- Strict schema validations help to improve data quality before loading data in the warehouse
- Supports updates and deletes using simple SQL commands; as RDBMS is the underlying technology, data warehouses are ACID-compliant, ensuring data operations do not leave any inconsistent, messy data
- It is easier to optimize standalone cloud data warehouse performance using features like indexes, partitions, and materialized views.

Standalone cloud data lake

- Spark-skilled data engineers can implement data pipelines quickly but SQL support is limited
- The schema is not applied, while storing the data can reduce data quality
- Uses underlying storage technologies that are immutable; these do not support direct updates or deletes; custom code is needed to perform any updates or deletes
- Not ACID compliant; data engineers must take extra measures to handle concurrency and data consistency

Combined architecture

- Complex to implement data pipelines; need additional jobs to constantly sync the data within the two storage tiers
- Strict schema validations make processing and storing quality data in the warehouse easier; schema on read approach reduces the quality of data stored in the lake but avoids data loss
- Data in the warehouse can be updated using simple SQL commands; data in the lake needs custom code for implementing updates and deletes
- Data warehouse is ACID compliant; data lake does not support ACID features; additional efforts required to maintain consistent data in data lakes

Lakehouse architecture

- All data resides in a single storage tier, making development activities much easier than the two-tier combined approach

- Schema validation and evolution are supported to ensure data consistency across systems and flexibility to support frequent schema changes, avoiding any data loss

- Quality improves as data moves to higher zones of the lakehouse; data engineers can apply various rules to validate and cleanse data before storing it in higher zones (we will discuss this in more detail in Chapter 7)

- Supports updates and deletes like the warehouse system using the features provided by underlying open table format technologies

- ACID properties enabled by underlying open table formats make it easier for data engineers to implement data pipelines, resulting in consistent data

- A lakehouse helps to unify batch and stream processing, reducing implementation and code-maintenance efforts

Lakehouse architecture helps the data engineering teams build platforms much more easily than other architectures by leveraging features like direct updates and deletes, ACID transactions, and schema evolution. Its unified approach is its most significant advantage over the combined architecture, which helps to reduce the implementation efforts and code complexity.

Administration and Management

Here are the key points that administrators should consider when implementing administration and management processes for each architectural style.

Standalone cloud data warehouse

- Administrators must invest efforts to back up data regularly and restore it when required

- There are no native features to track every transaction; administrators and support engineers have to implement custom solutions by using features like triggers or change data capture (CDC) for audit tracking at a record level

- Some cloud warehouse products can retain all versions of records and support time travel, but most of the cloud native data warehouse services do not offer this feature

Standalone cloud data lake

- Like standalone cloud warehouses, administrators must perform regular backups (snapshots) of data lakes; features like versioning can help maintain history at the object level but add to overall maintenance overhead
- Transaction-level audit tracking is not supported; only file- or object-level tracing is possible
- Administrators must implement lifecycle policies to archive or delete data for cost optimizations

Combined architecture

- Additional administration efforts needed to manage two storage tiers, provision users, and sync permissions
- As data resides in two storage tiers, support engineers must monitor the pipelines for syncing data and metadata
- Out-of-box feature for transaction-level audit tracking is not possible

Lakehouse architecture

- Single storage tier reduces monitoring activities to validate data and metadata sync between different storage tiers
- Time travel feature helps quickly retrieve older versions of records, reducing the need for ad hoc backups
- Audit tracking is easy because the transactional layer tracks changes at the transaction level
- Some open table formats also offer cloning features for incrementally replicating data
- Helps to reprocess and replay data easily for rectifying any erroneous data loads

With lakehouse architecture, you don't need to invest additional efforts to maintain data in two fundamentally different storage tiers. With the built-in transaction-level tracking, auditing within the lakehouse becomes much easier. Lakehouse architecture enables you to build platforms that are easier to manage, maintain, and that can roll back to earlier states of data using the time travel feature.

Business Outcomes

The most important aspects of the data platform are to ensure that it helps achieve the desired business outcomes, reduce overall cost, and provide good return on investment (RoI) for the business sponsors and leaders. Here is a quick comparison of business outcomes for each of the four architectures:

Standalone cloud data warehouse

- Faster implementation cycles than data lakes; helps achieve quick time to market for products
- Use proprietary storage formats and native processing engines, resulting in higher costs due to proprietary storage and compute
- Proprietary storage makes sharing data with consumers using different vendor products difficult; this reduces the benefits associated with data sharing and exchange
- Due to a lack of support for unstructured data, the business loses the opportunity to leverage its data for performing predictions, recommendations, and forecasting

Standalone cloud data lake

- Organizations can reduce their overall costs since all data can reside in the lake, which is much cheaper than the proprietary warehouse storage
- Open-source compute engines like Spark and Presto help reduce the compute cost
- There is no vendor lock-in; anyone can access data stored in the lake without specific proprietary software, enabling data-sharing opportunities
- Lacks data governance and quality, thus reducing consumers' trust in data

Combined architecture

- Additional costs for managing data movement between the lake and the warehouse; the data warehouse's proprietary storage and compute engine increases the overall cost
- Other vendors and data consumers can access the data stored in the data lake; the data stored in the warehouse uses proprietary storage formats, making it difficult for consumers on other vendor platforms to access it
- Inherits the data-sharing limitations of warehouses

Lakehouse architecture

- Quick and easy data discovery for business users with the help of data catalogs that hold technical and business metadata

- Cheap, scalable cloud storage houses all the data, reducing the overall storage cost; open-source compatible processing engines help further bring down compute costs

- Operational expenses minimized compared to two-tier storage systems

- All data resides in data lakes using open technologies, making it easier for any data consumer to access the data, irrespective of the vendor product platforms

- Open storage formats enable enhanced, secured, and open data-sharing mechanisms with the outside world, increasing business opportunities associated with data-sharing and exchange initiatives

Lakehouse architecture is beneficial not just from a technical perspective, but also from a business perspective. It helps reduce overall costs by using open technologies and by employing a single storage tier. It also provides multiple avenues to leverage business data by enabling secure data sharing. Lakehouse architecture also has various features that can reduce overall time to market for business products.

Lakehouse Architecture: The Default Choice for Future Data Platforms?

Four types of organizations might consider implementing a new data platform or changing their existing one:

- Organizations that do not have an enterprise-wide data platform and are looking to implement a central data repository

- Organizations with a data platform on their on-premises infrastructure that want to migrate to the cloud

- Organizations that use standalone cloud data warehouses or standalone cloud data lakes and want to implement a combined approach to support different use cases

- Organizations that use the combined approach to implement their data platforms and are now looking for a simple, unified approach

Considering the expectations from a modern data platform and after studying the benefits and limitations of each architectural style, you would probably agree that moving to lakehouse architecture could benefit all of these organizations. Whether building a new data platform from scratch or planning to redesign an existing landscape, lakehouse architecture is becoming a top contender.

The rise in products and services that support lakehouse architectures from Microsoft, AWS, Databricks and many others indicates its growing popularity among vendors and data practitioners.

Though its popularity is rising slowly, lakehouse architecture may soon become the default choice for implementing modern data platforms.

Key Takeaways

Table 2-1 shows a quick summary of the comparison of various architectures used for implementing a data platform.

Table 2-1. Comparison summary of different architectures

Architecture pattern	Features
Cloud data warehouse	• **Architecture:** Simple, single storage tier • **Data formats:** Mostly structured and semi-structured • **Use cases:** BI reports, MIS, DSS • **Workload frequency:** Batch • **Implementation features:** Supports SQL, ACID features, easy updates/deletes • **Data quality:** Good data quality, strict schema validations • **Access control:** Well-governed, fine-grained access control • **Data sharing:** Internal or external consumers using same vendor platform • **Performance:** Excellent BI performance • **Cost:** High cost due to proprietary storage and engine • **Risks:** Vendor lock-in, difficult to migrate to other vendor platforms
Cloud data lake	• **Architecture:** Simple, single storage tier • **Data formats:** Structured, semi-structured, unstructured • **Use cases:** AI/ML, real time, BI (limited performance) • **Workload frequency:** Batch and real time • **Implementation features:** Support for Spark, no direct updates/deletes, no ACID support • **Data quality:** Reduced data quality, no strict schema validations • **Access control:** File/object level access control • **Data sharing:** Consumers get open, direct access to files in data lake • **Performance:** Limited BI performance • **Cost:** Cheaper as no proprietary storage • **Risk:** Without governance, can easily get converted into data swamps

Architecture pattern	Features
Combined architecture	• **Architecture:** Complex two-tier storage (data lake and data warehouse) • **Data formats:** Structured, semi-structured, unstructured • **Use cases:** BI, AI/ML, real time • **Workload frequency:** Batch, real time • **Implementation features:** Supports ACID, updates/deletes for warehouse data only • **Data quality:** Good data quality for warehouse data, reduced quality for data stored in lake • **Access control:** Fine-grained in warehouse, file level for lake data • **Data sharing:** Open for lake, limited for data in warehouse • **Performance:** Best BI performance for warehouse data, limited for data lake • **Cost:** High cost due to proprietary warehouse storage, additional syncing efforts between lake and warehouse • **Risks:** Data between storage tiers can get out of sync, vendor lock-in risk for the warehouse data
Lakehouse architecture	• **Architecture:** Simple, single storage tier, unified and open • **Data formats:** Structured, semi-structured, unstructured • **Use cases:** Supports all use cases—BI, AI, real time, ETL • **Workload frequency:** Batch and real time • **Implementation features:** Support for ACID, update/delete, schema evolution • **Data quality:** Improved quality in higher storage zones • **Access control:** Well-governed, fine-grained access control • **Data sharing:** Open, easy to share with consumers across vendor platforms • **Performance:** Good BI performance • **Cost:** Cheaper as no proprietary storage and compute engines • **Risk:** Relatively new architectural approach

In the first two chapters of this book, I've given you an overview of the traditional architectures and modern data platforms and introduced you to the lakehouse architecture. The next chapter focuses on the storage layer in lakehouse architecture. I'll explain the different file and table formats, their benefits, and the differences you should consider while making design decisions.

References

- Ralph Kimball's dimensional modeling techniques (*https://oreil.ly/-2X-k*)
- Data lake versus data warehouse versus lakehouse (*https://oreil.ly/6WjRa*)
- What Is a Data Mart? (*https://oreil.ly/Au5y_*)
- ACID guarantees (*https://oreil.ly/ZgfPD*)
- What Is a Data Lake? (*https://oreil.ly/ZN7dc*)
- What Is a Data Warehouse? (*https://oreil.ly/SQzJj*)

CHAPTER 3

Storage: The Heart of the Lakehouse

The storage layer is the heart of any data platform. In platforms based on lakehouse architecture, it plays a significant role in efficiently persisting all types of data and improving the performance of queries. The lakehouse storage layer consists of cloud storage, file formats, and table formats. In this chapter, we will focus on understanding these concepts and the available technologies to implement the lakehouse storage layer.

I'll explain the fundamental concepts related to lakehouse storage, the difference between row-wise and columnar stores, and how storage is closely associated with performance. We will then dive deep into the file formats used to store data for analytics use cases, the benefits of using each format, and the key features you should consider while building a data platform.

Once you understand these concepts, it will be easier to discuss this chapter's core topic—the open table formats. We will discuss the leading table formats, their features and benefits, and specific limitations that you should keep in mind when making any design decisions.

In the last section of this chapter, I'll discuss the key design considerations for choosing the right table format for your use case. This will help you to make better design decisions while working on your day-to-day projects.

Lakehouse Storage: Key Concepts

The storage layer is the backbone of a data ecosystem. When you implement a data platform, you need a durable, reliable, and highly available storage layer that can persist large volumes of historical data of all types. Lakehouse platforms need a storage layer that can also enable fast retrieval, support ACID features, and preserve older versions of data.

Before diving deeper into the specifics of the storage layer and its components, let's first discuss two important concepts that will be referred to often when we discuss the file and table formats: row versus columnar storage, and storage-based performance.

Row Versus Columnar Storage

Whenever you create a table or insert records into a table, the data physically gets stored as data files in the underlying storage hardware and disks. Modern data platforms use cloud storage for persisting data. There are two approaches to storing data:

- Row-based approach
- Column-based approach

Table 3-1 shows a sample product table. Let's consider this table to understand these two approaches.

Table 3-1. Sample product table

product_id	product_name	product_category
22	keyboard	computer accessory
12	headphone	computer accessory
3	mobile case	computer accessory

In a row-based approach, the data is stored row by row on the physical disk. Table 3-2 shows how the query stores the product data using a row-based approach.

Table 3-2. Row-based storage

22	keyboard	computer accessory	12	headphone	computer accessory	3	mobile case	computer accessory

When you execute a select query to retrieve the data, it reads the complete row from the disk. This is beneficial in cases where the query wants to read all columns from the data. However, analytical workloads generally consist of reading a few columns as aggregations or summarizations. Due to the nature of row-based storage, the query has to read all columns across many records, irrespective of the number of columns required by the query.

In the columnar format, the data is stored as columns on the physical storage. Table 3-3 shows how the data is stored (same product table from earlier example) based on its columns.

Table 3-3. Columnar storage

22	12	3	keyboard	headphone	mobile case	computer accessory	computer accessory	computer accessory

For analytical queries, columnar storage helps quickly retrieve the data by scanning only those disk blocks where these columns are stored. Unlike row-based storage, the query does not have to scan the full record for a few specific columns. This approach enables faster data retrieval, especially in cases where the tables have hundreds of attributes and the query needs only a few columns. Also, as the data from the same columns are stored together, it is much easier to apply compression on the same data types, thus reducing the overall file size.

Storage-based Performance Optimization

Storage is not just about persisting the data. It also enables the compute engines to retrieve the required result faster by reducing the data to be scanned. It's not only the compute engines that determine the performance, but also the underlying storage.

The data retrieval time for any analytical query is severely impacted by the amount of data scanned. The less data it scans, the less time it takes to fetch the result. Some file and table formats (discussed later in this chapter) help to minimize the data that a query needs to scan for retrieving the results. The process for minimizing that data is also known as data skipping or row skipping.

There are different approaches to skip unwanted data, including:

- Partition or file pruning, which helps in reducing the number of partitions or files that need to be scanned by the query
- Indexing and clustering, which helps in fetching the exact records required by queries instead of scanning the whole table
- Maintaining column-level statistics (like min and max values for each column), which helps to scan only the relevant data blocks where required records would be present

Different file and table formats employ these techniques to reduce data scans and retrieve results quickly. Instead of increasing the compute capacity to improve the query performance, always strive to first fetch only the relevant data by considering the following:

- Selecting only required attributes
- Partitioning or clustering tables
- Maintaining column stats
- Other similar data-skipping approaches

Now that you understand these key storage concepts, let's discuss the technologies and components used to implement lakehouse storage.

Lakehouse Storage Components

The lakehouse storage layer consists of three main components:

- Cloud object storage for storing the data
- Open file formats for compressing data and support distributed processing
- Open table formats for providing the transactional capabilities and efficient data retrieval

Let's first look at cloud object storage, which provides the storage capabilities.

Cloud Object Storage

The storage layer is responsible for persisting all the data in lakehouse architecture. Cloud storage is best suited for storing large volumes of data that varies in nature, type, size, and speed at which it is received.

Figure 3-1 shows the lakehouse storage layer with different cloud technologies that can be used for implementing it.

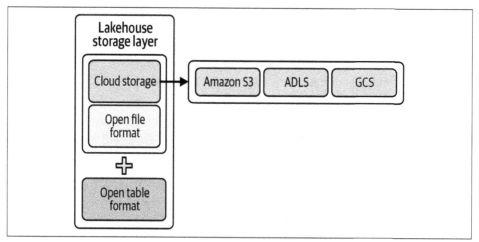

Figure 3-1. Popular technology options for cloud storage

Storage characteristics

The technology used to implement the physical storage should exhibit the following fundamental characteristics:

Durability
    Storage should be highly durable and able to persist data for as much time as required by the system. The underlying technology should ensure that the data does not get corrupted and that there are measures taken to avoid any data loss.

Availability

Data should always be available for its consumers whenever they want to use it. Even during any downtime of the service that provides the storage, it should have enough backups to present the required data to consumers.

Scalability

The data storage service should be easily scalable—able to scale up as the data growth demands without any manual intervention.

Cost

The storage should be available at cheaper cost (as compared to purpose-built storages like a data warehouse) and should also provide levers to optimize cost by moving data across hot and cold storage tiers.

Security

One of the most important characteristics of a storage layer is to provide built-in security. It should provide features to protect the data at rest within the storage layer.

Most of the cloud storages like Amazon S3 (*https://aws.amazon.com/s3*), ADLS Gen2 (*https://oreil.ly/m899p*) (referred as ADLS throughout this book), and GCS (*https://cloud.google.com/storage*) offer all of these as built-in features and are top choices for implementing a lakehouse platform. HDFS can also be used for implementing the storage layer but, as discussed in Chapter 1, we will restrict our discussion in this book to cloud technologies because they are most suitable for building the modern data platforms.

File Formats

The next component within the storage layer is the file format. The file formats define the approach to storing the data on the cloud storage. The data is stored using a row-based approach or a columnar approach. Modern file formats offer different encoding schemes for data compression and the ability to split the data files to support distributed processing.

Organizations have been using many popular file formats for storing and exchanging data, including CSV, JSON, and XML. However, these file formats have some key limitations for handling big data:

- They have limited compression capabilities, thus taking up more storage space.
- Data retrieval time is significantly higher and analytical queries often take a long time to fetch the required results.
- Data scanned is not limited to only required columns; queries often scan entire rows to process the result.

- Some do not have the built-in schema, which must be explicitly defined while reading these files.

- They need to be in their uncompressed, raw form to support splitting for distributed processing.

What Is a Splitable File Format?

In distributed processing, data is distributed across various clusters to support parallel processing. When a file is stored on these distributed storages, it needs to be stored into various data blocks, or chunks, so that multiple processes can read these blocks. The file format used to store data should support splitting the file into multiple blocks. The files in big data systems are often of large volumes and compressed to save storage and to perform better. They should be splitable in their compressed form to perform distributed processing. Big data file formats support such splitting when compressed using algorithms like Snappy, LZO, bzip2, and others. However, the traditional formats like CSV cannot be split when compressed using GZIP compression.

For storing and processing large volumes of big data, you need open file formats with good compression ratios, optimized data retrieval, and data-skipping capabilities. Considering the above limitations, various organizations and product vendors like Cloudera (*https://www.cloudera.com*) and Hortonworks have introduced purpose-built file formats for processing the big data workloads in Hadoop ecosystems. These formats have been widely adopted even in modern platforms built using cloud technologies.

This section will discuss these file formats, their benefits, and limitations. The three most popular open file formats are:

- Apache Parquet
- Apache ORC
- Apache Avro

Figure 3-2 shows the technologies used to implement the file format component. Parquet, Avro, and ORC are open file formats based on open technologies available as part of the Apache Software Foundation (ASF) ecosystem.

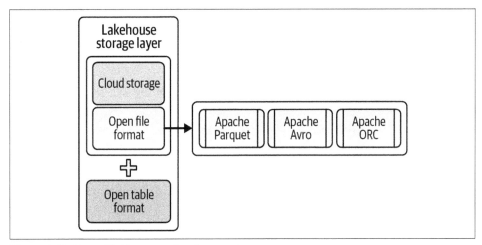

Figure 3-2. Open file format technology options

Parquet

Parquet, created in 2013, has been adopted by many organizations for their big data workloads. It is an open source file format that uses columnar storage to store and retrieve data efficiently. Parquet provides much better compression ratios than CSV and JSON file formats and provides enhanced performance for handling complex data.

File layout. Figure 3-3 shows a simplified version of the Parquet file format based on the ASF documentation (*https://oreil.ly/mM2TT*).

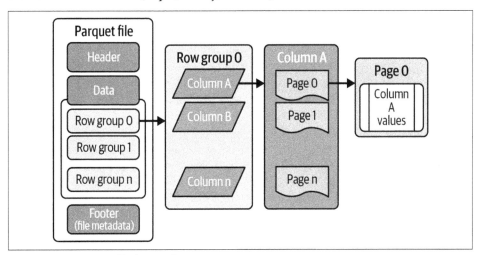

Figure 3-3. Parquet file format layout

The Parquet file structure is as follows:

- Every parquet file consists of a header, footer, and data block.
- The header has details that indicate the file is in Parquet format.
- The data block consists of multiple row groups that logically combine various rows within the file.
- The row groups consist of columns present in the file.
- The values within each column are stored as pages. Pages are the most granular data elements within Parquet.
- The file footer consists of metadata of row groups and columns. The metadata includes stats like min/max values. Compute engines use these min/max values from the footer for data skipping.

Key features. Parquet offers several features compared to file formats like TXT, CSV, and JSON:

- The compression it applies while storing the data reduces the file size significantly based on its *encoding* techniques on columnar data stores (see note about encoding at the end of this section).
- Parquet, being columnar storage, can retrieve only the required columns instead of scanning all the columns stored on disk. This helps improve the performance of analytical queries that often need only a few columns for aggregations.
- Parquet files have the schema information of the records, which helps load the data easily in tables and split the file for distributed processing using frameworks like Apache Spark.

Most organizations building an on-premises or cloud-based data platform use Parquet as their primary data format. It is the default format for Spark, the most widely adopted processing framework for big data workloads. Parquet has also become a top choice for leading vendor platforms like Microsoft Fabric (OneLake (*https://oreil.ly/ XHafh*)) and Databricks (Delta Lake).

Open file formats like Parquet convert the data into binary form before storing it on the disk. This binary conversion is known as encoding and can help in compressing the data considerably with respect to its raw, human-readable form. There are various encoding techniques including Plain, Dictionary, Bit Packing, and Run Length Encoding (RLE) that are used individually or in combination by the file formats for compressing data and supporting faster retrieval.

ORC

ORC (Optimized Row Columnar), like Parquet, is also a columnar file format and successor to Apache Hive's standard RCFile format. ORC provides ACID support, has built-in indexes for faster data retrieval, and supports complex data types like struct, lists, and maps.

File layout. Figure 3-4 shows a simplified version of the ORC file format based on the ASF documentation (*https://oreil.ly/mfoGA*).

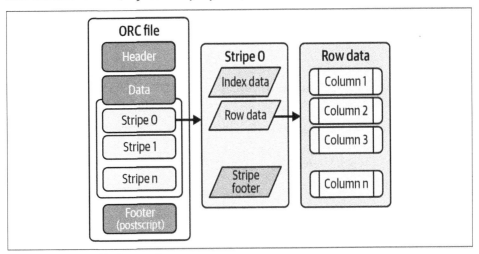

Figure 3-4. ORC file format layout

The ORC file format is as follows:

- Each ORC file contains the header, footer, and multiple data blocks known as stripes.
- The header has details to indicate that the file is in ORC format.
- Each stripe consists of index data, row data, and stripe footer.
- Index data holds the indexes for the stored data and stores the min and max values for row groups.
- Row data holds the actual data used in scanning.
- The stripe footer contains details related to each column, including encoding, location, min, and max values.
- The file footer contains statistics related to stripes in the files, the number of rows in each stripe, and other helpful information that can help skip data.

ORC has 3 levels of indexes:

- File level to store column statistics across the entire file
- Stripe level to store column statistics across for each stripe
- Row level to store column statistics across each set of 10,000 rows within a stripe

File- and stripe-level column statistics are stored in the file footer (similar to Parquet) to skip the rest of the file during scanning.

Key features.   ORC offers several features and benefits as compared to CSV, JSON, and TXT files:

- ORC has a deep integration with Hive. It was initially created as the file format for storing data in Hadoop that would be processed using Hive.
- Since ORC is a columnar file format, it offers better compression ratios than CSV and JSON.
- ORC is the only file format that enables Hive to offer ACID features for transactional processing.

ORC has been used mostly in Hadoop ecosystems that use Hive extensively for processing data. Most organizations implementing their data ecosystem using Hortonworks Data Platform (HDP) adopted ORC as their primary format.

Avro

Avro is an open source, row-based data serialization format for creating Avro data files. Avro is one of the most preferred formats for Hadoop ecosystems. Organizations use Avro extensively in modern data platforms for persisting large volumes of raw data for further ETL processing.

File layout.   Figure 3-5 shows a simplified version of the Avro file format based on the ASF Avro documentation (*https://oreil.ly/OwQOW*).

An Avro file consists of a header and one or more data blocks. The header consists of file metadata, including the schema, name of the compression code, and a randomly-generated sync marker that helps in splitting the file. Each data block consists of the following:

- Count of objects in that block
- Size of that block (post-compression)
- Data stored as serialized objects in its compressed form
- File's 16-bit sync marker

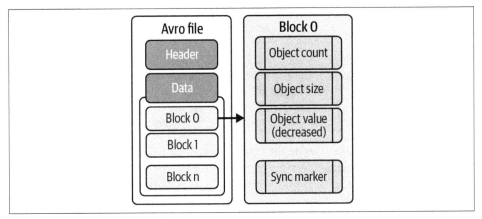

Figure 3-5. Avro file format layout

This layout helps to efficiently extract or skip data while also detecting any corrupt blocks.

Key features.   Like Parquet and ORC, Avro also offers some unique features that help in storing and processing large volumes of data:

- Its self-describing nature means it stores the schema along with the data, and any reader can access the schema while reading the data.
- The schema is stored as JSON or in Avro IDL (AVDL) format, which makes it human-readable, while the actual data is stored as binary to get better compression ratios.
- Avro supports schema evolution, making it an excellent choice for implementing ETL-like workloads to accommodate schema changes.
- Avro file is splitable, which means it can be used in distributed processing even in its compressed form, thus helping in faster data processing.
- It supports multiple languages, including JAVA, C, C++, C#, and Python.

Avro is best suited for implementing use cases like ETL pipelines for processing big data and in systems that need support for handling schema changes.

Similarities, differences, and use cases

All these file formats aim to efficiently store the data and improve query performance while reading the data. All three have similar features that help achieve these goals; however, they have key differences based on their approach to storing and compressing data.

Here is a summary of their similarities and differences which will help you compare and select one based on your use case:

Supported data formats

All three formats support storing large volumes of structured and unstructured data. Organizations have used these formats extensively for implementing Hadoop-based data platforms.

Compression

All three file formats offer higher compression than CSV, TXT, and JSON files. This helps in reducing the storage capacity and also helps in improving query performance. Parquet and ORC offer better compression as compared to Avro file formats.

Figure 3-6 shows a quick comparison of the compression ratios provided by these file formats for a 2 GB uncompressed CSV file.

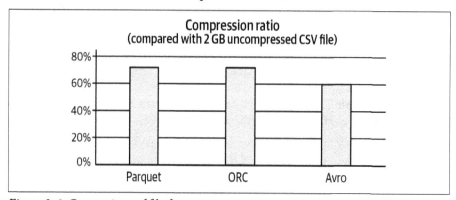

Figure 3-6. Comparison of file format compression ratios

As compared to an uncompressed CSV file, ORC and Parquet provided approximately 70-75% compression, while Avro provided around 55-60% compression. These are compared with uncompressed CSV files, as compressed CSV files are not splitable.

 I used Amazon EMR Spark for creating the output files used in this comparison without changing any default settings. In the above comparison, Parquet and ORC file sizes are post-Snappy compression.

Splitable

Parquet, ORC, and Avro are splitable and can support distributed processing without uncompressing the data, which results in fewer data scans and faster data retrieval.

Adoption and use cases

All three file formats are widely used for implementing big data workloads:

Parquet is widely used across organizations and is arguably the most popular format among the three. It integrates easily with Spark, one of the most popular processing frameworks.

ORC has deep integration with Hive and is the only format that supports Hive with ACID features.

Avro is great for ETL workloads where changing schema is a common scenario.

Being columnar, Parquet and ORC are better suited for analytics workloads where only a few columns are retrieved.

File format layout

Parquet and ORC follow the columnar format for storing data but have different approaches to implementation. While Parquet stores data as pages, ORC stores data as stripes. Avro follows the row-based approach and stores data in blocks. These different approaches impact their compression ratios and data-skipping abilities.

Data scanned

Avro gives better performance for write operations as compared to Parquet and ORC. Parquet and ORC perform better when reading a subset of columns for analytical purposes, as they can skip data based on column values.

Figure 3-7 shows the amount of data scanned for retrieving a single column from tables created using these file formats.

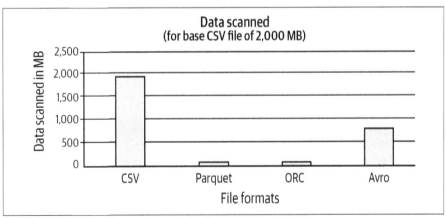

Figure 3-7. Comparison of file format data scans

Please note that queries running on tables created using CSV and Avro format scanned the complete data, while ORC and Parquet tables scanned much less data (corresponding to a single column) since they use a columnar format

Schema evolution

Avro supports schema evolution—columns can be added or modified. Parquet and ORC only support adding columns at the end (after the last column).

For analytics workloads, the columnar format is best suited for data retrieval. Both ORC and Parquet offer good compression levels and faster data retrieval. ORC best suits Hive implementations and Parquet works great with Spark. Considering most of the modern vendor data platforms have adopted Parquet, it could potentially be your first choice for storing data for analytics workloads. You can complement it with Avro for storing raw data used in the ETL process. Be sure to carefully review your use cases before selecting the file formats.

Table Formats

In Chapter 1, you learned about open table formats that help enable data lakes with data warehouse-like capabilities. A table format helps to organize the data files for each table. It consists of information related to data files like schema details, file create and update time, number of records in each file, and record-level operation types (addition and deletion). Table formats give data lakes ACID features, support for updates and deletes, and data-skipping capabilities, thus improving the performance of queries.

In this section, we will dive deep into these open table formats to understand their architecture and features. However, before we discuss the modern table formats, let's understand Hive, which is an earlier generation table format used in traditional Hadoop ecosystems.

Hive

Data lakes became popular with the rise of Hadoop technologies, which used HDFS as the primary storage. Hive provides the structure and the capabilities to execute analytical workloads on HDFS data. It is one of the most popular and widely adopted technologies for building data warehouse systems within Hadoop clusters.

Hive has key components like HiveServer2 (HS2), Hive Metastore (HMS), and Beeline (CLI for Hive) as part of its services. It uses HDFS to store the data and MapReduce to process it. This section will focus on how Hive, as a table format, stores and reads the data.

Hive has a central metadata repository known as Hive Metastore (HMS) for storing the schema details of Hive tables. It also stores the information related to partitions for each table. Many modern cataloging tools, like AWS Glue and Databricks, use HMS for storing metadata. We will discuss metastores and catalogs in more detail in Chapter 4.

Unlike other traditional data warehouses, you don't need to load the data in the Hive warehouse. The data resides within the data lake storage (HDFS, cloud object storage), and Hive provides the metadata layer on top of this data lake storage. This metadata layer provides the schema for Hive tables.

Figure 3-8 shows the Hive table directory structure.

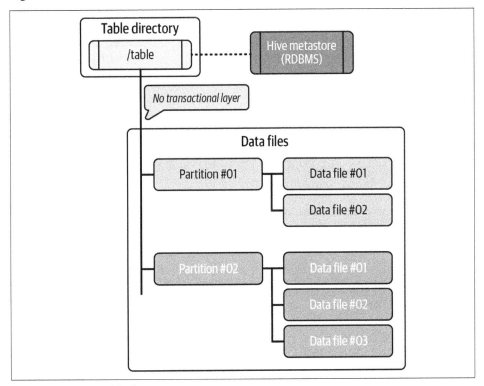

Figure 3-8. Hive table directory structure

When you create a table in Hive, it stores the data in HDFS and the schema in the HMS. The Hive table directory has all files under its root table folder. If you partition this table, it creates additional partitional-level directories and places the relevant data files under these directories.

The data always resides in the data lake (in this case, HDFS) and does not get loaded into any other dedicated warehouse storage, thus enabling users to build a system like a lakehouse with only a single storage tier. Some of Hive's key features include:

Partitioning

Hive supports partitions on tables, which helps optimize queries to scan only the required partitions instead of the complete table.

Supported file formats

Hive supports various file formats for storing data, including CSV, JSON, Parquet, ORC, and Avro, which increases its flexibility.

Supports multiple engines

You can access HMS through multiple compute engines, including Spark, Presto, and other commercial query engines.

Hive also has several limitations, however, that have influenced the evolution of modern table formats. Some limitations that restrict Hive from being used as a lakehouse table format include:

No ACID support

Hive does not support out-of-the-box ACID features, which leads to inconsistent data. Hive with ORC file format provides limited ACID support; however, there is no ACID support for formats like Parquet and Avro, which can lead to data corruption and concurrency issues.

Limited performance

Query planning often takes longer, as Hive does not maintain versions or snapshots of data. Hive has to list all files within a directory in order to identify the files required for data retrieval, adding to the overall performance overhead for larger tables.

No support for update and delete operations

You cannot directly update or delete any record present in the Hive table by executing a SQL command. Since the data resides on HDFS, which is immutable, there is no direct approach to update or delete records. If you want to modify a few records, you must first identify the partitions in which they reside, drop all these partitions, and re-create the partitions with modified and original non-impacted records. This results in longer processing time and unnecessary deletion and re-creation of large volumes of data.

All these limitations have led to the evolution of modern open table formats, which organizations have slowly shifted toward to implement their data ecosystems.

Figure 3-9 shows the three popular open table formats—Apache Iceberg, Apache Hudi, and Delta Lake—for implementing lakehouse architecture.

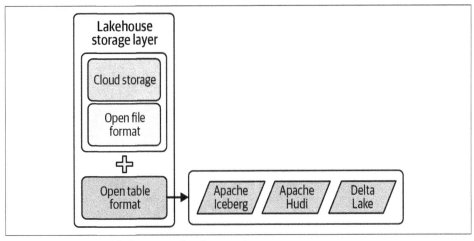

Figure 3-9. Open table format technology options

As we discussed earlier, the data is stored in the cloud storage as data files. A table format provides an additional transactional layer on top of these data files.

Let's now look at the three popular open table formats you can consider implementing in your data platforms.

Iceberg

Iceberg, started at Netflix, is one of the widely adopted open table formats—used by organizations like Apple, Netflix, and Airbnb—and is supported by various vendor platforms, including Dremio (*https://www.dremio.com*), Snowflake (*https://www.snow flake.com*), and Tabular (*https://tabular.io*). It has recently gained popularity due to its rich feature set and ability to support Parquet, ORC, and Avro file formats.

Table layout.   Figure 3-10 shows the Iceberg layout, based on the Apache Iceberg specification (*https://oreil.ly/z-y_J*). Iceberg consists of two major parts: a metadata layer and a data layer.

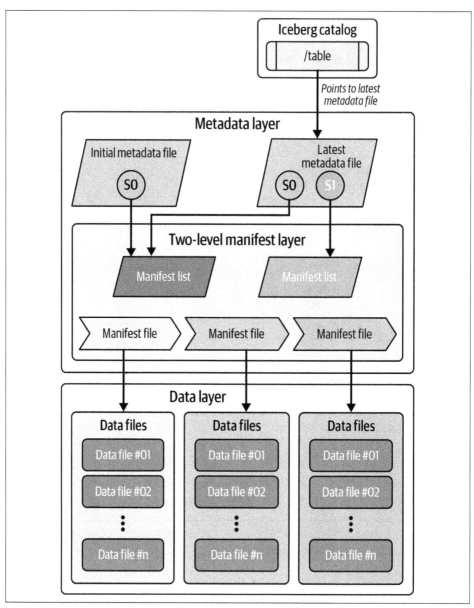

Figure 3-10. Iceberg table layout structure

The directory structure of Iceberg is as follows:

Iceberg catalog
Iceberg catalog gives the table location and points to the latest metadata file.

Metadata layer
The metadata layer consists of multiple elements:

- Like the Hive metastore, Iceberg stores the schema details partition information in a metadata file.
- There is a section in the metadata file known as Snapshot. Each snapshot points to a file known as a "manifest list." For every new transaction, a new snapshot is added to the metadata file.
- A manifest list points to all the manifest files that belong to specific snapshots.
- These manifest files store a list of data files and column statistics details.

Data layer
Iceberg supports Parquet, ORC, and Avro file formats for writing the data in files.

Key features. Now that you understand the underlying structure of Iceberg, let's discuss its features and benefits:

ACID support
ACID support is one of the most important features of a platform built with lakehouse architecture. Iceberg supports ACID properties and provides consistency and isolation for concurrent reads and writes.

Schema evolution
Iceberg supports schema evolution, which helps accommodate any schema changes at source systems to ensure no data loss when storing the data.

Hidden partitioning
In the earlier table formats, like Hive, to make effective use of partitions, you had to use the partition column in filter predicates. It was not possible to use any transformations on these partition columns. For example, a table partitioned on "date" (YYYYMMDD) cannot limit the data scans to specific months when you use only "month" in your filter conditions. Iceberg offers a feature known as hidden partitions. These help you to perform transformations on partition columns and limit the scans based on partition transformations.

Partition evolution

As the data increases with time, the existing partitions might need to be changed for better query performance. In such cases, the only option in Hive was to rewrite the table based on the new partitions. Iceberg offers a feature to evolve these partitions without the need to rewrite the data.

Time travel

Time travel helps in querying historical data and viewing previous versions of records that have been updated or deleted.

File format supported

At the time of writing this book, Iceberg is the only format that supports all three file formats—Parquet, ORC, and Avro—for storing data.

These are just some of the important features that Iceberg offers. If you plan to use Iceberg as a table format for implementing your lakehouse platform, you can refer to *Apache Iceberg: The Definitive Guide* by Tomer Shiran, Jason Hughes, and Alex Merced (O'Reilly) for a deeper understanding of this topic.

Hudi

Hudi (which stands for Hadoop Upserts Deletes and Incrementals) is a streaming data lake platform that brings data warehouse capabilities to data lakes. It can perform record-level upserts and deletes and support incremental data processing. Created at Uber, Hudi primarily aimed to provide an efficient, incremental data processing framework and later became open source under the Apache Foundation.

The overall Hudi stack is much more than just a table format. In this section, we will focus on the table format features of Hudi that you can use for implementing modern data platforms.

Table layout. Figure 3-11 shows the data layout for Hudi based on the official Apache Hudi documentation (*https://oreil.ly/Nxy_G*).

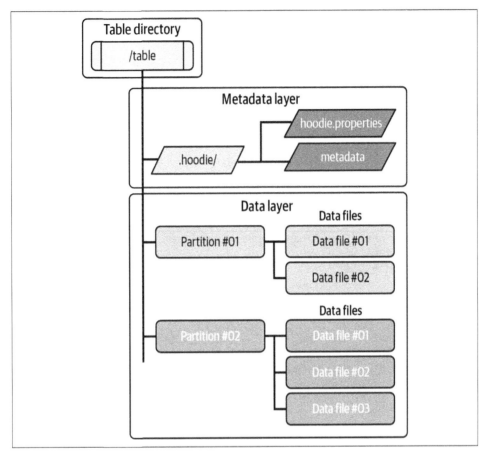

Figure 3-11. Hudi table directory structure

Metadata layer

Hudi stores the transaction logs in the *.hoodie* directory. The table metadata gets stored in the metadata directory under the *.hoodie* directory. Hudi also creates a *hoodie.properties* file to persist table-level configurations. The writers and readers of the table use this configuration file.

Data layer

Based on the columns used for table partitioning, sub-directories are created under the base path for distinct column values to store the data files. Hudi stores these data files as either base files or log files.

Let's look at the various directories and files that form the Hudi data management framework.

Key features. Hudi offers multiple features that can help implement a lakehouse platform:

Support for ACID, updates, and deletes
Hudi enables data lakes with ACID transaction guarantees and provides isolation between writer and reader queries. It also enables users to perform record-level upserts and deletes.

Time travel
You can query previous states of data using the time travel capabilities that Hudi offers. This feature can help you easily revert to older versions of the table, debug changes, and maintain audit history

Performance optimizations
Hudi offers various performance-optimization features including:

- Clustering, which helps to co-locate data next to each other
- Indexing, which enables efficient upserts and deletes
- Compaction, which helps to perform low-latency ingestion and faster reads

Commit timeline
Hudi maintains a timeline of all commits performed on the table with file information created as part of each transaction. Incremental queries use these commits to fetch records inserted and to update after a specific commit time.

Supported query types
Hudi supports three types of queries:

- Snapshot queries on real-time data, using a combination of columnar and row-based storage
- Incremental queries for change streams of records that are inserted or updated after a specific time
- Read-optimized queries, which provide enhanced query performance using columnar storage

Table types

For performance optimizations based on workloads, Hudi supports two types of tables: Copy On Write (COW) and Merge On Read (MOR).

COW writes the entire Parquet file again, even for a single record change. Whenever the user performs any transaction, Hudi creates a new Parquet file consisting of all the records from previous versions plus the changes from that transaction. This approach makes updates slower but query performance faster.

MOR does not create a copy of an existing file. It only maintains the changes performed in the transaction in another log file created using Avro format. When a reader executes a query to retrieve results, Hudi merges the change logs to create a new Parquet file that the reader can use to retrieve the data. MOR is best suited for frequent table updates but can impact query performance for large volumes of small-size change log files that have not been compacted.

If you plan to use Hudi as the table format for implementing your lakehouse-based platform, you must explore these concepts in more detail. For a further understanding of these concepts, refer to the Apache Hudi FAQs (*https://oreil.ly/JPhhm*).

Linux Foundation's Delta Lake

Delta Lake is another technology that is growing in popularity among data practitioners. It is an open technology, originally created at Databricks and later made open source as part of the Linux Foundation. It supports several compute engines, including Spark, PrestoDB, and Trino. Like Iceberg and Hudi, Delta Lake also offers transactional capabilities to data lakes to enable them to have data warehouse-like features.

Table layout. Figure 3-12 shows the underlying data management directory structure of Delta Lake.

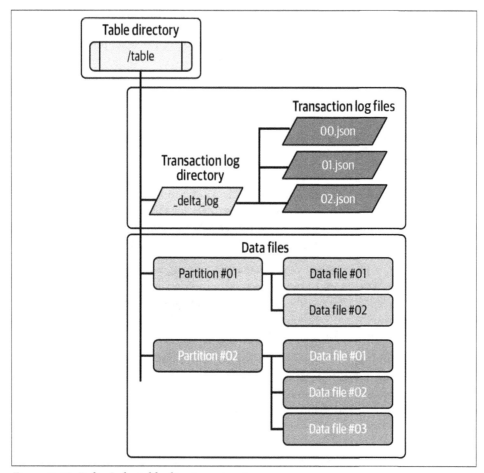

Figure 3-12. Delta Lake table directory structure

Like the other open table formats, Delta Lake consists of metadata and data layers:

Metadata layer

The metadata layer consists of a *_delta_log* folder that holds the JSON files that Delta Lake creates for every transaction. These JSON files within that folder contain metadata and transaction details. The metadata has details related to the table schema, including attribute name, type, and whether it is nullable. It also holds information about partitions. The transaction holds details of the data files, size, modification time, and min/max values in each attribute. The transaction log files in the *_delta_log* folder has an entry for every transaction, indicating whether a data file was added or removed as part of the transaction.

Data layer

Delta Lake uses the Parquet file format to store data and uses Snappy as the default algorithm for data compression.

Key features. Delta Lake offers several features that enable data lakes to perform like data warehouses:

ACID support

Multiple writers can modify a table simultaneously. Readers can continue viewing consistent data even if another job changes the table.

Update, Delete, and Merge support

You can quickly delete or update records to implement use cases like Slowly Changing Dimensions (SCD) or streaming upsert operations.

Time travel

You can maintain all versions of the records and get any previous versions based on timestamps or version numbers.

Schema enforcement and evolution

Schema enforcement features ensure that any records with schema variations get rejected during the data-insertion process. Delta Lake also supports schema evolution to accommodate source records with metadata variations to ensure no data loss.

Batch and streaming unification

Any delta table can be a batch table, streaming source, or sink, thus enabling users to implement a unified code for batch and streaming use cases.

Vacuum

The vacuum command helps to delete older versions of files and keep only the required versions, based on specific timestamps or version numbers.

Optimize and Z-order

The optimize feature helps reduce several "small" files by compacting them to create larger ones. Z-order reorganizes the data in storage to allow queries to read less data for faster processing. This also helps the queries to skip a large number of unwanted data files.

Deletion vector is another storage optimization technique employed by open table formats like Delta Lake. Whenever records are deleted in Delta Lake, it rewrites the Parquet file. Some of the delta operations can use these vectors to mark deleted records without rewriting the file. Subsequent read operators can skip these records based on these deletion vectors. At the time of writing this book, the deletion vectors feature is available in Delta Lake (*https://oreil.ly/Y7SIs*) in experimental support mode.

Cloning

"Shallow" cloning of delta tables creates copies of specific table versions without copying the source files. The Databricks Delta Lake also provides "deep" clones that make a copy of source files in the clone table directory. Clones can help in activities like taking regular backups and creating data for testing, which enables users to work with specific table versions.

All the above features—its deep integration with Spark and support from Microsoft and Databricks—makes Delta Lake one of the top table format choices for implementing a lakehouse platform. If you want to do a deeper dive into Delta Lake, see *Delta Lake: The Definitive Guide* (O'Reilly).

Similarities, differences, and use cases

Now that we have discussed the underlying structure and features of the three table formats, let's compare them based on key design parameters. We will only focus on the practical design aspects that can help you make design decisions while selecting the table formats:

ACID support

Iceberg, Hudi, and Delta Lake all provide ACID guarantees for transactions. They also enable data lakes to support update and delete operations at a record level. This one feature makes these technologies suitable for implementing lakehouse architectures and sets them apart from the previously adopted Hive format for querying data in data lakes.

Time travel

Time travel is one of the critical features of a lakehouse platform and all three table formats support it. Each of these table formats can preserve older versions of data and restore them based on the version number or timestamp.

Schema evolution

All three formats support schema evolution features. You can easily add, drop, or rename a column without rewriting the data again.

Support for incremental data processing
  Incremental processing is an important feature for building ETL pipelines:

  - Hudi supports efficient, incremental processing by tracking appends, updates, and deletes as change streams. It has record-level indexes to process these streams efficiently.

  - Delta Lake has a similar feature known as change data feed (*https://oreil.ly/ X7xYG*), which is in experimental support mode at the time of writing this book.

  - Iceberg has a similar feature but only supports append (*https://oreil.ly/ DLQvP*). Support for replace, overwrite, and delete is not yet available.

Partitioning and clustering
  Partitioning and clustering are common techniques often used for performance optimization:

  - Iceberg has a unique feature for supporting partition evolution. It helps you to update the partitions without rewriting the data.

  - Delta Lake has a feature known as liquid clustering (*https://oreil.ly/SxQqV*) (in experimental support mode at the time of writing) that can help change clustering columns without rewriting the data.

  - Along similar lines, Hudi uses clustering to improve query performance and adjust the data layout as data evolves.

Support for file formats
  All three table formats support Parquet, which is one of the most adopted file formats by the modern data platforms:

  - Iceberg supports the Parquet, ORC, and Avro.

  - Hudi supports Parquet and ORC.

  - Delta Lake only supports Parquet.

Data quality validations
  Data quality validations help to validate source data and reject any erroneous records:

  - Delta Lake supports constraints to ensure data quality and integrity. It provides a `NULL` constraint to validate `NOT NULL` values and `CHECK` constraints to validate if the specified Boolean expression (for example, `product_id > 10`) is true or false for each input record.

  - Hudi also has a feature called pre-commit validators to check the data quality while writing data.

  - Iceberg does not yet have a feature for such validations.

Adoption and use cases

All three formats are best suited for implementing lakehouse-based platforms. Various product vendors have started supporting these formats as part of their services:

- Delta-Parquet is a popular combination that organizations use to implement use cases on Azure. Delta Lake exhibits excellent performance with Spark and is one of the top choices for Spark-heavy ecosystems.

- Organizations using AWS have started adopting Hudi as AWS has deep Hudi integration.

- Many organizations are considering Iceberg because it supports multiple file formats, partition evolution features, and support from many vendor products, including Dremio, Tabular, Starburst, and Snowflake.

Interoperability

As these table formats evolve, you might see platforms using different formats for different use cases and interoperability between these open formats. Delta Universal Format (UniForm) (*https://oreil.ly/UTk5d*) and Apache XTable (*https://xtable.apache.org*) could be just the start of such initiatives. This will further help to bring openness to lakehouse platforms and allow users to avoid making tough choices to decide on a single table format for their platform. We will discuss these interoperability features in more detail in Chapter 9.

We've covered some of the key features that you can consider while designing your lakehouse platform. There are multiple other features that you can explore based on your use case. However, I recommend avoiding making the final design decisions based only on available features in the latest and the greatest version. All these formats are evolving and might start supporting the missing features sooner or later. There are other critical factors that you should consider while designing your system. We'll discuss these design considerations in the next section.

Key Design Considerations

So far, we have discussed the file and table formats and their key features. It's time to discuss the key considerations for selecting one of the open table formats for implementing your platform.

Making a design decision is not easy. And if the choice is between new technologies with similar features, it becomes even more challenging. In this section, I'll discuss specific factors you can consider while deciding. Use these considerations as a guide while evaluating the technologies for your use case, based on your organization's approved tech stack.

Ecosystem Support

While deciding the table formats, it is essential to consider the complete ecosystem you are planning to build. Are you implementing a multi-cloud system? Do you plan to implement the data platform using only one of the cloud systems? Do you plan to complement it with other vendor products?

For example, if your tech landscape uses Azure, and there is already investment in Databricks, it would make sense to use Delta-Parquet as a combination as it has deep support within the Microsoft ecosystem.

You can consider Hudi for AWS-based implementations because multiple AWS services like Glue, EMR, Athena, and Glue Catalog have deep integration with Hudi. You can consider Iceberg if you need write support in Athena SQL. At the time of writing, Iceberg is the only format supporting the write operations in Athena SQL.

Always go through the CSP documentation to understand if there are any limitations. A good example is Azure Synapse Serverless SQL limitations (*https://oreil.ly/hTkVQ*) or Amazon Athena limitations (*https://oreil.ly/olyMd*) for using Delta Lake format.

Community Support

For open source technologies, community contributions and support are crucial for resolving issues, implementing changes, and continuing to innovate. Iceberg, Hudi, and Delta Lake have vibrant communities, Slack channels, and other initiatives where the community has regular discussions.

Figure 3-13 shows a simple comparison of Git repositories of these technologies. Git repositories have three key parameters: Stars, Forks, and Watchers. These parameters let you compare and understand their popularity and adoption.

If you only consider the Stars for the repository, Delta Lake is the most popular, though Databricks made Delta Lake open source much later than Hudi and Iceberg. Forks and Watchers for Hudi are much more than the other two. As seen in these charts, this trend has been the same after a year-long period between mid-2023 to mid-2024.

These charts are generated by referring to the individual repositories of these three table formats:

- GitHub—apache/iceberg (*https://github.com/apache/iceberg*)
- GitHub—apache/hudi: Upserts, Deletes And Incremental Processing on Big Data (*https://github.com/apache/hudi*)
- GitHub—delta-io/delta (*https://github.com/delta-io/delta*)

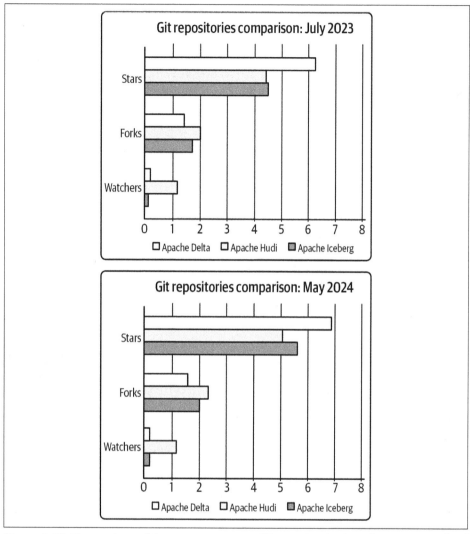

Figure 3-13. Comparison of three parameters on Git repositories (numbers are in scale of 1,000)

Supported File Formats

The file formats supported by these open table formats can significantly influence your design decisions, especially if you want to migrate your existing big data workloads to a lakehouse platform.

For example, consider a use case where your existing on-premises landscape uses the Hortonworks Data Platform (HDP), and most data storage files are in ORC format. In this case, you can consider Iceberg or Hudi, as they support ORC format.

However, if you use the Azure or Databricks platform with Delta Lake, it will not support the ORC file format. In that case, you must convert all your existing ORC files to Parquet, as Delta Lake only supports the Parquet file format. This conversion of ORC to Parquet for large volumes of historical data can be a significant activity and a key factor in making design decisions. Consider the existing data storage formats while designing the new lakehouse platform.

Supported Compute Engines

As the table formats are still evolving, they don't yet have the full support of all the compute engines. Iceberg, Hudi, and Delta Lake support the widely adopted open source compute engines like Spark, Trino, Presto, Flink, and Hive. However, in most cases, you might use some of the native services of leading CSPs like Amazon Athena, Google BigQuery, or Azure Synapse Analytics. Table formats might have some limitations while working with these commercial compute engines. Be sure to carefully evaluate these limitations before making design decisions.

As an example, consider a scenario where you use Azure as your cloud platform and would like to use Iceberg due to its support for various file formats and partition-evolution features. However, Synapse has native support only for the Delta Lake format. In this case, you will have to manually install and configure Iceberg libraries in Synapse Spark notebooks or use an alternative approach like HDInsight cluster to process Iceberg files on ADLS.

The compatibility between compute engines and table formats is a significant consideration while making design decisions. As the table formats and compute engines evolve, they will start supporting other technologies. We will discuss the compute engines in more detail in Chapter 5.

Supported Features

Each open table format offers standard features like ACID support, schema evolution, and time travel. However, some provide unique features, as follows:

- Iceberg provides partition evolution and hidden partitioning.
- Hudi offers bulk loading optimizations, efficient incremental processing, and COW and MOR table options.
- Delta Lake offers data sharing, converting existing Parquet files to Delta, and built-in data quality validations.

If any of these features play an extensive role in your use case, consider the specific table format that offers them. As these technologies evolve further, it might be worth considering a mix of table formats based on relevant use cases and not restricting the platform users to only a single format.

Commercial Product Support

Most open source technologies have an equivalent managed offering provided by the CSPs or other product vendors. Databricks (*https://www.databricks.com*) created Delta Lake and offers it as a core component within its lakehouse platform. The creators of Hudi have founded Onehouse (*https://www.onehouse.ai*), a commercial offering for the Hudi platform. Dremio (*https://www.dremio.com*) and Tabular (*https://tabular.io*) offer managed Iceberg for building lakehouses. The commercial offerings often help the community to grow by adding contributions and new features. Evaluate these products if you want to go with the commercial offerings for implementing your lakehouse architectures. Some of the key points to consider are multi-cloud support, ease of use, implementation features, performance optimizations, and (the most significant consideration for commercial products) total cost of ownership (TCO).

Current and Future Versions

One table format might not have all the features available in other table formats. The absence of these features from their latest version should not be the only reason to reject a specific format. As the formats evolve, these missing features might be made available in future versions.

For example, consider a case where the latest Delta Lake version is unavailable in Azure Synapse Spark pools. If you want to use features from the latest version, you must wait until it is made available in Azure or look for alternative implementation approaches. Make a choice based on the time sensitivity and criticality of your use case.

Performance Benchmarking

Performance benchmarking is a debatable parameter and might not be the best approach to deciding on a specific technology. Many vendors and System Integrator (SI) partners do benchmarking exercises based on Transaction Processing Performance Council (TPC) standards and publish the comparison results.

Benchmarking exercises to compare different technologies require a good understanding of all configurations and settings of these technologies. Product vendors would have good knowledge of their own products but might not be aware of the critical settings of the competing products to get the best performance, which might result in inconsistent observations across the executions. *TPC* gives guidance for standard queries and datasets but cannot provide the technology-specific configurations that differ from tool to tool.

The other option is to perform a benchmarking exercise independently, in a controlled environment, by carefully considering all the configurations and settings. In that case, you must invest a lot of time and effort. In today's fast-moving world, you won't have the time (and budget) to learn all technologies and perform the benchmarking exercise!

Benchmarking exercises done by third parties can be considered better, unbiased, and more reliable. A practical approach is to use these benchmarking reports as a reference to validate the performance of your preferred table format but not make a final decision based only on the benchmarking results.

What Is TPC?

TPC (*https://www.tpc.org*) is an organization formed by member companies and associates that provide guidance for performing tests for benchmarking the performance of various tools and technologies.

TPC provides a couple of benchmarking frameworks for decision support systems, known as TPC-H and TPC-DS. Many product vendors use TPC-DS for performance benchmarking of modern data platforms. TPC-DS provides a set of 99 queries that differ in complexity and amount of data scanned, which users can execute on a large volume dataset based on a standard data model provided by the benchmarking framework. You will find TPC-DS benchmarking results for most of the vendor platforms that you can use as a reference.

Comparisons

Before you make a final decision on the table format, be sure to review various comparisons, blogs, and articles from the platform vendors you plan to use for implementing your data platform.

Most of the time, you would have already decided on the cloud platform before deciding on the table formats. Native cloud services might work much better with one format than the others, so be sure to reference their documentation to understand limitations (if any) with table formats and to make the call.

For example, AWS has published a detailed blog (*https://oreil.ly/7-qgf*) to compare the three formats and their integration with AWS. Look for the information that focuses on the AWS integrations with the table format of your choice.

Sharing Features

One of the key drivers for implementing lakehouse architecture is its ability to easily share data with consumers. There is no need to copy or replicate the data in a lakehouse. Also, the consumers don't need to be on the same vendor platform as producers. Lakehouses help to implement platforms that offer data democratization and sharing features via data marketplace. When deciding the underlying table formats, consider the sharing features that they provide. Delta Lake supports data sharing via its delta sharing feature as well as fine-grained access controls.

When evaluating the different table formats, you can consider these points. For making final decisions, the best approach is to take a holistic view of your data platform, considering the overall tech stack of your organization and the use cases that you plan to implement.

Key Takeaways

Here is a quick summary of the file formats and table formats that we've discussed in this chapter. Tables 3-4 and 3-5 summarize the comparison between the file formats and table formats.

Table 3-4. Comparison of file formats

File format	Features
Parquet	• **Storage type**: Columnar storage • **Best suited for**: Analytical queries, Spark workloads • **Compression**: Better compression than Avro, CSV files • **Data scanned**: Much less, only related to column selected • **Adoption**: Widely adopted, used as default file format for Spark
ORC	• **Storage type**: Columnar storage • **Best suited for**: Analytical queries, enables ACID features in Hive • **Compression**: Better compression than Avro, CSV files • **Data scanned**: Much less, only related to column selected • **Adoption**: Popular among HDP users
Avro	• **Storage type**: Row-based storage • **Best suited for**: Row-level transactions, frequent inserts/updates, write-intensive workloads • **Compression**: Better compression than CSV files, not as good as Parquet and ORC • **Data scanned**: Much more as compared to Parquet and ORC • **Adoption**: Widely used for Kafka messages due to its compact format and schema-evolution features

Table 3-5. Comparison of open table formats

Table format	Features
Iceberg	• **File format support**: Parquet, ORC, Avro • **Suitable use cases**: Workloads that need changing partitions, support for multiple file formats, non-Spark compute engines • **Key features**: ACID compliant, time travel, partition evolution • **Limitations**: No data quality constraints • **Has deep integrations with**: AWS, GCP, Dremio, Tabular, Snowflake

Table format	Features
Hudi	• **File format support:** Parquet, ORC • **Suitable use cases:** Incremental processing, AWS implementations, multiple file formats • **Key features:** ACID compliance, time travel, incremental processing, indexes • **Limitations:** No partition evolution, no support for Avro • **Has deep integrations with:** AWS, Onehouse
Delta Lake	• **File format support:** Parquet • **Suitable use cases:** Workloads using Spark engines, Azure implementations • **Key features:** ACID compliance, time travel, cloning, Z-ordering, sharing • **Limitations:** Works only with Parquet • **Has deep integrations with:** Azure, Databricks, Microsoft Fabric

Remember these points:

- Any single file or table format cannot offer all the best features or easy integrations that you might need. You will either have to compromise on some features or plan to have more than one format within your data platform.

- You should perform a proof of concept, or implement a pilot phase, to understand which format best suits your use case and integrates well with your cloud platform.

- All these formats are evolving. Any missing features might come sooner than later. Don't reject a table format just on the basis of a missing feature.

I hope this chapter has given you a better understanding of the storage layer and its components. In the next chapter, we will discuss the metastore and data catalogs and their significance in lakehouse architecture.

References

File Formats
- Apache Avro (*https://avro.apache.org*)

- Apache Parquet (*https://parquet.apache.org*)

- Apache ORC (*https://orc.apache.org*)

- Avro Data (O'Reilly conference video) (*https://oreil.ly/PcgBa*)

- ORC Indexes (*https://orc.apache.org/docs/indexes.html*)

Iceberg
- Documentation (*https://iceberg.apache.org/docs/latest*)

- Tabular (*https://tabular.io*)

- Dremio (*https://www.dremio.com*)

- GitHub—apache/iceberg (*https://github.com/apache/iceberg*)

Hudi
- Onehouse (*https://www.onehouse.ai*)
- GitHub—apache/hudi: Upserts, Deletes And Incremental Processing on Big Data (*https://github.com/apache/hudi*)
- Build Your Apache Hudi Data Lake on AWS Using Amazon EMR – Part 1 (*https://oreil.ly/kg4iR*)
- Spark Guide | Apache Hudi (*https://hudi.apache.org/docs/quick-start-guide*)
- Apache Hudi vs Delta Lake vs Apache Iceberg - Data Lakehouse Feature Comparison (*https://oreil.ly/jYVAb*)

Delta Lake
- Delta Lake (*https://delta.io*)
- Delta Lake Time Travel (*https://delta.io/blog/2023-02-01-delta-lake-time-travel*)
- GitHub—delta-io/delta (*https://github.com/delta-io/delta*)
- Databricks (*https://www.databricks.com*)

Others
- Apache Hive (*https://hive.apache.org*)
- Apache Spark (*https://spark.apache.org*)
- *The Cloud Data Lake* by Rukmani Gopalan (O'Reilly)

CHAPTER 4

Data Catalogs

The storage layer within the lakehouse architecture is important, as it stores the data for the entire platform. To search, explore, and discover this stored data, users need a data catalog. This chapter will focus on understanding a data catalog and the overall metadata management process that enables lakehouse platform users to search and access the data.

In the first section of this chapter, I'll explain fundamental concepts like metadata, metastore, and data catalogs. These are not new concepts; organizations have long been implementing data catalogs in both traditional data warehouses and modern data platforms. I'll explain these core concepts first in order to set up our discussion of the advanced features later in the chapter.

We will discuss how data catalogs differ in lakehouse architecture, as compared to the traditional and combined architectures, and how they help users get a unified view of all metadata. We will also discuss the additional benefits of data catalogs in lakehouse architecture that allow users to leverage metadata to implement a unified data governance, permission control, lineage, and sharing mechanism.

In the last section of this chapter, I'll discuss some of the popular data catalog technology options available across cloud platforms. You'll learn about design considerations and practical limitations that can help you make an informed decision while designing the data catalogs in your lakehouse platform.

Understanding Metadata

Just as we need processes to manage the data within the platform, we also need well-defined approaches to manage the metadata. A sound metadata management process helps to simplify data search and discovery for platform users.

Metadata is often defined as "data about data." It is as significant as the data itself. Metadata helps define the data by providing additional information that describes the data like attribute name, datatype, filename, and file size.

Metadata provides the required structure and other relevant information to make sense of data. It helps users discover, understand, and find the exact data they need for their specific requirements.

Metadata is broadly categorized as technical metadata and business metadata.

Technical Metadata

Technical metadata provides technical information about the data. A simple example of technical metadata is the schema details of any table. The schema comprises attribute names, datatypes, lengths, and other associated information. Table 4-1 lists the schema of a product table with three attributes.

Table 4-1. Product table schema

Attribute name	Attribute type	Attribute length	Attribute constraint
product_id	integer		Not Null
product_name	string	100	Null
product_category	string	50	Null

Similar to tables, other objects (like files) also have metadata. File metadata provides details like the filename, creation or update time, file size, and access permission. Files like CSVs sometimes have a header record that defines the attribute names of the data. JSON and XML files also have attribute names within them. As seen in Chapter 3, file formats like Apache Parquet, Apache ORC, and Apache Avro also carry metadata information.

Business Metadata

Business metadata helps users understand the business meaning of data. Business metadata augments the technical metadata to give a business context to the data. Table 4-2 lists the business metadata of the product table.

Table 4-2. Product table business metadata

Attribute technical name	Attribute business name	Attribute business meaning
product_id	Product identifier	Unique identifier of the product
product_name	Product name	Name of the product
product_category	Product category	Category of the product

In this example, the technical attribute names are self-explanatory and you can easily understand their business meaning. However, this is not always the case.

Consider a scenario where you are using SAP as a source system and the SAP logistics module Materials Management (MM). MARA, which holds the general material data, is one of the widely used tables in this SAP module. As shown in Table 4-3, the technical names of these attributes are not self-explanatory and you would need to add a business context for users to understand what data each attribute holds.

Table 4-3. SAP MARA table business metadata

Attribute technical name	Attribute business name	Attribute business meaning
MANDT	Client	Client name
MATNR	Material number	Unique identifier of material
ERSDA	Created on	Date when the material entry was created

Technical and business metadata are essential to better understand the data in your platform. A sound *metadata management process* should provide capabilities to maintain and manage technical and business metadata. It should support governance and security features like access control, sensitive data handling, and data sharing, which we will discuss later in this chapter.

What Is Metadata Management?

The metadata management process is a set of activities that are carried out in order to:

- Create or ingest metadata from external and internal systems
- Add business context to the technical metadata
- Update and maintain various versions of metadata
- Organize the metadata for easier user discovery

The key objective of the metadata management process is to treat metadata like a first-class citizen within the data ecosystem, managing and maintaining its entire lifecycle.

How Metastores and Data Catalogs Work Together

While metadata management is a process to manage the metadata and make it available to users, we need solutions and tools to implement this process. Metastores and data catalogs are the solutions that help to build a sound metadata management process.

A metastore is a repository within the data platform where the metadata is physically stored. It acts as the central metadata storage system. You can access all metadata from this central storage.

A data catalog provides a mechanism to access the metadata stored within the metastore. It provides the required user interface to explore the metadata and search for various tables and attributes.

Figure 4-1 shows how metastores and data catalogs are related, and how they enable users to access metadata.

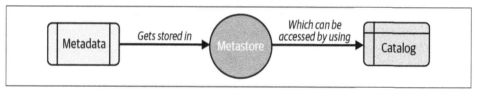

Figure 4-1. Metadata flow diagram

For example, in the traditional on-premises Hadoop ecosystems, Hive provided Hive Metastore (HMS) for storing metadata (for Hive tables created on top of HDFS data) and Hive catalog (HCatalog) to access the HMS tables from Spark or MapReduce applications.

Modern data catalogs provide a mechanism to manage metadata in a more organized way. They enable you to provision the right access controls to the right users so that they may access your data securely. You can logically divide the catalogs into databases or schemas that hold tables, views, and other objects. You can manage user access permissions at catalog-level or at the more granular schema- or table-level.

Figure 4-2 shows a real-world scenario of how a user might access specific catalogs based on their roles and permissions.

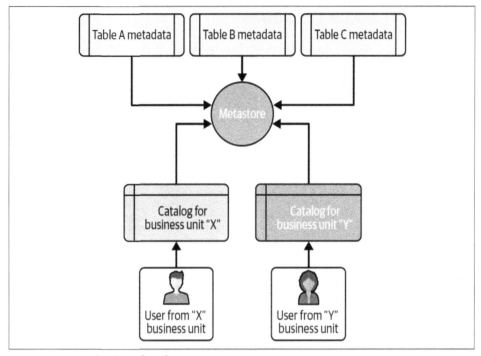

Figure 4-2. Catalog based on business units

As shown in Figure 4-2, users from "X" business unit can access only the catalog for business unit "X", and users from "Y" business unit can only access the catalog for business unit "Y."

It is not always necessary to categorize the catalogs based on business units. There can be various approaches and you can select what works best for you. You can create catalogs based on the various environments—like dev, test, and prod—or you can create one single catalog and control permissions at the schema- or table-level.

Many data practitioners use the terms metastores and data catalogs interchangeably to describe metadata storage systems. Most of the modern cloud services that offer data catalog capabilities abstract the physical storage of metadata and only expose the data catalogs for users to browse and access schema, tables, and attributes. Behind every catalog, there is a physical storage where the actual metadata is stored.

Features of a Data Catalog

Data catalogs provide several key features that help platform administrators organize, manage, and govern data. The features discussed in this section help platform users search, explore, and discover the relevant data quickly.

Search, Explore, and Discover Data

Data catalogs provide users with an easy mechanism to search the required data and to understand where (which schema, table, or attribute) data exists so that they can query it. Data catalogs also offer features to add business descriptions to the tables and attributes.

Users can traverse the catalog, understand the business context, and discover data that might help them in further analysis.

Data Classification

Classification is the process of categorizing attributes based on certain specifications or standards. You can classify attributes based on domains (like customer, product, and sales) or sensitivity (like confidential, internal, or public). Classification helps users to more fully understand and leverage the data. For example, an attribute classified as "internal" indicates that users should not share the data outside their organization.

As part of the classification process, you can add tags to your metadata. For example, consider a scenario where you are implementing a lakehouse for an insurance provider. You would have several tables with data related to customers—like customer name, date of birth, and national identifier. All such attributes are personally identifiable information, or *PII,* attributes. You can tag these attributes as "pii_attributes" in your catalog and use these tags to implement governance policies to abstract this sensitive data from non-eligible or external users. We will discuss how to handle sensitive data in more detail in Chapter 6.

PII attributes are portions of data that can be used to identify a particular individual and include national IDs, email IDs, phone numbers, and date of birth.

For compliance purposes, it is mandatory to abstract such information from data consumers. You should give access to PII attributes only to a specific set of users based on their organizational role.

You should also implement data governance policies to hide or mask such PII attributes from non-eligible users who are not authorized to see the values in the PII attributes.

Data classification helps in managing data, implementing governance policies, and securing data within the platform.

Data Governance and Security

Data catalogs act as gatekeepers of data and help in implementing the data governance and security policies necessary to manage, govern, and secure the data across the organization.

Data catalogs provide following governance and security features:

- Support for implementing standard rules and constraints for maintaining data quality
- Implement the audit process, like tracking users accessing specific tables or attributes, required for compliance reporting
- Support for fine-grained permission control for users who access the data
- Secure the platform data by providing capabilities to filter or abstract sensitive data stored within the platform
- Enable secure data sharing with data consumers

Data governance is a broad topic, and we'll cover it in more detail in Chapter 6.

Data Lineage

Any data and analytics ecosystem consists of multiple jobs that ingest the data from source systems, transform it, and finally load it to the target storage for users' consumption. Within this storage, there can be hundreds of tables with thousands of attributes, through which the data flows across various components. As the system grows, the data assets keep increasing. To track the data flow across components in your platform, you need a tracking mechanism to give end-to-end details about how the data navigates through these attributes. Data lineage is a process that provides information about this data flow across various components.

Data lineage can also help to perform impact analysis whenever any attribute name, type, or length changes. And it can help you to audit data assets, like tables, that are redundant or not used by any consumers. Data catalogs help you implement a data lineage solution to track the relationship between source and target attributes. We will discuss this in more detail in Chapter 6.

The features of a data catalog enable collaboration between different data teams and data personas within an organization, enabling business users to perform self-serve analysis by discovering and leveraging the data that they need to make better decisions.

Unified Data Catalog

As discussed in Chapter 2, the combined architecture faces several limitations because it uses two different storage tiers—one for data lake and one for data warehouse. In such systems, you also face challenges associated with managing separate, siloed metastores and catalogs for the data lake and the data warehouse.

Challenges of Siloed Metadata Management

Most of the challenges associated with the siloed, individual data storage tiers in the combined architecture also apply to metadata management. These challenges include:

Maintenance
> You need to maintain separate metadata for data lake objects and data warehouse tables, which adds to the overall maintenance efforts. You have to frequently replicate metadata between the two systems to sync changes from one system to another.

Data discovery
> Data discovery becomes challenging in combined architecture as users have to browse two different data catalogs. Some objects, like summarized tables and aggregated views, might be available only in the data warehouse. In such cases, the platform users should know which system holds the data that they seek.

Data governance and security
> Due to siloed storage tiers, implementing data governance and security policies like access control, sensitive data handling, and secure sharing becomes challenging. In such environments, you cannot have a unified data governance policy that is easy and practical to implement and maintain.

Data lineage
> For any change in name, datatype, or length of a specific column, you need to perform an impact analysis to identify the tables where the specific column is present. In combined architectures, the lineage view is limited to individual ecosystems (data lake or data warehouse); you can't get an end-to-end understanding of the data flow.

Considering these challenges, it is beneficial to use a unified data catalog that can simplify the metadata management, data discovery, and governance processes. Lakehouse architecture enables you to implement this unified data catalog.

What Is a Unified Data Catalog?

A unified data catalog is a catalog that can hold metadata of all data assets like tables, views, reports, functions, as well as AI assets like ML models and feature tables. A

---

unified data catalog enables its users to govern all their data and AI assets from a single, central platform. In lakehouse architecture, all the assets across data and AI workloads reside within the single cloud storage layer, enabling platform administrators to implement a unified data catalog to manage and govern the entire ecosystem.

Figure 4-3 shows a unified data catalog within a lakehouse platform and the key features that it provides.

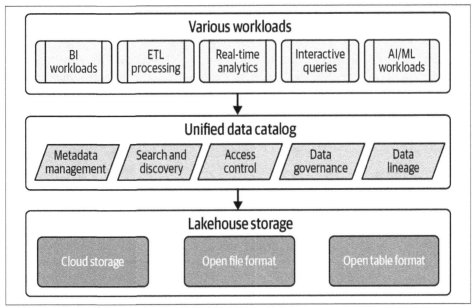

Figure 4-3. Unified data catalog in a lakehouse platform

As discussed earlier, a data catalog offers key features like search, discovery, governance, and lineage. In a unified data catalog, organizations can implement these features across all data objects like tables, views, and reports as well across all assets like models and feature stores used in AI workloads.

A unified data catalog provides a single interface for different data personas—like data engineers, analysts, and scientists—to collaborate efficiently and work together to explore and leverage data. It acts as a central repository for technical as well as business users to search and discover data.

To summarize, as a data consumer, a unified data catalog is your window to explore the entire data and AI assets within the platform, browse the technical metadata of these assets, and understand the business context of data.

Benefits of a Unified Data Catalog

The key benefits of a unified data catalog are as follows:

Unified search and data discovery

In lakehouse architecture, you can implement a single metastore layer to hold all the metadata across the ecosystem. Unlike the combined architecture, users can browse and explore the metadata of all data assets using a unified data catalog. This enables users to search the required tables or attributes quickly without knowing where the data physically resides within the system.

Data catalogs also provide features to augment technical data with business context. Data owners can add business descriptions and business meanings to attributes. This enables business users and technical users to easily discover data.

Consistent access controls

Managing and maintaining access to data is difficult. It becomes more challenging when you want to implement consistent access levels across your platform. Unified data catalogs help implement a consistent access control mechanism across the data ecosystem.

You can implement a consistent access control mechanism for different persons, irrespective of which compute engines they use. Consider a scenario where you want your sales team's data engineers and data scientists to be able to access their business unit-specific data assets. Data engineers might use notebooks, while data scientists might want to query the feature store tables to access the data. Using the unified access control mechanism, you can provide the same access levels to both personas.

Unified data governance and security

With a unified data catalog, you can implement unified data governance and security policies that apply to all assets including tables, files, functions, ML models, and feature tables. You can secure your data by applying the consistent masking policies to sensitive data within the lakehouse. Any persona, irrespective of the tool used for accessing the data, can only see the data that they are eligible to access.

End-to-end data lineage

With a lakehouse employing a unified metastore and catalog, you can easily see the end-to-end lineage across all components. Some of the advanced data catalogs also provide capabilities for implementing federated catalogs, which can show the metadata for sources outside your data platform, as well as lineage that includes these sources.

Unifying various aspects of data management processes across all assets gives lakehouse platform users a consistent experience from wherever they access the data.

Implementing a Data Catalog: Key Design Considerations and Options

There are multiple tools and platforms that can help you implement data catalogs in a lakehouse. Every cloud provider has their own native services and most of the leading third-party products have features to implement data catalogs.

You can design and implement a unified data catalog based on your use case and the overall technical landscape. In this section, I'll discuss some of the leading data catalog tools, design considerations, possible design choices, and key limitations to implementing a data catalog in a lakehouse platform.

We will discuss the widely adopted Hive metastore; cloud native data catalogs from AWS, Azure, and GCP; and data catalog offerings from third parties like Databricks.

Using Hive metastore

Hive has been popular since the Hadoop days. Many organizations have adopted Hive metastore (HMS) to support their metadata management needs while implementing Hadoop ecosystems or modern data platforms. Traditional Hadoop ecosystems used MapReduce as a compute engine and HCatalog as the data catalog for accessing HMS. Spark also has a data catalog API to access metadata stored in HMS.

You can consider using HMS for storing the metadata for your data platform. HMS provides users the flexibility to use an external RDBMS to store metadata like table types, column names, and column datatypes. It serves as the central repository for storing and managing the metadata of tables created using different compute engines like Hive, Spark, or Flink. Native cloud services like AWS Glue and third-parties like Databricks, and many others, offer options to use HMS for storing metadata.

Though many organizations have adopted HMS as their primary metastore, it has a couple of key challenges:

- You have to provision and manage a separate RDBMS to store the metadata, adding to the maintenance overhead.

- Since it is not a native cloud service, you have to spend extra effort for its integration, compared to cloud native data catalog services.

Considering these challenges, CSPs have introduced native cataloging services for implementing easy and simple metadata management processes.

Using AWS Services

AWS offers two options for storing metadata—HMS and Glue Data Catalog.

Glue Data Catalog, a native AWS service, integrates easily with services like AWS Glue ETL, Amazon EMR, Amazon Athena, and AWS Lake Formation. You would use most of these services while implementing a lakehouse platform in AWS.

> Here is a quick description of the AWS services just mentioned. I'll discuss these in detail in subsequent chapters of this book:
>
> - AWS Glue ETL is a serverless data integration service to create Spark jobs for data processing.
> - Amazon EMR provides a big data platform to execute frameworks like Spark, Hive, Presto, HBase, and other big data frameworks for data processing, interactive analytics, and machine learning.
> - Amazon Athena is a serverless service for interactive analysis of data stored on S3.
> - AWS Lake Formation provides capabilities to secure and govern data in S3.

Figure 4-4 shows a simple flow diagram of how you can create Hudi files in S3, parse them to create metadata in the Glue Data Catalog, govern Hudi tables using Lake Formation, and query them using the Amazon Athena engine. You can also use other open table formats, like Iceberg or Delta Lake, instead of Hudi.

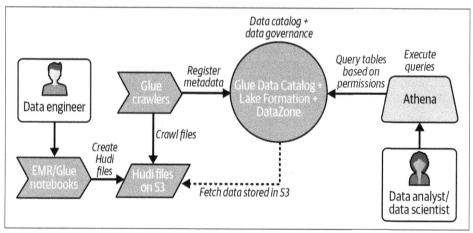

Figure 4-4. Lakehouse data flow in AWS ecosystem

As shown in the diagram, the Glue Data Catalog plays a significant role in lakehouse architecture to enable different personas to create, access, and query data residing on S3.

Like HMS, Glue Data Catalog also provides a central metadata repository for all data assets. Key features of AWS Glue Data Catalog are as follows:

- It has deep integrations with other AWS services.
- It is a fully managed, serverless service that does not need to be deployed or maintained by the user.
- You can use Glue crawlers to parse the data files from S3 to create metadata within the catalog.
- Its integration with Amazon Athena provides a UI to easily explore the schema, tables, and attributes.
- Tables created using open source frameworks like Spark, Hive, and Presto within the EMR cluster can use Glue Data Catalog to store their metadata.
- It integrates with AWS Lake Formation to provide users with fine-grained access control.

Amazon also offers a service called Amazon DataZone, which can help you implement a data catalog that has capabilities to augment the technical metadata with business metadata. You can import the metadata stored in Glue Data Catalog into DataZone and add business descriptions to the technical attributes to give them business context. You can further govern and share your data using DataZone, which internally uses Lake Formation for permission management and data sharing.

Consider following key points when using AWS services to implement a data catalog for your lakehouse platform:

Glue Data Catalog instead of HMS
   Glue Data Catalog is an alternative to HMS. You can use Glue Data Catalog as a metastore to metadata of the tables that are created using query engines like Hive, Spark, and Presto within the Amazon EMR cluster. Glue Data Catalog supports storing metadata for Hudi, Iceberg, and Delta Lake tables. Ability to support your preferred open table format is one of the most important considerations when selecting a data catalog service.

Glue crawlers for automated metadata creation
   You can use AWS Glue crawlers to crawl the data files in S3 and fetch (parse) the metadata. Glue crawlers store the metadata in the Glue Data Catalog and create the tables based on the records parsed from the files. You can use crawlers to generate the metadata for all your files stored in S3. Glue crawlers can also detect

schema changes in the S3 data store. You can configure the crawlers to either update or ignore the table changes in the data catalog.

Table format support
Glue crawlers now also support Hudi, Iceberg, and Delta Lake files to automatically create tables in the Glue Data Catalog. Depending on your choice of table format, you can select the relevant option while creating the crawlers.

Lake Formation for data governance
Glue Data Catalog is well-integrated with Lake Formation, which helps you implement fine-grained access controls and other data governance features like role-based data filtering and secure data sharing.

Athena for data exploration
Glue Data Catalog has deep integration with Amazon Athena, a service for querying data in the S3 data lake. We will discuss this in detail in Chapter 5. Athena allows you to explore all databases, tables, and columns in the Glue Data Catalog.

Using Azure Services

If you plan to implement a lakehouse using the Azure ecosystem, you will use services like Azure Synapse Analytics as the compute layer and ADLS as the storage layer.

Synapse Analytics offers two compute engines to process the data stored in ADLS: Synapse Spark pools and Synapse serverless SQL pools. Data engineers familiar with Spark programming can use the Spark pools. For data analysts who are more comfortable with SQL, Synapse offers serverless SQL pools. You can use either of them to process data stored in ADLS. We will discuss these compute engines in more detail in Chapter 5.

Figure 4-5 shows the two options that Synapse Analytics offers to maintain and manage the metadata for the data stored in ADLS—the lake database and the SQL database:

Lake database
Synapse Spark pools manage the lake databases. You can use lake databases for storing the metadata of the objects created using the Synapse notebooks. This includes the metadata of delta tables created using Spark pools.

SQL database
Serverless SQL pools manage the Synapse SQL databases. You can create tables using Synapse serverless SQL pools in the SQL database, and you can use the serverless SQL endpoints to connect Management Studio or Power BI to the tables within the SQL database and query data.

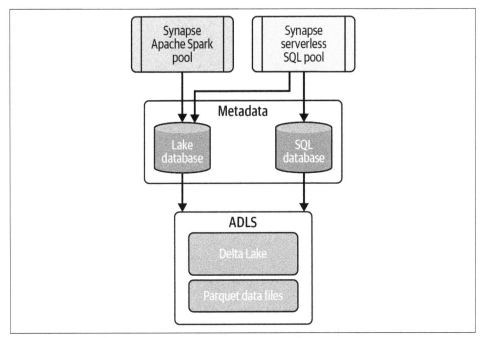

Figure 4-5. Metadata management using Synapse Analytics

 The Synapse SQL database is different from the Azure SQL database (relational database) service. The Synapse SQL database holds the metadata of tables created using the Synapse serverless SQL pools. It does not hold the actual data, as the data resides on ADLS.

Depending on which compute engine you use, you can select lake database (for Spark pools) or SQL database (for serverless SQL pools). As shown in Figure 4-5, the advantage of using the lake database is that you can access it from Synapse notebooks, as well as Synapse serverless SQL pools.

Figure 4-6 shows how you can create delta tables in ADLS, metadata in a lake database, and implement a unified catalog using *Microsoft Purview* to query it securely using Synapse serverless SQL pools for further analysis.

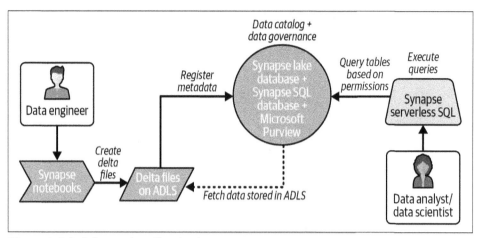

Figure 4-6. Lakehouse data flow in Azure ecosystem

As shown in Figure 4-6, you can create delta tables using Synapse notebooks, and then use serverless SQL pools endpoint to query the data using Power BI or any other database query editors like SQL Server Management Studio (SSMS).

While the Synapse lake database and SQL database persist the metadata, they are not full-fledged cataloging solutions. Azure provides a service called Microsoft Purview that provides catalog capabilities. You can consider using it to implement a data catalog for your lakehouse.

Microsoft Purview offers support for unified data governance across on-premises, Azure native, and multi-cloud platforms, as well as support for data classification and the handling of sensitive data. It also offers features like data lineage, access control, and data sharing, as well as features to create and maintain a business glossary for business users. You can import the metadata from the Synapse SQL database into Microsoft Purview and leverage these features in your platform.

> Microsoft Purview also supports importing metadata from Data-bricks. This is a useful feature if you are processing data using Databricks compute and want to maintain a data catalog using Microsoft Purview.

Using GCP Services

Like AWS and Azure, you can follow a similar pattern for creating your data catalog in GCP and using it as a central, unified layer for metadata management.

Figure 4-7 shows how you can create Iceberg tables in GCS and metadata in BigLake, centrally govern the metadata using Dataplex, and query it securely using BigQuery for further analysis.

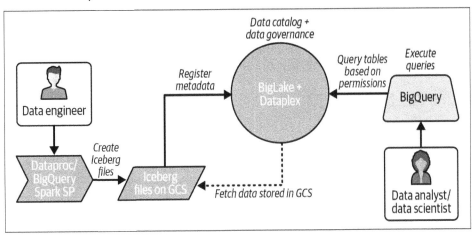

Figure 4-7. Lakehouse data flow in GCP ecosystem

Here is a quick description of the compute services shown in Figure 4-7, which I'll discuss in subsequent chapters in detail:

- Dataproc is a GCP-managed service to run Spark and Hadoop clusters.
- BigQuery is a serverless data warehouse service that offers built-in BI and ML features.

BigLake

BigLake is a GCP service that enables BigQuery and other open source frameworks like Spark to access data stored in GCS with fine-grained access control. It supports the Iceberg open table format and enables BigQuery users to query Iceberg data stored in GCS as BigLake tables with controlled permissions.

Key features of BigLake are:

- It provides a metastore to access Iceberg tables from BigQuery.
- It can sync Iceberg tables created in Dataproc or BigQuery and make these available to users via BigQuery SQL interface.
- It enables administrators to implement fine-grained access control for Iceberg tables.

BigLake currently only supports Parquet data files for Iceberg and has a few more limitations (*https://oreil.ly/bKs96*).

Dataplex

> Dataplex is a GCP service that enables organizations to discover and govern their data assets. It provides capabilities to explore data, manage data lifecycle, and understand the data flow using end-to-end lineage.

BigLake integrates with Dataplex to provide a central access control mechanism for BigLake tables. You can consider Dataplex for your platform if you want to manage all your data assets from a single pane of glass.

Using Databricks

With the notion of *multi-cloud* picking up, many organizations have started looking for third-party products that integrate well with their multi-cloud strategy. Databricks offers one such product that enables organizations to adopt a multi-cloud strategy, as it can leverage AWS, Azure, and GCP infrastructure for compute and storage.

> Multi-cloud strategy is an approach to use multiple cloud platforms to get the best features and cost advantages provided by different CSPs. Many organizations now opt for more than one cloud provider to implement their data ecosystems.

Databricks offers a couple of options for cataloging metadata. You can use HMS or a native service known as *Databricks Unity Catalog* for managing, maintaining, and governing metadata. Unity Catalog helps implement a unified governance solution across the data and AI assets on a lakehouse.

Similar to AWS Glue Data Catalog, Unity Catalog, being a native service within Databricks, provides easy integrations with Databricks features like Notebooks (*https:// oreil.ly/YTCcT*) and Databricks SQL (*https://oreil.ly/smElf*).

> Databricks SQL is a serverless compute engine within the Databricks lakehouse platform. You can use it to execute interactive queries in the lakehouse. When combined with a query editor (a service available within the Databricks UI for query authoring), you can easily browse data assets from the HMS or Unity Catalog and execute queries using SQL commands.

Figure 4-8 shows a simple flow diagram within a lakehouse implemented using Azure Databricks. You can create the delta files using Databricks Notebooks and access the delta tables from Databricks SQL.

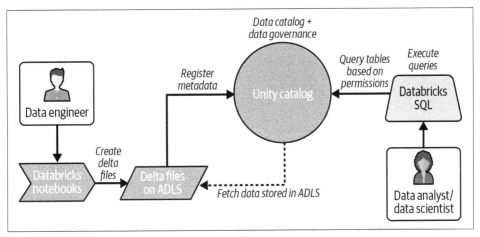

Figure 4-8. Lakehouse data flow in Databricks ecosystem

Unity Catalog plays a significant role by providing capabilities to manage metadata at a central location that is accessible by Databricks Notebooks as well as Databricks SQL. It also provides the central access control mechanism for implementing data governance policies.

Key features offered by the Unity Catalog are as follows:

- Capability to manage and govern all your data and AI assets like tables, views, notebooks, ML models, feature tables, and dashboards
- Ability to add business context, resulting in easy search and data discovery
- Ability to provide federated catalogs (in preview at the time of writing this book) for external sources like MySQL, PostgreSQL/Postgres, Snowflake, and Redshift
- End-to-end data lineage across the Databricks ecosystems, including AI components
- Secure data sharing by providing fine-grained access controls on data shares
- Any schema and metadata changes done in Notebooks are reflected immediately in Databricks SQL without any lag (compared to Azure Synapse Analytics with Delta Lake)

Unity Catalog has recently been open sourced by Databricks (*https://oreil.ly/e8iJQ*) and will soon start supporting various data and AI products.

Unity Catalog is an excellent option for implementing a lakehouse within the Databricks ecosystem. However, if you want to access and govern metadata outside Databricks, you can also consider other enterprise-grade catalogs that can ingest data from Databricks Unity Catalog and make it available to users outside Databricks for easier discovery and central governance.

Many features and services discussed in this section are relatively new or still in preview mode. These will evolve and mature gradually, and workarounds or solutions will be offered for some of the limitations we've discussed here. When exploring these tools for your use case, please consult the latest documentation and evaluate the latest versions.

Along with the cloud native catalogs, there are open source catalogs like Project Nessie (*https://projectnessie.org*) and enterprise cataloging tools like Alation (*https://oreil.ly/-o1j4*), Collibra (*https://oreil.ly/ktCFq*), and Atlan (*https://atlan.com*) that provide additional features and benefits that you can explore for specific requirements.

What Is a Catalog of Catalogs?

In the previous sections, we discussed various cloud native cataloging services. Organizations can use multiple clouds or implement a hybrid data ecosystem that spans on-premises, private, and public clouds. Such organizations need enterprise-grade cataloging tools that can integrate with different CSPs, ingest or federate data from different source systems, and connect to various on-premises or private cloud platforms to provide a single view of the entire organization's metadata. An enterprise-grade catalog is also known as a "catalog of catalogs." Collibra is one product that provides such features.

Key Takeaways

In this chapter, we discussed how you can store the metadata for all of your data assets in a metastore and access it using data catalogs based on access permissions. Lakehouse architecture enables you to implement a unified data catalog to manage, govern, and share all your data and AI assets.

Table 4-4 summarizes the various services available across the cloud platforms for implementing metadata management processes.

Table 4-4. Metadata management services across providers

Provider	Technical metadata management	Business metadata management and data governance
AWS	HMS, Glue Data Catalog	DataZone
Azure	Synapse Lake Database, Synapse SQL Database	Microsoft Purview
GCP	BigLake	Dataplex
Databricks	HMS, Unity Catalog	Unity Catalog

Table 4-5 summarizes the key design considerations, per ecosystem, when implementing a data catalog in lakehouse architecture.

Table 4-5. Key points for data catalog implementation

Ecosystem	Key design considerations
AWS	• Consider implementing a unified data catalog using services like Glue Data Catalog, Lake Formation, and DataZone. • You can manage, govern, and share data using these services. • Use DataZone to add the business context to the technical metadata. • Glue Data Catalog and Lake Formation integrate with DataZone. • Organizations can store metadata from Hudi, Iceberg, or Delta Lake in the Glue Data Catalog and query the data stored in S3 using Athena.
Azure	• You can use Azure Synapse Analytics for implementing lakehouse architecture. • Use Synapse notebooks to create delta files in ADLS and metadata in the Synapse Lake database. • Synapse serverless SQL pools can query data from the Lake database as well as the SQL database. • Organizations can use Microsoft Purview to catalog technical and business metadata and apply governance policies.
GCP	• BigLake stores the metadata for tables created in GCP. • BigLake supports Iceberg tables natively and BigQuery can use BigLake tables to query data. • Organizations can use Dataplex to implement a unified catalog within GCP for governing data.
Databricks	• Organizations can use Unity Catalog to implement a unified catalog. • Unity Catalog offers features to implement fine-grained access controls across all data and AI/ML assets. • Databricks has recently open sourced Unity Catalog and can now be used outside Databricks.

In this chapter, we focused our learning on metastores and data catalogs, and their features and benefits in lakehouse architecture. In the next chapter, we will discuss the different compute and data consumption options within lakehouse architecture, and how they help different personas perform data and analytics workloads efficiently.

References

AWS

- What Is Amazon DataZone? (*https://oreil.ly/3n8iV*)
- Data Lake Governance: AWS Lake Formation FAQs (*https://oreil.ly/hFz2J*)
- Crawl Delta Lake Tables Using AWS Glue Crawlers | AWS Big Data Blog (*https://oreil.ly/b_dmH*)
- Introducing AWS Glue Crawler and Create Table Support for Apache Iceberg Format | AWS Big Data Blog (*https://oreil.ly/mppD9*)
- Get Started with Apache Hudi Using AWS Glue by Implementing Key Design Concepts – Part 1 | AWS Big Data Blog (*https://oreil.ly/vL7Ha*)
- Use the AWS Glue Data Catalog as the Metastore for Spark SQL | Amazon EMR (*https://oreil.ly/dt0Ow*)

Azure

- Azure Synapse Analytics | Microsoft Learn (*https://oreil.ly/hD5ZE*)
- Access Lake Database Using Serverless SQL Pool in Azure Synapse Analytics | Microsoft Learn (*https://oreil.ly/mxFvJ*)
- Bringing ML Assets to the Microsoft Purview Data Map (*https://oreil.ly/ NMUUY*)
- Organizing lakehouse structure in Synapse Analytics (*https://oreil.ly/otuc7*)
- Azure Synapse lake database concepts (*https://oreil.ly/G8vf8*)
- Connect To and Manage Azure Databricks in Microsoft Purview | Microsoft Learn (*https://oreil.ly/wBPlo*)
- Connect To and Manage Azure Databricks Unity Catalog in Microsoft Purview | Microsoft Learn (*https://oreil.ly/F40Oa*)
- Azure Synapse Analytics Shared Metadata | Microsoft Learn (*https://oreil.ly/ aRTJR*)

GCP

- BigLake support for building Apache Iceberg lakehouses is now GA (*https:// oreil.ly/PBpk0*)
- Open Data Lakehouse on Google Cloud (*https://oreil.ly/wE9Ax*)
- Table format projects now available on Dataproc (*https://oreil.ly/hbq8X*)
- Automating data governance with Google Cloud Dataplex & BigLake (*https:// oreil.ly/3CCtv*)
- Create Apache Iceberg BigLake Tables | Google Cloud Documentation (*https:// oreil.ly/4VL_k*)
- Building a Data Lakehouse on Google Cloud Platform (*https://oreil.ly/8swP6*)

Databricks

- What Is Unity Catalog? | Microsoft Learn (*https://oreil.ly/A2TH9*)
- Cataloging Data for a Lakehouse | Databricks (*https://oreil.ly/EatYq*)
- Discover Features in Unity Catalog | Microsoft Learn (*https://oreil.ly/SuTjY*)
- Open source Unity catalog (*https://www.unitycatalog.io*)

Other

- Atlan (*https://atlan.com*)
- AWS Glue Data Catalog | Apache Hudi (*https://oreil.ly/Ayybv*)
- HCatalog UsingHCat (*https://oreil.ly/T26oe*)
- Collibra: Catalog of Catalogs (*https://oreil.ly/WBYDb*)

CHAPTER 5

Compute Engines for Lakehouse Architectures

If storage is the heart of the lakehouse, then the compute engine is the brain that performs all of its computational activities. You need a performant compute engine to ingest, process, and consume data from a data platform. A compute engine enables platform users like data engineers, data analysts, data scientists, business users, and others to access and use data per their needs.

In this chapter, we will first discuss the various data computation benefits you get when implementing lakehouse architecture. We will explore how lakehouses enable unified batch and real-time processing, enhance the performance of BI workloads, and offer the freedom to choose any processing engine.

We will also discuss the various compute engines that are available via open source tools, cloud platforms, or other third-party platforms. Every CSP offers data and analytics services that provide compute resources. We will discuss some of the most adopted services that data engineers and analysts use in modern data platforms, and their varying levels of support for open table formats. The examples we discuss will help you understand the integration challenges between cloud services and open table formats.

Finally, we will examine the key considerations when choosing a compute engine, and when designing and implementing your platform's data ingestion, processing, and consumption processes.

Data Computation Benefits of Lakehouse Architecture

As we discussed in Chapter 1, lakehouse architecture is based on decoupled storage and compute tiers. This decoupling provides multiple benefits for data computation activities like data ingestion, processing, transformation, and consumption.

Independent Scaling

Decoupled compute helps scale the platform's compute capacity, independent of its storage. Such independent scaling of compute was impossible in traditional Hadoop and data warehouse systems, where you had to add new nodes with additional storage to increase the compute capacity. Lakehouse architecture allows you to scale your storage and compute capacities independently.

Cross-region, Cross-account Access

The decoupled compute layer of a lakehouse enables you to use compute engines across cloud regions and across accounts to access data. For example, you can implement a lakehouse using AWS and store data in one of the S3 buckets in a specific region (to maintain *data sovereignty*) and perform analysis using analytics services from any other region.

Data sovereignty refers to the compliance policies restricting data from being stored outside a specific country or region. Many countries have data protection laws and regulations that restrict their residents' data from being moved or copied outside the country. Organizations that collect, process, and store data must comply with these laws and regulations, and ensure that data is not stored on cloud servers outside that specific country.

Unified Batch and Real-Time Processing

In lakehouse architecture, you can unify your batch and real-time processing. This unification helps maintain the code base and allows you to easily make changes only in a single place. Consider building your code using a real-time approach with controlled execution frequency and configuring it to execute every 24 hours (batch), a few hours (micro-batches), or even a few minutes (near-real time). This approach of unified data processing is possible in lakehouses because there is only a single storage tier for persisting data for both batch and real-time workloads.

Enhanced BI Performance

SQL/BI on Hadoop was a common approach in the Hadoop ecosystem for performing BI workloads. Data analysts would execute Hive queries on HDFS data to explore and analyze data. The most challenging aspect of this approach was performance. Hive (with the MapReduce engine) was extremely slow and created major performance bottlenecks within the ecosystem.

BI performance will be a highly discussed and debated topic within any organization that plans to implement lakehouse architecture. The major area of concern is the compute performance of queries running over data stored in cloud object storage like S3, ADLS, or GCS. Lakehouse architecture does not use purpose-built, proprietary storage like data warehouses. So, how does it address the performance issues that traditional Hadoop architectures face?

The open table formats and lakehouse compute engines employ the following techniques to address these performance challenges:

Maintaining statistics

File formats like Apache Parquet maintain stats such as min and max column values within each file. When you query data on Parquet files, the compute engine uses these stats to skip data records. However, this process needs to read every Parquet file. The open table formats maintain these stats from the data files in a central place (the metadata layer) so that the query doesn't need to scan individual data files. This helps in data skipping and improves the overall query response time.

File compaction

Frameworks like MapReduce and Spark use distributed processing for computing. The performance of these frameworks gets impacted when data gets stored in smaller file sizes (few KBs/MBs). Open table formats provide features to compact smaller files into large ones, thus improving the overall query performance. The reduced file count means fewer data scans and faster retrieval of query results.

Partitioning, clustering, and Z-order

You can partition the data stored in the lakehouse storage layer. When you use the right predicates in your queries, the engine skips the unwanted partitions, thus helping to improve the query performance.

Some open table formats have specific features that aim to improve performance by using partitioning, clustering, or Z-ordering. Some examples are as follows:

Iceberg supports hidden partitions and partition evolution (as discussed in Chapter 3). As the data grows with time, partition evolution can help change the partitions without rewriting the complete dataset.

Delta Lake offers a feature known as liquid clustering (*https://oreil.ly/cTrty*) (available in Delta Lake 3.1.0; in experimental support mode at the time of writing), which enables users to redefine clustering columns without rewriting existing data.

Some open table formats also support the Z-ordering feature, which involves co-locating data in the same set of files. Z-ordering rewrites the data files, which is costly but helps improve performance.

Apart from these techniques, here are some examples of the commercial products that offer optimized compute engines to enhance BI performance:

- Databricks offers a next-generation Photon (*https://oreil.ly/MuZg6*) engine, developed using C++, with improved query performance over the Databricks Runtime (DBR) that is based on Spark.

- Dremio, another leading lakehouse platform, offers a feature called Reflections (*https://oreil.ly/c1nF1*) that uses various optimization techniques for accelerating query performance.

- Snowflake uses various levels of caching to improve query result performance.

Freedom to Choose Different Engine Types

Several compute engines support open table formats like Iceberg, Hudi, and Delta Lake. Various open source engines, cloud native services, and third-party products support writing and reading from these open table formats. You can use different types of processing engines to process data stored in a lakehouse.

Figure 5-1 shows a lakehouse compute tier with different types of compute engines like Spark, Apache Flink, and Presto.

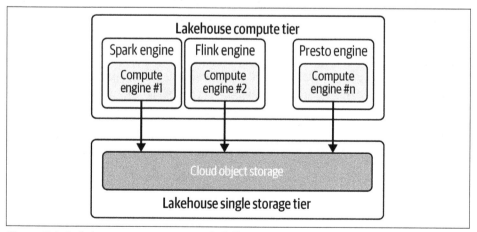

Figure 5-1. Lakehouse compute tier with different engine types

Consider a scenario where data engineers want to ingest data in a lakehouse. They can use Spark to execute a PySpark code to ingest data from the source system. Data engineers are generally more comfortable writing Spark code and can use the Spark engine for ETL-like workloads. If data analysts want to access this same data for further analysis, they can use SQL-based engines like Presto or Trino to query the data from the lakehouse. These engines can also update or delete records based on compatibility with the open table formats. We will discuss this in more detail in the later sections of this chapter.

The freedom to use your preferred compute engine helps reduce vendor dependency. In cases where the data consumers of your platform are using a different vendor's product, they can use their product's compute engine and pay according to their compute capacity and utilization. You don't need to provide them access to your compute engine and bear the cost of their data consumption.

Cross-zone Analysis

Lakehouse architecture enables you to perform data processing operations across various storage *zones* within the lakehouse storage.

What Are Storage Zones?

When you store lakehouse data in a cloud storage like Amazon S3, ADLS, or GCS, you will often create separate zones. These zones physically separate data within the lakehouse and indicate the purpose of data usage.

A standard lakehouse architecture would have a minimum of three data zones:

Raw zone
    Stores data "as is" from source systems

Cleansed zone
    Stores data after performing the data quality checks and validations

Curated zone
    Stores data that is modeled per business processes for easy querying and analysis

There are additional zones that help in overall data management. We will discuss these zones in detail in Chapter 7.

Consider a combined architecture where the raw data is stored in a data lake and the curated data is stored in a warehouse, for performing BI workloads. In such architectures, you have to use two different compute engines:

- A compute engine that can access the data within the data lake

- A proprietary compute engine provided by the warehouse to query the data stored within the warehouse

In such cases, you cannot directly join the data from the lake and warehouse using any open source engine. You need to either copy the data lake data into the warehouse or rely on a proprietary, purpose-built engine provided by the warehouse that can access data from the lake. For example, Amazon Redshift Spectrum (*https://oreil.ly/Dcbj3*) is a service that can help you query data present in the S3 data lake and Redshift warehouse.

Since lakehouse architecture uses only a single storage tier, you can use any open source compute engine to join data from raw and curated zones. You don't have to depend on any proprietary service for cross-zone analysis.

Compute Engine Options for Lakehouse Platforms

Figure 5-2 shows the two broad categories of activities you typically perform on a data platform: data engineering and data consumption.

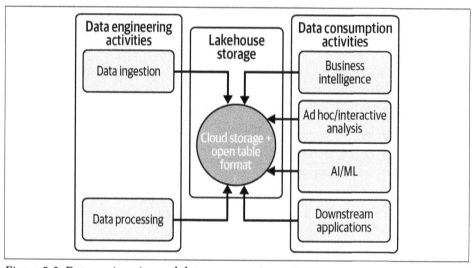

Figure 5-2. Data engineering and data consumption activities

Data engineering activities involve data ingestion, validation, cleansing, processing, transforming, and curating data before storing it in the platform. These activities ensure you store clean, valid, accurate, and complete data within the platform—data that users can trust and consume easily. Data engineers are responsible for these data engineering activities. They implement code that connects to several source systems to ingest and store data in the data platform.

Data consumption activities involve various use cases like interactive analysis, BI, AI/ML, and sharing with downstream applications. Data consumers leverage the data from the platform for interactive analysis, insight generation, predictions, recommendations, or even sharing or monetizing the data. Data analysts, BI engineers, ML engineers, data scientists, and business users are some of the different personas that consume data stored in the platform. There are also downstream applications that can consume data from the platform.

Lakehouse architecture provides the flexibility to use different compute engines that different personas can use to perform their work. In this section, we'll explore various open source tools, cloud services, and third-party products that offer computational capabilities for a lakehouse.

Open Source Tools

There are various open source compute engines available that you can use for multiple data engineering and data consumption activities.

Tools for data engineering

Spark is the most popular and widely adopted big data processing framework used for data engineering activities. Flink is another option.

Spark. Spark is a distributed, in-memory processing framework. It has no storage component but rather uses distributed storage like HDFS or cloud object storage like S3, ADLS, or GCS to store data.

Key features, benefits, and limitations of Spark are listed below:

- Spark offers high reliability and scalability while processing large volumes of data.
- Unlike its predecessor, MapReduce (which stores data on disk), Spark supports in-memory processing.
- Spark supports Python, Java, Scala, and R languages.
- Spark is best suited for ETL workloads that process large volumes of data.
- You can perform real-time processing using Spark Structured Streaming.
- You can also use SQL queries using Spark SQL, which makes it possible for data engineers with SQL skills to write transformation logic in SQL and execute using Spark engine.
- Latency can be an issue for streaming workloads with sub-second latency expectations.

In lakehouse architecture, you can use Spark for ETL workloads, including data ingestion, transformation, validation, cleaning, and loading into the lakehouse. You can use managed cloud offerings like Amazon EMR, Azure HDInsight, or GCP Dataproc to run Spark clusters to process data and write them using suitable open table formats.

Spark is one of the most feature-rich engines for the open table formats. It supports Iceberg (*https://oreil.ly/1KkDG*), Hudi (*https://oreil.ly/U5gXa*), and Delta Lake (*https://oreil.ly/4zyFU*). You should consider the compatibility of the latest version of Spark and the chosen open table format before finalizing the tech stack for your platform.

Flink. Spark might not be the best choice for low-latency streaming operations where you need millisecond-level latency. In such a case, Flink is another open source framework that you can use to implement streaming ingestion and processing.

It offers the following features:

- It is a distributed, in-memory processing framework.
- It supports low latency, high throughput, and real-time processing.
- It also has SQL support, similar to Spark SQL, for writing SQL-like queries.
- It has support for Iceberg (*https://oreil.ly/MErk-*), Hudi (*https://oreil.ly/md6ad*), and Delta Lake (*https://oreil.ly/LRBkf*).

Flink is a widely adopted processing framework for implementing streaming use cases. Before using it in your platform, be sure you understand its features and compatibility with various open table formats.

Tools for data consumption

Just as many data engineers are more comfortable writing Spark programs for performing ETL operations, most data analysts prefer working with good old SQL commands for analyzing data. SQL is one of the most popular languages used by business users and analysts to access and query structured data.

Presto and Trino. Presto and Trino are widely adopted, open source, distributed SQL engines used for running fast analytical queries on lakehouse platforms. They have the following characteristics:

- They support ANSI SQL dialect for querying data.
- They support *pushdown optimization* for enhancing query performance by pushing the queries at source or target databases.

- They leverage decoupled architecture for independent scaling of compute capacity.
- They support federated querying from heterogeneous data sources.

Are Presto and Trino the Same Engine?

Meta (formerly Facebook) created Presto (formerly PrestoDB) for running interactive queries on a large data warehouse. Presto later became an open source tool. PrestoSQL was forked from PrestoDB but later rebranded as Trino in late 2020.

Presto and Trino have the same core query engine and similar architectures. While they have several common features, both engines offer some unique features that you can further explore for your specific requirements.

There are also managed offerings available, like Starburst (*https://www.starburst.io*) (based on Trino) and Ahana (*https://docs.ahana.cloud/docs*) (based on Presto) that you can consider.

When selecting Presto or Trino as a compute engine for your lakehouse platform, be sure to check the compatibility of the latest versions of these engines with Iceberg (*https://oreil.ly/4VDwa*), Hudi (*https://oreil.ly/95h3z*), and Delta Lake. (*https://oreil.ly/YhieY*) Presto and Trino have native support for Delta Lake, but there might be some limitations for other table formats. These are evolving technologies and you should always study the latest version features, supported connectors, and limitations before using them.

Cloud platforms like AWS, Azure, and GCP also offer managed services (based on Spark or the Presto/Trino engine) that support open table formats, which you can consider when implementing a lakehouse. We'll look at these services in the next section.

Cloud Services

CSPs offer cloud native and managed services, based on open source technologies, for various computation activities related to data engineering and consumption. In this section, we will discuss these services, their key features, and their support for the open table formats.

AWS

AWS has several services for data processing. Figure 5-3 shows some of the key AWS services you can use for processing and consuming data. Please note that this section covers only a few key services that most data projects use. There are several other purpose-built AWS services that you can consider based on your use cases.

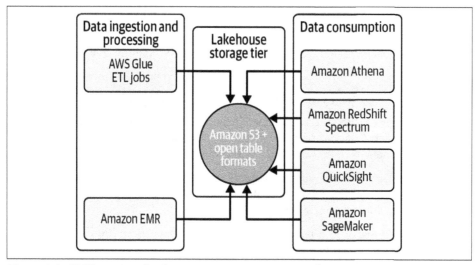

Figure 5-3. AWS services for data ingestion, processing, and consumption

AWS Glue. AWS Glue (*https://aws.amazon.com/glue*)is a serverless data integration service based on the Spark framework. You can use it for data ingestion, processing, and transformation activities. It provides a GUI with a low-code or no-code approach for implementing ETL jobs.

Glue 3.0 and higher supports creating Iceberg, Hudi, and Delta Lake open table formats. You can select one of these formats while creating the target files in the Glue ETL jobs.

Amazon EMR. Amazon EMR (*https://aws.amazon.com/emr*) offers several open source big data processing frameworks like Spark, Hive, Presto, Flink, and TensorFlow. With EMR, you can deploy a cluster on an Elastic Compute Cloud (EC2) machine or containers, or run a serverless EMR cluster.

EMR supports creating Iceberg, Hudi, and Delta Lake open table formats using frameworks like Spark. One of the key advantages of EMR over Glue is that you can use EMR as a single service for data engineering (using Spark), data analysis (using Presto), and ML (TensorFlow) workloads.

EMR also provides a feature to sync the metadata (created using Hive, Spark, and Presto) to the Glue Data Catalog so that the Iceberg, Hudi, or Delta Lake tables can be accessed using other services like Amazon Athena. This is an important feature for lakehouse implementations—you get the flexibility of querying tables across different compute engines.

Amazon Athena.   Amazon Athena (*https://aws.amazon.com/athena*) is a serverless query service for interactive analytics. You can analyze the data stored in S3 using standard SQL in Athena.

The latest version of Athena (version 3) offers two different engines for data processing:

- A Spark engine with notebook support for executing code using Spark clusters
- An open source Presto/Trino engine for executing SQL queries

Both engines now support Iceberg, Hudi, and Delta Lake formats.

Athena is used by data analysts and business users for data consumption workloads, like interactive analysis, or as a compute engine for BI workloads. Some data analysts might be well-versed with Spark and prefer writing Spark code for their analyses. They can use Athena Spark notebooks for data processing activities. Athena can act as a single service for executing Spark or SQL code, based on the user's preference.

If you are implementing a lakehouse using the AWS cloud platform, consider using Athena (for compute) and Iceberg (as open table format). Athena version 3 provides better integration with Iceberg than other table formats. It supports update and delete operations using the SQL engine so analysts can perform read and write operations. At the time of writing this book, the update and delete operations are not available for Hudi and Delta Lake open table formats using Athena SQL engine. Iceberg offers unique features, like hidden partitioning, that help further optimize Athena queries by reducing the amount of data scanned to fetch the required results.

You can refer to the blog post "Choosing an open table format for your transactional data lake on AWS" (*https://oreil.ly/_YicI*) from AWS to understand the read/write support offered by different AWS analytics services for Iceberg, Hudi, and Delta Lake.

Other AWS services.   Amazon Redshift (*https://aws.amazon.com/redshift*) is a cloud data warehouse service within AWS and offers a feature known as Amazon Redshift Spectrum (*https://oreil.ly/04xJp*). You can use it to read data from S3 that is stored using open table formats like Iceberg. AWS also has a service called Amazon QuickSight (*https://aws.amazon.com/quicksight*) for creating BI reports and dashboards, as well as Amazon SageMaker (*https://aws.amazon.com/sagemaker*) for implementing ML models that you can use for your lakehouse platform.

Azure

Azure offers several services for data computation, shown in Figure 5-4.

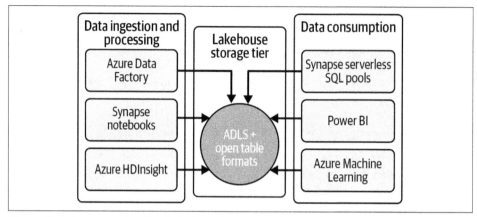

Figure 5-4. Azure services for data ingestion, processing, and consumption

Azure Data Factory (ADF).   Azure Data Factory (ADF (*https://oreil.ly/gvz4r*)) is a fully managed, serverless data integration service that you can use to ingest data from several source systems into Azure cloud storage. It offers GUI-based, low-code and no-code programming for data engineers to build ETL jobs using a drag-and-drop approach. ADF supports the Delta Lake format as a source to read delta files and as a target to create delta files. At the time of writing this book, there is no direct support for other open table formats within ADF.

Azure HDInsight.   Azure HDInsight (*https://oreil.ly/epfpc*) offers use of Hadoop, Hive, Spark, Kafka, and other big data processing frameworks. It is the easiest way to use these open source frameworks without spending any effort on provisioning and managing the hardware and software updates.

Data engineers can use the HDInsight Spark framework to create Iceberg, Hudi, and Delta Lake files. Other Azure services like ADF and Synapse Analytics support only Delta Lake files.

Azure Synapse Analytics.   Azure Synapse Analytics (*https://oreil.ly/urtAU*) offers a complete platform for implementing a data analytics solution. It provides two different compute engines for processing data stored within the ADLS storage.

Data engineers can use Synapse notebooks to write Spark code to perform data engineering activities. To execute the code, you can create Spark pools in Synapse and attach them to your notebooks. Synapse Spark pools support writing files in Parquet-Delta format and creating delta tables. As discussed in Chapter 4, the metadata of these notebooks gets stored in the lake database.

Data analysts can use Synapse serverless SQL pools to write and execute SQL queries. You can write the standard T-SQL commands and execute queries on the serverless SQL pools. You can browse the SQL database to explore the delta table metadata to use in your queries. Synapse Serverless also supports querying the Delta Lake files (*https://oreil.ly/7PTth*). Synapse Serverless SQL is based on an engine called Polaris (*https://oreil.ly/xBOUi*) and is different from Presto/Trino and Spark engines.

Synapse Analytics has native support for the Delta Lake format, and Delta Lake libraries are available as part of the Synapse Spark environment. For other open table formats, like Iceberg or Hudi, you will need additional configurations like importing required jars and configuring Spark SQL extensions within the Spark environment.

 Synapse also offers another compute engine based on dedicated SQL pools. However, it only works on data you load into the purpose-built storage of a dedicated SQL pool (data warehouse). If you implement lakehouse architecture, avoid loading the data in the dedicated SQL pool storage. Instead, have a single storage tier (ADLS, in this case) which can be accessed using any compatible compute engine. Use the serverless SQL pools for provisioning a SQL engine to query data present in ADLS.

ADF and Synapse are the most widely adopted services within Azure for implementing a lakehouse. You can also consider using open source engines like Spark or Presto on HDInsight to get a managed offering for these open source frameworks. Microsoft has recently launched Microsoft Fabric, which offers a SaaS platform for implementing data and analytics use cases. We will discuss Microsoft Fabric more in Chapter 9.

Along with these Azure services, you can also use Power BI (*https://powerbi.micro soft.com*) for implementing BI workloads and the Azure Machine Learning (*https://oreil.ly/QwQC9*) service for building ML models at scale.

GCP

Like other cloud platforms, GCP offers services for performing data ingestion, processing, and consumption, shown in Figure 5-5.

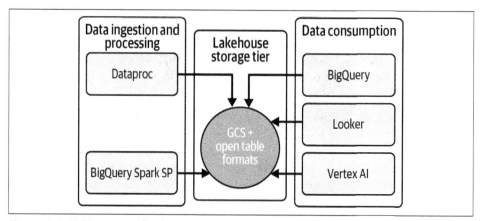

Figure 5-5. GCP services for data ingestion, processing, and consumption

Dataproc. Dataproc (*https://cloud.google.com/dataproc*) is a fully managed service for running big data frameworks like Spark, Hadoop, Presto, and Flink in GCP. It has out-of-box integration with other GCP services like BigQuery, Dataplex, and Vertex AI.

Dataproc 1.5.x Spark clusters support Iceberg, Hudi, and Delta Lake table formats. You need to import the required jars and configure SQL extensions to make the necessary configurations and integrations with data catalogs. Be sure to check the documentation (*https://oreil.ly/f0V3r*) to see which open table format versions are supported by Dataproc.

BigQuery. BigQuery (*https://cloud.google.com/bigquery*) is a serverless query service for executing complex analytical queries for data stored within BigQuery or GCS. For lakehouse implementations with data stored in GCS, you can use BigQuery as a compute engine for data computation activities.

BigQuery supports the Iceberg table format. You can use the BigQuery stored procedure (for Spark) to create an Iceberg BigLake table (as discussed in Chapter 4). BigLake tables can be accessed using the BigQuery SQL engine for executing analytical queries.

There are other GCP services, like Looker (*https://cloud.google.com/looker*) and Vertex AI (*https://cloud.google.com/vertex-ai*), that you can explore for your BI and AI/ML needs, respectively.

Third-Party Platforms

Third-party platforms offer benefits like infrastructure abstraction and multi-cloud support that reduce the complexity of data platform setup and management. Many organizations prefer third-party products over native cloud services because: (1) these organizations don't have the cloud experts to manage their cloud infrastructure or (2) they need platforms that can support their multi-cloud strategy.

Most of these platforms now support open table formats for implementing lakehouse architecture. Some platforms, like Databricks and Snowflake, are widely adopted, while others are relatively new.

Databricks

Databricks (*https://www.databricks.com*) is one of the leading platforms for implementing lakehouse architecture. It is also the creator of Spark and Delta Lake—the two high-impact technologies for implementing a lakehouse. Databricks has separate compute engines (based on Spark) for data engineering and analysis workloads. Figure 5-6 shows some of the Databricks services used for data engineering and consumption activities.

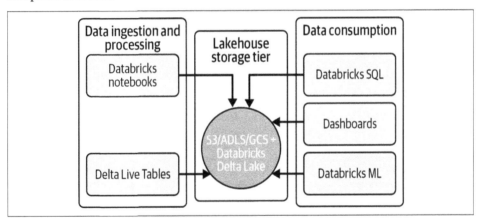

Figure 5-6. Databricks services for data ingestion, processing, and consumption

Databricks offers a notebook-based interface for data engineers and scientists to write and execute Spark code. The compute cluster uses Databricks Runtime (DBR), based on Spark, with several additional updates that improve Spark's performance.

Databricks has built-in support for Delta Lake (their proprietary Delta Lake, not the OSS Delta Lake), as well. Unlike some of the managed offerings by cloud providers, you don't have to spend any effort to configure or set up Delta Lake within Databricks.

Data analysts can use Databricks SQL for interactive analysis or for running interactive queries. Databricks provides a compute engine known as SQL Warehouse for running the SQL commands. You can provision the required capacity or use the serverless offering and compatible BI tools like Power BI, Looker, or Tableau to connect to the Databricks warehouse for executing BI workloads. Databricks also provides native dashboards for creating visualizations and reports.

Databricks has an improved compute engine (compared to existing DBR), known as Photon (*https://oreil.ly/JGu7y*), which we introduced earlier. Photon can provide extremely fast query performance across various workloads. It is compatible with the Spark APIs and you do not need to make any code changes for running the Spark workloads using Photon.

There are other Databricks services like Delta Live Tables (DLT) (*https://oreil.ly/iG2Uu*) with declarative ETL features that you can explore for your use cases. DLT provides features like incremental processing, data quality and error handling, cluster management, pipeline observability, and orchestration—all within a single interface.

Snowflake

Snowflake (*https://www.snowflake.com*) Cloud Platform is well-known for its revolutionary architecture, performance, and ease of use for implementing cloud data warehouses. Many organizations have adopted it for their BI needs. It's a SaaS platform and does not require any effort for infrastructure provisioning and maintenance. Though organizations have mainly used Snowflake for implementing data warehouse architectures, you can also use it as a compute engine in a lakehouse platform.

Figure 5-7 shows how you can use Snowflake to create native Iceberg tables (governed by Snowflake) with data stored on customer-supplied cloud storage.

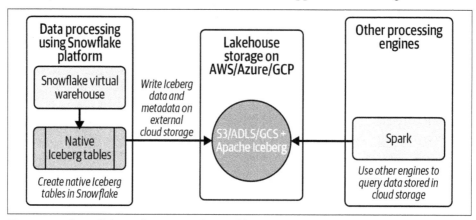

Figure 5-7. Snowflake with native Iceberg tables

Snowflake has a feature known as external tables, which allows you to read data directly from cloud object storage without loading it in its proprietary format. In such cases, you can use its compute engine for reading data but cannot update or delete data present in cloud storage.

Snowflake now has a new feature (*https://oreil.ly/OQ_h_*) (still in preview at the time of writing) to create native Iceberg tables, similar to Snowflake managed tables. Using this feature, you can store your data in customer-supplied cloud storage, like S3, and create Iceberg tables in Snowflake. This will enable benefits like enhanced performance, strong governance, and support for update and delete operations. You can also configure other engines like Spark to access and query this data from the cloud object storage. The Iceberg support means Snowflake's powerful query processor is an excellent compute option for your lakehouse.

In addition to Databricks and Snowflake, other platforms like Dremio (*https://www.dremio.com*), Ahana (*https://docs.ahana.cloud/docs*), and Starburst (*https://www.starburst.io*) also offer compute capabilities for performing various data computation activities within lakehouse architecture. While these platforms all address the basic compute needs, each product and platform has unique offerings, additional features, and performance optimizations you should consider when selecting a compute engine for your lakehouse.

Key Design Considerations

As discussed in the previous section, there are multiple compute engines that you can use in your lakehouse platform. But how do you decide which one to use?

Your choice of compute engine largely depends on your overall data ecosystem. However, another critical factor is the data persona(s) using the compute engine. Your platform should have the flexibility to enable different users to use different types of engines based on their skills and preferences.

Some of the important questions that a data architect should answer when choosing a lakehouse compute engine are:

- Does the compute engine support the chosen open table format and the features that I need?
- Does it support the required version of open table format?
- Do these compute services integrate well with other services within my cloud ecosystem?
- Do the compute resources suit all the data personas using our platform?
- Do the cloud native engines offer acceptable BI performance, or do I need other third-party products?

- Do they support various data consumption workloads like BI reporting and machine learning?

Consider a scenario where you are evaluating the compute options available in the AWS cloud platform that support Delta Lake open table format. Figure 5-8 shows a simple exercise you might go through to evaluate different AWS compute options based on key considerations, available services, and their limitations (if any). I've considered AWS analytics services like Glue, EMR and Athena for this analysis. These observations are based on the latest versions of the various AWS services at the time of writing.

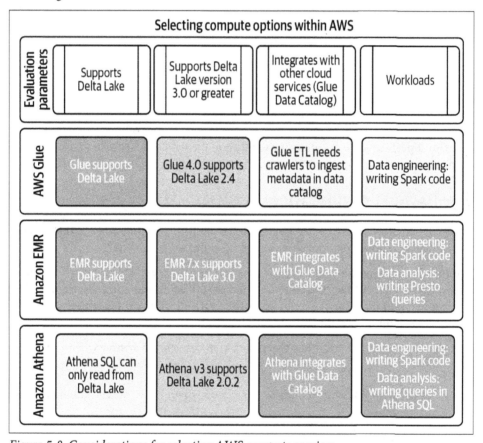

Figure 5-8. Considerations for selecting AWS compute services

The key observations from this exercise are:

- Glue 4.0 supports Delta Lake but not the latest version. We will also have to create Glue crawlers to ingest metadata in the Glue Data Catalog. You can use Glue mainly for data engineering workloads.

- EMR 7.x supports Delta Lake 3.0. It integrates with the Glue Data Catalog and can be used for both data engineering and data analysis workloads by leveraging the various open source frameworks it offers.
- Athena v3 engine supports Delta Lake 2.0.2. Athena SQL provides read capabilities for Delta Lake. You can use Athena Spark for writing Spark code.

You can also use these compute options individually or in combination. For example, consider using EMR for data engineering and Athena SQL for data analysis. You should do a similar exercise based on your cloud ecosystem and evaluate the several compute options carefully.

Let's discuss some of these key considerations for selecting the compute resources for your lakehouse platform.

Open Table Format Support

The most important design consideration when selecting a compute engine is its support for the chosen open table format that will be used to implement your lakehouse. As seen in the previous sections, several open source, cloud, and third-party compute engines are available to consider. However, not all these engines have deep support for Iceberg, Hudi, and Delta Lake table formats.

For example, consider a lakehouse implementation using the Azure cloud platform. Most of the Azure services, like Synapse Analytics, have native support for Delta Lake but not for other open table formats. For other formats, like Iceberg or Hudi, you will need additional configurations within the Synapse Spark environment. You may also consider using HDInsight with Spark to create a lakehouse using Iceberg—but you won't get native support for other table formats to query data from Synapse serverless SQL pools. You will have to use other open source engines, like Presto in HDInsight, to query the Iceberg tables. This can add complexity to your architecture and restrict you from using some native cloud services and their features.

Supported Version and Features

Once you have checked the compute engine's support for a specific table format, you should also check whether it supports the *latest version* of the open table format. Not every compute engine or cloud service will support the latest versions of the open table formats. In such cases, study the features that are unavailable in the supported (lower) version. If the missing features are not important to you, then you can use the compute engine. If the missing features are important to you, then explore other compute options or cloud services that support the latest versions.

For example, the latest Azure Synapse runtime for Spark supports Spark 3.4 (*https://oreil.ly/w3kmi*) and Delta Lake version 2.4.0 (*https://oreil.ly/MrTMo*). In such a case, you will lose the latest Delta Lake (*https://oreil.ly/HxuVV*) (v3.1 at the time of writing) features. You can wait until the Spark version that supports the latest Delta Lake is made available in Synapse Analytics, or you can explore other options like hosting a self-managed, open source Spark cluster where you can install the latest Spark and Delta Lake versions. You can check the latest Delta Lake version and compatibility with Spark at the Delta Lake website.

 Azure Synapse Analytics offers Spark pools, serverless SQL pools, metadata management features, and easy integration with other Azure services. It is much easier to use Synapse Analytics to implement a Delta Lake-based lakehouse platform than using HDInsight or running self-managed Spark clusters on virtual machines or containers.

There can be scenarios where the latest Azure Synapse Runtime for Spark does not support the latest Delta Lake version. In such cases, you might lose on some of the newest Delta Lake features—for example, liquid clustering, available from Delta Lake 3.1.0 on. If you don't have a high dependency on these latest features, it might be worth waiting for the latest Spark or Delta Lake versions to be made available within Synapse Analytics. After all, Synapse Analytics reduces the manual efforts required to set up, maintain, and manage Spark clusters while also reducing the complexity of integrating with other Azure services.

Always refer to the latest product or service documentation to understand which version it supports and design your system accordingly. You can also check with the product vendors about the availability dates (based on product roadmap) of the latest versions of these open source technologies in their products.

Ecosystem Support

Most of the time, the compute engine you choose will depend on the cloud ecosystem you use for your data platform. You must check for integration between these compute engines and other services.

For example, consider a scenario where you are implementing a lakehouse platform based on Delta Lake format on AWS. You have these two options for data ingestion and processing:

- Glue ETL jobs
- EMR

Glue ETL (GUI-based) does not automatically create the metadata in the Glue Data Catalog for Delta Lake format (at the time of writing). You will have to perform an additional step of creating a metadata table in the Glue Data Catalog using Glue crawlers. If you use EMR, you can directly sync Spark metadata with Glue Data Catalog so delta tables are immediately available, and you don't need to create and execute crawlers.

Another critical point is to check the open table format versions supported by two services within the same cloud platform. These can be different and may cause compatibility issues.

Case in point: Glue 4.0 supports Delta Lake 2.1 (*https://oreil.ly/P--1f*), while the latest version of EMR (*https://oreil.ly/C73R2*) (emr-7.x at the time of writing) supports Delta Lake 3.0. Similarly, when using the Azure ecosystem, check the Delta Lake version of delta files created by ADF and Synapse Analytics Spark pools, and study any compatibility issues. Delta Lake features are always backward compatible (tables written by lower Delta Lake versions can be read and written by higher Delta Lake versions) but some features can break forward compatibility (*https://oreil.ly/1OtDo*).

When working with the open table formats, ensure you check the supported open table format version and always use the latest versions of cloud services. As these are evolving technologies, every new version of a cloud service might add many new features.

Persona-Based Preferences

As discussed earlier, your choice of compute engine also depends on the data persona(s) using the engine. Figure 5-9 shows the preferred engines by data engineers and other personas.

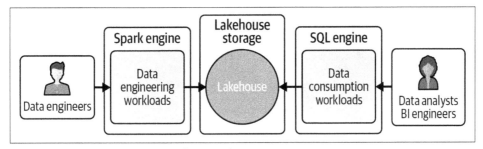

Figure 5-9. Processing engine preferences for various personas

To perform data processing activities, data practitioners use different cloud compute services based on their skills, expertise, and preferences. Data engineers prefer to use Spark notebooks, while data analysts prefer to use SQL editors.

Since lakehouse architecture uses a single storage tier and can support several engines, you can use different compute engines. Data architects should ensure that they design a flexible platform that can provision various compute engines (and a shared data catalog) so that different personas can use their preferred compute engine and collaborate.

A good rule of thumb is to provide a Spark-based notebook service for data engineers and a SQL engine for data analysts.

Managed Open Source Versus Cloud Native Versus Third-Party Products

Most cloud platforms offer managed open source services and their own cloud native purpose-built services for data computation activities. There are also third-party products that provide optimized compute engines for lakehouse platforms.

Table 5-1 provides a summary of pros and cons of using managed open source and cloud native offerings to implement a lakehouse platform.

Table 5-1. Managed open source versus cloud native services

	Managed open source services	Cloud native services
Pros	• Support for writing custom Spark code using notebooks (like EMR with Jupyter notebooks) • More control over the compute cluster and its scaling options • Ability to support different versions of open source frameworks • Flexibility to add libraries and configure Spark SQL extensions • Code can be easily migrated to other cloud platforms using the same open source services	• Easy integration with other cloud services like catalogs • GUI-based drag-and-drop programming (like Glue, ADF) • Built-in support for open table formats without any additional configuration efforts • No efforts required for cluster provisioning or initial setup • Deep integrations with other services like authentication and logging within the platform
Cons	• Requires effort for initial provisioning of clusters • Might need custom configurations for integration with other platform services • Latest open source updates might be slow and may take days or months to be available	• Uses proprietary platform services, so it is not easy to migrate to other cloud platforms • More expensive compared to managed open source
Examples	• Amazon EMR • Azure HDInsight	• AWS Glue • ADF

Based on the key design considerations discussed in previous sections and points mentioned in Table 5-1, carefully evaluate and select the services that meet your requirements.

Third-party platforms like Databricks, Snowflake, and Dremio provide an excellent alternative to cloud services. They offer some unique features to implement your data processing workloads. Since performance plays a significant role in selecting your compute resources, you can consider these third-party platforms if the cloud services do not provide the expected performance. Table 5-2 lists some of the benefits of leading third-party platforms.

Table 5-2. Benefits of third-party platforms

Third-party platform	Benefits
Databricks	• Offers an optimized Spark engine that can be used for notebooks and SQL query execution • Good alternative to Azure Synapse Analytics or Amazon EMR; provides deeper Spark-Delta Lake integration • Latest and consistent Delta Lake versions across data engineering and consumption services
Snowflake	• Data platforms built using Snowflake can share data with non-Snowflake consumers by storing data as native Iceberg tables (preview feature); consumers can use preferred compute engine to query data stored as Iceberg files in cloud storage
Dremio	• Dremio lakehouse platform offers a SQL engine called Dremio Sonar (*https://oreil.ly/_Zlf5*) that provides data warehouse-level performance on lakehouses

You can also consider other options, like using self-managed virtual machines or containers, for installing and managing compute engines. This approach provides the highest level of flexibility and customization but needs more effort and expertise for its implementation.

Data Consumption Workloads

Multiple data consumption workloads use the compute engines for their data computation needs. These workloads range from creating dashboards to running ML models for predictions or forecasting. Your choice of compute engine for these workloads largely depends on your cloud platform.

BI workloads

Popular tools like Tableau (*https://www.tableau.com*), Power BI, and Looker help you create reports, visualizations, and dashboards as per business needs. Deciding which of these tools to use is mainly driven by the cloud platform you use or by an organization-level strategic decision to adopt one or many of them.

When selecting the compute engine for these tools, look for the available connectors and supported features. Using tools from the same cloud ecosystem will reduce integration efforts—like authentication, cataloging, and security—with other services.

For example, Power BI can use Synapse serverless SQL pool to connect to Delta Lake tables and query data. Power BI can also read Delta Lake tables natively without any Spark or Synapse cluster running. You can study the Power BI—Delta Lake connector (*https://oreil.ly/aMnIJ*) to understand which features are supported.

Amazon QuickSight helps to create modern interactive reports and dashboards within AWS. You can use the Athena engine with QuickSight to execute queries and fetch data from the lakehouse with fine-grained access control implemented using the AWS Lake Formation service.

AI/ML workloads

Lakehouse architecture provides a unified platform for all your data and AI/ML use cases. You can use AI/ML cloud services or third-party products to implement these use cases. Most of these services use Spark as a processing engine and can benefit from Spark and open table format integration.

Amazon SageMaker is a service within AWS that builds, supports, and trains ML models. It supports Iceberg for creating feature tables and registering metadata in the Glue Data Catalog. SageMaker also supports reading/writing Delta Lake files using the Delta-Spark (*https://oreil.ly/YPsch*) library (PyPI package based on Python APIs).

Databricks ML (*https://oreil.ly/OWqXF*) offers out-of-box integration of MLflow (*https://mlflow.org*) with Delta Lake, enabling data scientists to perform experiments easily. You can consider Databricks clusters for ML workloads that need MLflow-Delta Lake integrations.

Always be sure to check available connectors, supported table formats, and features available when selecting an ML service for your lakehouse.

The open table formats provide features to unify data engineering, data analysis, and data science workloads. You should choose compute resources that can help to leverage these features and enable all types of personas to perform their activities efficiently. There might not be a single compute engine that can offer all the features you need.

The best part of the lakehouse architecture is that you don't have to choose just one compute service. You get the freedom to use any compute service within your cloud ecosystem. Use the questions below to evaluate and select a compute engine:

- Is there a cloud native service that supports the preferred open table format and required versions?
- If I need more customization, is there a managed open source service I should consider?
- Is there a third-party product or platform that can provide more significant benefits?
- If nothing works, do I want to use virtual machines or containers to manually install the required compute engines and other compatible technologies?

Key Takeaways

Lakehouse architecture gives you the freedom to choose compute engines. You aren't restricted to a single engine or a single cloud service. This opens up many opportunities to provision multiple engines in your lakehouse, enabling different data personas to perform their data computation activities.

There are several options for provisioning the compute resources within a lakehouse. Table 5-3 summarizes the key compute options available across open source tools, cloud services, and third-party platforms.

Table 5-3. Compute options summary

Platform	Compute engine options
Open source (self-managed)	Spark, Presto/Trino, Flink
AWS	Glue ETL, EMR, Athena
Azure	ADF, HDInsight, Synapse Analytics
GCP	Dataproc, BigQuery
Third-party	Databricks, Snowflake, Dremio

While provisioning compute engines for your lakehouse, remember these key points:

- Before selecting any compute engine, check its support for the open table formats you have chosen for your lakehouse.

- Read the cloud services documentation to check which version of the Spark or Trino/Presto engine they support. Also, check the version of the open table format they support and whether it has all the necessary features you need.

- If the compute engines are not based on open source technologies, check if the engine supports your preferred open table format. For example, Azure Serverless SQL is based on the Polaris engine. Study all limitations and implement the workarounds to overcome the critical ones.

- You will face fewer integration challenges when implementing platforms that use the same compute engine for data engineering and analysis. For example, Spark is used for data engineering, and Spark SQL is used for data analysis in Databricks.

- Communities and commercial vendors are constantly working on creating new connectors for different compute engines to support open table formats. Keep an eye on these and leverage them in your platforms as required.

- There are purpose-built, third-party products that offer optimized compute engines with features that can enhance the BI performance of your queries. Consider these when evaluating the overall tech stack.

In this chapter, we discussed the different compute options within a lakehouse platform and the key considerations when selecting them. In the next chapter, we will discuss the best practices and practical challenges for implementing data governance and security processes within a lakehouse platform.

References

AWS

- Using the Iceberg Framework in AWS Glue (*https://oreil.ly/S80Ij*)
- Using the Hudi Framework in AWS Glue (*https://oreil.ly/8726O*)
- Using the Delta Lake Framework in AWS Glue (*https://oreil.ly/PmrCx*)
- Iceberg | Amazon EMR (*https://oreil.ly/Dd5u6*)
- Hudi | Amazon EMR (*https://oreil.ly/D3IWe*)
- Delta Lake | Amazon EMR (*https://oreil.ly/UxGs2*)
- Build a High-Performance, Transactional Data Lake Using Open-Source Delta Lake on Amazon EMR | AWS Big Data Blog (*https://oreil.ly/Q_GHP*)
- Querying Across Regions | Amazon Athena (*https://oreil.ly/8615o*)
- Choosing an Open Table Format for your Transactional Data Lake on AWS (*https://oreil.ly/b1aeF*)
- Using Apache Iceberg Tables with Amazon Redshift (*https://oreil.ly/600kr*)
- Load and Transform Data from Delta Lake Using Amazon SageMaker Studio and Apache Spark | AWS Machine Learning Blog (*https://oreil.ly/gUvDB*)
- Presto, Trino, and Athena to Delta Lake Integration using manifests (*https://oreil.ly/n5RVQ*)
- Querying Linux Foundation Delta Lake Tables | Amazon Athena (*https://oreil.ly/-6TpL*)

Azure

- Delta Format in Azure Data Factory (*https://oreil.ly/0hniA*)
- Delta Lake on HDInsight | Microsoft Community Hub (*https://oreil.ly/uViyf*)
- HDInsight - Iceberg Open-Source Table Format | Microsoft Community Hub (*https://oreil.ly/TDWQx*)
- Use Delta Lake in Azure HDInsight on AKS with Apache Spark Cluster (*https://oreil.ly/Y-u1c*)
- Apache Hudi on Microsoft Azure (*https://oreil.ly/Sjz5Q*)
- Connect to Serverless SQL Pool with Power BI Professional (*https://oreil.ly/0D_3R*)

- Update-AzSynapseSparkPool (Az.Synapse) | Microsoft Learn (*https://oreil.ly/mbcSs*)

GCP
- Dataproc | Google Cloud (*https://oreil.ly/ykt0b*)
- 1.5.x release versions | Dataproc Documentation (*https://oreil.ly/TtN05*)
- Create Apache Iceberg BigLake Tables | BigQuery (*https://oreil.ly/qVkho*)
- Work With Stored Procedures for Apache Spark | BigQuery (*https://oreil.ly/U_fdM*)

Databricks
- Data Skipping for Delta Lake | Databricks on AWS (*https://oreil.ly/2jTtD*)
- Productionizing Machine Learning with Delta Lake | Databricks Blog (*https://oreil.ly/C1M4W*)
- Databricks Pricing (*https://oreil.ly/v2Ff4*)

Snowflake
- Iceberg Tables: Powering Open Standards with Snowflake Innovations (*https://oreil.ly/y8iMq*)
- Unifying Iceberg Tables on Snowflake (*https://oreil.ly/UHXii*)
- Iceberg Tables: Catalog Support Now Available (*https://oreil.ly/lQqLk*)

Delta Lake
- Delta Lake Small File Compaction with OPTIMIZE (*https://oreil.ly/kESHn*)
- Building a More Efficient Data Infrastructure for Machine Learning with Open Source using Delta Lake, Amazon SageMaker, and EMR (*https://oreil.ly/ufrX-*)
- [Feature Request] Liquid Clustering, Issue #1874 | delta-io/delta GitHub (*https://oreil.ly/UE5kN*)
- Delta Lake Z Order (*https://oreil.ly/kl4-J*)

Dremio/Iceberg
- How Z-Ordering in Apache Iceberg Helps Improve Performance (*https://oreil.ly/ugoC8*)
- Compaction in Apache Iceberg: Fine-Tuning Your Iceberg Table's Data Files (*https://oreil.ly/hhCjY*)
- Unleash Data-Driven Innovation with Unified Analytics and Collaborative Governance | Dremio Documentation (*https://oreil.ly/ZorX6*)
- Reflection | Dremio Documentation (*https://oreil.ly/Th9t8*)

Other
- Presto SQL query engine, Presto versus Trino (*https://oreil.ly/gV5rd*)

CHAPTER 6

Data (and AI) Governance and Security in Lakehouse Architecture

A data platform revolves around three key pillars: people, process, and technology. In the previous chapters, we discussed various technologies for implementing a lakehouse. This chapter focuses on the people and process aspects of lakehouse implementations. This chapter will help you understand how lakehouse architecture implements unified governance and security processes across all of your data and ML/AI assets.

You need sound governance and security processes to enable those who work on lakehouse data to collaborate, exchange data securely, and maintain trust in the data. These governance and security processes lay the foundation of a robust data ecosystem.

I'll first introduce you to the key governance concepts and explain why governance is required and how it helps improve overall data management activities. We will focus on data quality, auditing, lineage, sharing, and different compliances you should consider while designing the data governance strategy for your platform. We will discuss why data security is essential for modern data platforms and how to secure your data when it is at rest, in transit, and in use by consumers. We will also explore the various options to identify and protect the sensitive data within your platform.

The last section of the chapter will guide you through your responsibilities in terms of governance and security, based on your role in the lakehouse implementation program.

What Is Data Governance and Data Security?

Data practitioners sometimes use the terms *data governance* and *data security* interchangeably. Although they are different concepts, they complement each other to manage and protect data within the data platform.

As briefly discussed in Chapter 1, data governance is an umbrella term that comprises various standards, rules, and policies to ensure that all data management processes follow formal guidelines. These guidelines are meant to assure and improve compliance, data quality, data trust, and value. Data governance provides guidance for both data and metadata ingestion, integration, storage, ownership, consumption, and sharing.

Data security deals with data protection—wherever it resides and whenever users access it. Security ensures that only the right people have the right levels of access to the right data. It ensures that your data will only be shared and accessed by authorized consumers (internal or external).

Figure 6-1 shows the different data governance and data security processes.

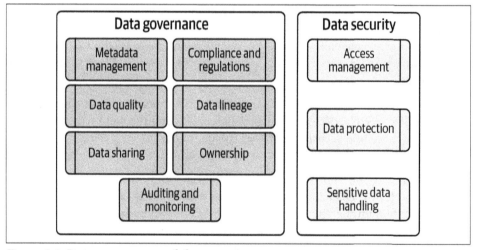

Figure 6-1. Data governance and data security processes

As shown in Figure 6-1, data governance and security are both essential functions and comprise different processes.

Data governance includes:

- Metadata management of all objects stored within the data ecosystem
- Compliance processes to follow industry- or country-specific rules and regulations

- Data quality to measure, monitor, and maintain the quality of data stored within the lakehouse
- Data lineage to track how data flows from source to target systems
- Secure data sharing with external consumers and downstream applications
- Assigning the right owners who are accountable for data
- Auditing and monitoring to track data access, frequency of access, and other audit use cases

Data security includes:

- Managing fine-grained access control for internal and external users
- Data protection when data is at rest or when it moves across systems
- Sensitive data management for protecting personal and private information

Benefits of Data Governance and Data Security

Data governance and security are essential functions that enable your platform users to perform search and discovery, conduct self-service analytics, collaborate with other users, and share data with third parties without compromising the quality and security of data stored within the platform.

The combined benefits that data governance and data security processes offer include:

- Reduced *data downtime* and increased consumer trust in data by improving data quality
- Compliance with regulations like HIPAA, SOX, PCI DSS, GDPR, and other similar laws avoids severe penalties
- Tracking end-to-end data flow, user activities, and unauthorized data access by implementing data lineage, auditing, and monitoring
- Ability to share, monetize, and exchange data with external partners and customers
- Protecting your data and avoiding data breaches and the associated reputational risk
- Ability to identify sensitive data and add required controls to mask it

Data downtime, as described by data observability platform Monte Carlo (*https://www.montecarlodata.com*), is a period when your data is erroneous or incomplete. If you don't implement data quality validations in your pipelines, you will often end up with data you cannot trust for accuracy or completeness.

In the modern data world, data governance and security have become mandatory for any organization that wants to be data-driven. Data governance initiatives enable such organizations to leverage their data not just to get the right value out of it but also to use it as a tool for collaborating with the outside world.

Unified Governance and Security in Lakehouse Architecture

In traditional data warehouses, governance was restricted to data assets, while platforms built using a data lake architecture did not employ robust governance processes. However, lakehouse architecture is built not just for data assets like tables, views, or BI reports; it's also built for AI assets like feature stores and ML models. Lakehouse architecture enables you to implement a unified data and AI governance strategy, holistically covering all of your data and AI assets.

Figure 6-2 shows unified governance across data and AI assets in lakehouse architecture.

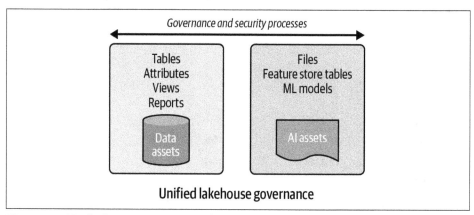

Figure 6-2. Unified governance across data and AI assets in a lakehouse

Unified governance provides several benefits, including:

- Central metadata management for data and AI assets that enables users to search and discover tables, views, reports, and ML models from a single interface

- Reuse of data quality rules, access permissions, and other governance policies (created in data pipelines) in ML data prep activities

- Tracking end-to-end lineage across data and AI assets to understand the impact of any source attribute changes on BI reports and ML models

- Ability to share tables, datasets, BI reports, and ML models with partners, customers, and external users

- Consistent access control policies across BI and AI use cases

- Monitoring end-to-end data flow from ingestion to report and model consumption

Governance and Security Processes in Lakehouse Architecture

Governance and security processes are an integral part of your lakehouse platform. In this section, we'll discuss the ten key areas in which you should implement these processes.

Metadata Management

In Chapter 4, we discussed the significance of data catalogs in metadata management, quick search, and easy discovery. Metadata management helps you control and govern metadata across data and AI assets in your lakehouse.

Lakehouse data governance policies around metadata provide guidance for:

- Ingesting metadata from different data systems into the central metadata repository

- Managing metadata of tables, views, files, reports, feature stores, and ML models

- Adding and maintaining the business context of assets for easy discovery and self-serve analysis

- Providing the right levels of access to users and enabling them to perform quick and easy data discovery

You should treat your metadata as a first-class citizen within your data ecosystem. Metadata is the backbone of lakehouse data governance, and you should implement it carefully, considering the following best practices:

- Assign data administrators to manage the metadata and its ingestion process, and to enforce the access policies.

- Auto-schedule the metadata ingestion process to keep metadata up-to-date.

- Frequently review metadata to identify tables without a business description and notify the respective data stewards.

Compliance and Regulations

Governance ensures that the data management processes align with the relevant compliance and regulations. You must follow country- and industry-specific compliance criteria when implementing a data platform. These rules also apply to AI assets, so be sure that your ML models comply with all the applicable regulations.

What Are the Different Compliances?

General Data Protection Regulation (*https://gdpr-info.eu*) (GDPR) protects European Union (EU) consumers' data and provides them the right to request their information be deleted.

Health Insurance Portability and Accountability Act (*https://oreil.ly/pVf9T*) (HIPAA) defines various regulations for protecting individual medical records and personal health information, known as Protected Health Information (PHI) data.

Payment Card Industry Data Security Standard (*https://oreil.ly/UOpqQ*) (PCI DSS) is a global data security standard that regulates the data generated, processed, and stored during payment transactions using cards.

These are just a few of the key compliances and regulations data practitioners need to be aware of and design for when implementing a data platform. There are many others, like the California Consumer Privacy Act (*https://oag.ca.gov/privacy/ccpa*) (CCPA), Sarbanes-Oxley Act (*https://sarbanes-oxley-act.com*) (SOX), Federal Risk and Authorization Management Program (*https://www.fedramp.gov*) (FedRAMP), and more that many organizations must follow based on their country of operation, industry, and the products and services that they provide.

In lakehouse implementations, you can leverage the features of open table formats and other technologies to comply with such regulatory mandates. One example is the "Right to be forgotten" as part of GDPR compliance, which mandates that customer data should be deleted when requested by the customer. You can implement this requirement in a lakehouse by deleting the customer record stored in cloud storage using Delta Lake's update/delete (soft delete) and vacuum (permanent delete) features.

While selecting tools, cloud platforms, regions, or cloud services, check if they comply with such regulations. For example, not every cloud service has a secondary site in the same country. Having a secondary site (to back up data) within the same country is a common compliance requirement.

While implementing ML models, consider all applicable laws and regulations. Remember these key points:

- Avoid using any sensitive data for model training without masking the values.
- Ensure that the data used for training is collected ethically and does not invade individual privacy.

 As a consultant, I've worked on projects across industries like banking, insurance, telecommunications, and pharmaceuticals. It is difficult to have deep knowledge of all the compliances associated with these industries. So, I try to collaborate with the compliance and security teams within the organizations to understand these compliances and their impact on the data platform. As a data architect, knowing the relevant compliances and working with other teams to understand the applicable rules and regulations is essential.

Data and ML Model Quality

Data quality is one of the most critical parameters that impacts users' trust in data. Good-quality data helps increase the consumer's trust in data; inferior data quality affects the accuracy of reports, predictions, and overall business decisions that are based on data.

Measuring data quality and using processes to improve should be a key part of your data governance strategy.

You can measure data quality based on the following five key dimensions (though, there can be more):

Accuracy
    Ensures that the data in the lakehouse is accurate and error-free

Consistency
    Ensures that the data is always consistent and does not return any inconsistent or conflicting values when accessed by different users

Freshness
    Ensures that the latest data is always available for processing

Uniqueness
    Ensures that there are no duplicate values in data

Completeness
    Ensures that you store complete data in target tables without any partial records

Similarly, you must also measure the quality of your ML models. With time, some models might not give the best possible results due to data drift or bias. Data drift can be caused by model degradation, as data sent by source systems or external data providers changes. ML models can develop bias over time that skews the results, which are unrealistic or away from the ground reality.

Implement processes to identify issues with your ML models that can degrade their results and overall performance.

To ensure sound data governance within your lakehouse, keep data quality at the core of all your data processes by following these best practices:

- Add technical and business validations at all layers within the lakehouse storage. When data moves between the raw, cleansed, and curated layers of lakehouse, perform data reconciliation to identify any data leakages.

- Leverage technology features, like constraints (Delta Lake) (*https://oreil.ly/Wh7PL*) and pre-commit validators (Apache Hudi) (*https://oreil.ly/TRrv9*), that add data quality checks during data processing. Automate these as much as possible.

- Always maintain rejected data in tables and share it with the source systems for their analysis and rectification.

- Generate data quality dashboards daily to get a quick view of data health. Take appropriate actions to improve data quality.

- Implement data observability features to decrease data downtime.

Lineage Across Data and AI assets

Data lineage provides information about how the data navigates your data platform.

Since all the data is on a single storage tier in lakehouse architecture, you can get end-to-end lineage from source systems to the target tables, reports, and models. Figure 6-3 shows how attributes are propagated from a source table cust_details to lakehouse dimension tables, BI reports, and ML models.

Lineage helps you understand the data flow, perform impact analysis, identify redundant objects, and track sensitive data.

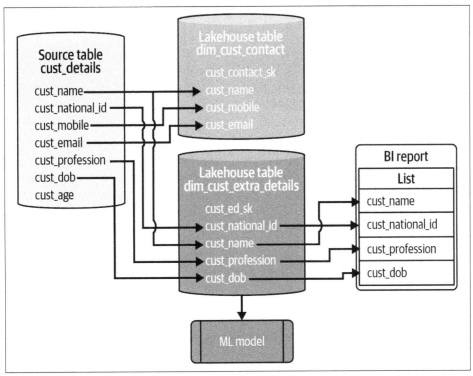

Figure 6-3. Attribute-level lineage in lakehouse architecture

Understanding data flow

Data lineage helps to track the flow between source and target table and attributes. Table-level lineage gives information on source tables, which populate the target tables, and enables you to understand the entities involved in the processes carried out in the data pipeline. Attribute-level lineage enables you to easily track how the attributes are populated and which downstream tables use these attributes.

Performing impact analysis

As we've discussed, lakehouse architecture provides end-to-end lineage—from source systems to BI reports and ML models. Use this end-to-end lineage for analyzing the impact of source schema changes, which is one of the most common and frequent scenarios faced by data teams. For example, as shown in Figure 6-3, cust_profession is one of the attributes in the cust_details table. If the name of this attribute changes to cust_occupation, lineage can help you understand the impact of this change by identifying the downstream tables, reports, and ML models that are using this attribute.

Identifying unused objects

Data lineage helps identify tables or attributes not used by downstream applications or other consumers. As shown in Figure 6-3, none of the target tables, reports, or models use the cust_age attribute from the source table. All downstream systems are using cust_dob to calculate age, if required. Lineage can indicate such redundant tables or attributes that are no longer needed.

Tracking sensitive data

If PII data is present within your lakehouse, lineage can help identify the systems producing it and the consumers using it. You can track all tables, reports, or models using PII attributes and take appropriate action to remove or abstract the sensitive data. For example, consider the attribute cust_national_id, shown in Figure 6-3. This attribute holds the customer's sensitive data and so must be handled accordingly.

Data and AI Asset Sharing

Multiple consumers access and use the data stored in a lakehouse. These consumers can be internal users, external users like customers and partners, or downstream applications. These consumers might be on different data platforms. For example, let's say your lakehouse platform is on Azure but your consumers are using AWS. In such cases, the open table format enables you to share data with others using its data-sharing features.

Traditionally, organizations would extract data from data warehouses as files and share them with external parties. This activity added replication and resulted in data redundancy. In lakehouse architecture, you don't have to extract data; consumers can directly access data stored in open formats. For example, consider the Delta Sharing (*https://delta.io/sharing*) protocol by Delta Lake, which is an open protocol for data sharing. It enables sharing of live data (in real time) without making a copy of the data. It also provides features to track and audit the access of shared data assets.

Lakehouse data sharing with well-governed processes help you to:

- Share data with various external consumers (including BI tools, governance products, analytics platforms) and let them leverage their own compute engine based on the products and platforms that they use.

- Explore opportunities to collaborate and exchange data with the outside world through secure data-sharing initiatives.

- Monetize your data and AI assets on marketplaces.

- Create clean rooms to share raw data with customers and partners to get more insights into your data without losing the data privacy.

A clean room is a controlled environment often used by organizations for sharing data securely with partners to perform collaborative analysis, like advertising agencies for targeted marketing.

However, sharing does not mean you compromise on data security. Remember these recommendations:

- Share only the required tables or attributes and not the complete schema.
- Review the shared objects and permissions regularly.
- Ensure sensitive data is not shared—even with internal users—with consumers who are not supposed to access sensitive information.

Data Ownership

As part of the data governance process, you must identify and assign the correct data owners for your data assets. Data owners are accountable for the data and can provide the business descriptions of the datasets. You should also have processes to identify data stewards, who can help maintain the data, add business context, classify data, highlight any sensitive information, and take required actions to maintain its quality and sensitivity. Both these roles are essential to persist good-quality data in the lakehouse.

You may be wondering: What is the difference between a data owner and a data steward?

While both of these roles come from business teams, they have different responsibilities.

The *data owner* is accountable for data and is best suited to describe data, define business descriptions of the data, and make strategic decisions related to the data. They are mainly in executive-level roles and are not involved in day-to-day operational activities.

The *data steward* is also from the business functions but works closely with IT to get data in the right shape, as defined by the data owner. They are the subject matter experts for specific datasets and understand their data better than the IT teams. They also know how to use data catalogs to explore data and how to use various features to classify and profile data. You can identify and assign data stewards based on their usage of specific tables or datasets.

To summarize, data owners provide strategic guidance while data stewards implement the required policies to govern, secure, and manage data.

You should consider assigning those users who run the most queries on a specific table as data stewards and involve them in data quality discussions when collaborating with the source system owners.

Auditing and Monitoring

As part of the data platform audit process, you can track various activities that users, or applications perform while accessing the data. You can use audit logs for different use cases related to data security, compliance, and other data governance processes. As part of your data governance initiatives, you should audit and monitor various data management processes, ML experiments, and models deployed in your lakehouse platform.

Auditing and monitoring can help you to answer questions like:

- How many users accessed a specific table or attribute in the last x days?
- Which tables are queried the most on a daily or monthly basis?
- Are there any tables not accessed in the previous x months?
- Which users accessed attributes that hold sensitive data?
- Which users tried to access tables that they were not authorized to access?
- Is there any data leakage as the data flows from source to target?
- Is your model's quality degrading over a period of time?

In a lakehouse, you can implement an end-to-end auditing of data. You can track all user activities, including query execution, table access, and API requests. Some of the approaches to using audit logs effectively are:

- Use the audit logs to identify the most commonly used datasets and publish these in your list of most used datasets within the organization. This can help users perform self-serve analytics.
- Identify users who frequently access specific datasets. Promote these users to be the data stewards of these datasets to certify the data, maintain its quality, and answer other user queries related to that dataset. Enterprise-grade catalog tools (like Alation) can help you identify and assign data stewards based on their access patterns.
- Based on the encryption keys access logs (like AWS KMS), identify unauthorized access attempts to data in order to spot attempted breaches or accidental access requests by internal users; be sure to educate them.

Access Management

Access management is part of the data security processes and enables data administrators to restrict access to the data stored in the lakehouse. In traditional architectures like data lakes, users could only implement a coarse-grained access control compared to the fine-grained access control employed by lakehouses. Table 6-1 lists the differences between coarse-grained and fine-grained access controls.

Table 6-1. Coarse-grained versus fine-grained access

Coarse-grained access management (data lake)	Fine-grained access management (lakehouse)
You can grant the access permissions only at the file level.	You can grant access permission at the table-, column-, or row-level.
You cannot restrict the access to specific attributes or records within the files.	You can restrict users to access specific attributes or records within a table.
It often requires tedious workarounds like creating views with selective attributes or selective records.	Modern data catalogs often provide out-of-box features to implement fine-grained access controls.

You can manage fine-grained access across tables, views, and reports using the central data catalog in a lakehouse, based on the user roles, user attributes, metadata tags, data sensitivity, or data classification.

For efficient access management in a lakehouse, follow the three Rs process—restrict, review, and revoke—shown in Figure 6-4.

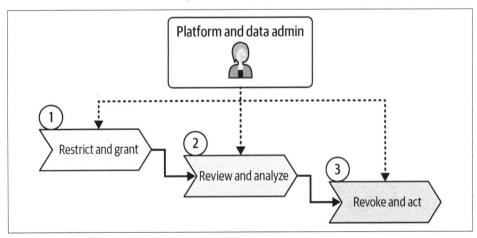

Figure 6-4. Three Rs access management process in a lakehouse

Restrict (and grant)
> Restrict access to all tables and grant only the least-required privileges to selective tables.

Most of the catalogs we discussed in Chapter 4 provide features to manage access to users, groups, or roles. Leverage these features to provide limited access.

When providing access to external consumers, give time-bound access for a few hours or days, as requested.

Review (and analyze)
Granting access is just half the process. Periodically reviewing the provided access is critical for maintaining the lakehouse security.

Cloud platforms provide services to perform "access analytics" that you can leverage to find frequently accessed tables and attributes.

Monitor the audit logs and access logs to check which users and roles are accessing specific attributes like PII or PHI data. Review whether they still need that access.

Revoke (and act)
Post-review, revoke any access that is no longer needed.

Take appropriate actions against any unauthorized access attempts.

Based on your use case, you can consider using third-party products like Immuta (*https://www.immuta.com*) or Privacera (*https://privacera.com*) for fine-grained access controls across the entire data ecosystem. These products can help simplify data access management overall.

Data Protection

Always protect your data—when it is at rest and in transit. You should never compromise data security to enhance performance, simplify management, or reduce costs. Figure 6-5 shows protection techniques for data while it is stored inside a lakehouse as well as when it moves in or out of the lakehouse.

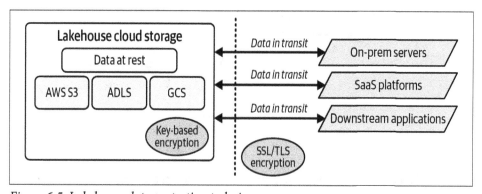

Figure 6-5. Lakehouse data protection techniques

Data at rest

In a lakehouse architecture, all data is stored in the cloud storage. This data, known as "data at rest," should always be encrypted. Every cloud provider offers services for encrypting data stored in its cloud storage. For example, if you are using Amazon S3 to store your lakehouse data, you can encrypt data using one of the following approaches:

- Use AWS managed keys (*https://oreil.ly/_Z5TK*) for server-side encryption (SSE-KMS).
- Use customer-managed keys for server-side encryption (SSE-C).
- Encrypt the data (client-side encryption) before loading it to cloud storage.

Similarly, other cloud providers offer key management services for encrypting data stored in their cloud object services.

Data in transit

It's also important to encrypt data that is moving, or "data in transit." You can use the services provided by cloud platforms to ensure that you securely move the data in and out of the lakehouse storage. Most cloud providers offer Secure Sockets Layer (SSL) or Transport Layer Security (TLS) encryption when data is moving in and out of the platform.

Some other alternatives for securing data in transit are:

- AWS Direct Connect (*https://oreil.ly/qN29Q*), Azure ExpressRoute (*https://oreil.ly/TCo10*), or GCP Cloud Interconnect (*https://oreil.ly/O_ak2*). These tools provide direct connectivity and additional security while moving data from on-premises systems.
- Use virtual private networks between the CSPs and on-premises networks.
- Third-party providers like Snowflake (*https://oreil.ly/IXp97*) and Databricks (*https://oreil.ly/PMuUM*) offer private links when moving data from the cloud to their platforms. They also offer enhanced data security features.

When implementing data-protecting features for your lakehouse, follow these best practices:

- For encrypting data at rest, use a customer-managed key with key rotation policies for more security.
- Consider using different keys for different buckets in your cloud storage based on the purpose of the bucket. For example, use separate keys for buckets that external users can access and other keys for buckets used by internal data engineering teams.

- Tokenize or mask data while storing (if required) for additional security. In such cases, even if someone gets accidental access to the bucket holding this data, they won't be able to see the actual raw data.

- Implement data movement through intranet, VPN, or other secure channels wherever possible and avoid moving data through the internet. This might increase costs but will give an additional layer of security.

Handling Sensitive Data

Data platforms generally deal with a variety of sensitive data. It can be related to PII, PHI, or other attributes like credit card numbers. Implement security checks for handling sensitive data stored in your lakehouse platform. The sensitive data handling process has two main steps: identify sensitive data and anonymize sensitive data.

Identify sensitive data

Source systems, external third-party applications, manual data uploads, and other similar data producers can introduce sensitive data to your platform. When you build your lakehouse system, be sure to implement processes to identify sensitive attributes. You can implement manual or automated techniques that run frequently to identify sensitive data. Modern catalogs or third-party security platforms can help identify sensitive attributes and alert data administrators.

Anonymize sensitive data

Once you identify any sensitive data, you must anonymize or abstract this data to ensure limited access to it in its raw form. There are several methods that you can implement to anonymize sensitive data, including:

- Use features like dynamic data masking that abstracts sensitive data based on who is accessing it. Eligible users can see the data in its raw form, while others can see the abstracted data. Products like Databricks and Snowflake offer such dynamic masking features.

- If you want to anonymize key columns and use them to join other tables, consider hashing or tokenizing the data. These are the standard methods used in data ecosystems to abstract key columns while retaining their uniqueness (as joining keys) to perform SQL join operations.

- The above two approaches use "data on read" masking, or masking that is applied when users read the data. However, you should also check if specific compliance requirements restrict storing unmasked sensitive data. For example, PCI DSS compliance has particular mandates for storing cardholder data. In such cases, you can consider tokenizing the data or using third-party services specializing in tokenizing card data before storing it in the platform.

Unauthorized access to PII can cause several compliance issues. Consider the below points when implementing processes for handling sensitive data:

- Automate the process to identify sensitive attributes. The best approach is to raise alerts when the system detects any PII during metadata ingestion.
- Use lineage features of modern data catalogs to find upstream and downstream tables, reports, feature store tables, or ML models that use sensitive attributes.
- Automate the PII anonymization process to abstract the data as soon as it is detected and send alerts to respective stewards.
- Use audit and monitoring to raise alerts in case unauthorized users try to access sensitive data.
- Always consult your compliance and security teams before deciding on encryption, masking, or tokenization approaches for storing sensitive data in your lakehouse.

This section discussed the essential governance and security processes you should apply across ten key areas. Implementing these processes will enable you to implement a well-governed and secure lakehouse platform.

What's Your Role?

Data governance is a team sport, and every data persona plays a significant role in ensuring the governance and security of the platform.

Figure 6-6 shows the different data personas from business and IT functions. I'll summarize these personas, and their responsibilities in terms of data governance and security, in this section:

Business sponsors
> These are executives from business teams and have the following governance-related responsibilities:
>
> - Provide budget approvals for data teams to work on data governance and security initiatives right from the program's start.
> - Support onboarding of governance committee members to advocate data governance initiatives and perform periodic reviews of processes.

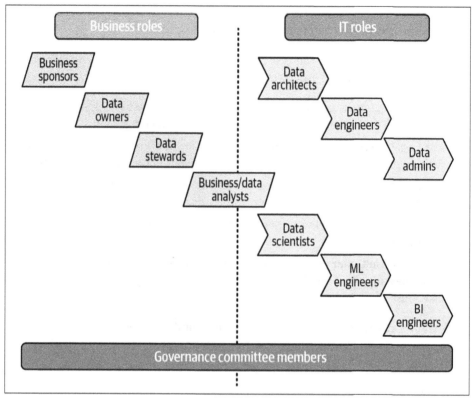

Figure 6-6. Personas using the data platform

Data owners

Data owners are business executives and should take up the following responsibilities:

- Define the business meaning of the data and work with data stewards to add the business descriptions to data catalogs.

- Take ownership and accountability for their data and make strategic decisions to support governance policies.

Data stewards

Data stewards are part of business teams and have in-depth knowledge of data for their domains. They should take up the following responsibilities:

- Profile the data loaded by data engineers, using tools like data profilers, to find any outliers or data issues.

- Analyze any sensitive data alerts and take action to abstract them.

- Work with the source systems and data owners to rectify erroneous data.

- Add business context to technical metadata to enable non-technical and business users to perform self-serve analytics.

Business analysts and data analysts

Analysts can be from a business team or they can be an experienced person from IT who has a good understanding of the domain. They have the following governance responsibilities:

- Be cautious when querying the data and query only the data they are authorized to access. Remember, any unauthorized access gets tracked and reported.

- Inform lakehouse data administrators of changes to their roles or departments for revoking or changing access levels.

- In case of accidental access to sensitive data, inform lakehouse administrators to implement the suitable abstraction mechanism.

Data architects

Data architects are part of the IT team and are responsible for the following activities when designing the lakehouse:

- Treat data governance and security as "day 0" (right from the beginning of your lakehouse project) activities, ensuring they are core design principles.

- Design all processes—including data ingestion, transformations, storage, and consumption—to comply with the governance and security policies.

- Collaborate with business, compliance, security, and cloud infrastructure teams to understand compliance and security requirements.

- Document governance and security guidelines and conduct sessions with data engineers, scientists, administrators, analysts, and other personas to explain how to incorporate these guidelines while working with platform data.

Data engineers

Data engineers are part of the IT team and play a vital role in implementing a well-governed lakehouse by owning these responsibilities:

- Keep data quality at the core of each data pipeline that they implement. Add validations to reject erroneous records and persist good-quality data in the higher storage zones of the lakehouse.

- Use the lakehouse features like constraints in Delta Lake to enforce data quality rules. Leverage the schema enforcement and evolution features to perform schema validations or to evolve schema.

- Always secure data when storing in the cloud storage. Anonymize any sensitive data before storing the data in the higher storage zones of the system.

- Inform data administrators about any accidental access to sensitive data they should not be exposed to.

Data administrators

Data administrators are the gatekeepers of the data ecosystem and are responsible for the following:

- Ingest metadata from different systems regularly and make it available for search and discovery.

- Implement the granular levels of access controls by restricting attributes based on user roles or tags. Grant only relevant access to data consumers based on their roles or departments within the organization.

- Manage the technical metadata and assign data stewards to data assets and owners for ML models and BI dashboards.

- Review the access permissions to internal and external or downstream consumers frequently.

Data scientists, ML engineers, and BI engineers

These are the internal data consumers and have the following governance-related responsibilities:

- Manage the ML models and BI reports and dashboards according to the organization's data governance policies.

- Follow DataOps and MLOps processes, maintaining code and model versions, and tracking access using audit processes.

Data governance committee members

The data governance committee members can be from various departments including IT, business, legal, and compliance. These members have the following responsibilities related to governance:

- Plan and document various data governance requirements, including compliance mandates, industry- or country-specific regulations, and data residency rules.

- Review the governance policies at regular intervals and measure the maturity levels periodically.

- Advocate and promote governance so that governance initiatives are embraced by data teams, instead of being seen as a bottleneck for deliverables.

What Is an Analytics Engineer?

The role of an analytics engineer has grown in popularity among modern data teams. Their work is a mix of data engineering and data analysis and brings in some best practices from the software engineering world, such as code modularity, reusability, versioning, continuous integration, and documentation. Analytics engineers create reusable and clean datasets that other data consumers can easily use for their requirements. dbt (*https://www.getdbt.com*) (data build tool), for example, is one of the leading products that analytics engineers use to implement complex transformations on data loaded in a warehouse.

In the context of lakehouse architecture, analytics engineers can use dbt to transform data loaded in the lakehouse by creating models (SQL queries). Analytics engineers should take on the governance responsibilities listed for data engineer and data analyst roles.

Key Takeaways

In this chapter, we've discussed how to apply data governance and security processes across ten key areas for our platform. Table 6-2 provides a quick summary of the benefits of employing these processes.

Table 6-2. Benefits of unified governance and security processes in lakehouse architecture

Governance and security process	Benefits in lakehouse architecture
Metadata management	• Helps to perform easy search and discovery across tables, views, reports, and ML models
Compliance regulations	• Ensure adherence to mandatory rules and regulations
Data and ML model quality	• Maintains data trust and reduces data downtime • Helps to reduce bias within ML models
Lineage across data and AI assets	• Helps to perform end-to-end impact analysis for any changes • Provides capabilities to identify the flow of sensitive attributes across assets
Data and AI asset sharing	• Helps to share tables, reports, and models with partners, customers, and external consumers • Monetize data on the marketplace
Data ownership	• Maintains data quality and raises alerts for any data issues
Auditing and monitoring	• Highlights unauthorized access, model performance degradation, and data leakages
Access management	• Helps to minimize unauthorized access to lakehouse data
Data protection	• Protects data wherever it resides and whenever it is moved or accessed
Sensitive data handling	• Protects customers' sensitive data

Remember these two critical points:

- When it comes to compliance and security, always ask when in doubt! The compliance and security teams are best suited to guide you during the design process for your lakehouse platform.
- Implementing lakehouse governance and security functions is not a one-time project. These initiatives run parallel with your data programs and are part of the overall data strategy. Data leaders should embrace and advocate these initiatives with their data teams from day 0 of the lakehouse program. It's a journey that will enable organizations to be truly data-driven and will make them industry leaders.

References

- What Is Data Governance? (*https://oreil.ly/9mXN0*)
- Data Governance vs Data Security: Nah, They Aren't Same! (*https://oreil.ly/Dzrfs*)
- Apache Hudi: Data Quality (*https://oreil.ly/EiiHX*)
- Apply Pre-Commit Validation for Data Quality in Apache Hudi (*https://oreil.ly/9JJTV*)
- What Is Data Governance? (*https://oreil.ly/5qNvE*)
- Introducing Delta Sharing: An Open Protocol for Secure Data Sharing | The Databricks Blog (*https://oreil.ly/I1aEh*)
- Protecting Data with Encryption | Amazon Simple Storage Service (*https://oreil.ly/Vw2NO*)
- What Is Data Downtime? | Monte Carlo (*https://oreil.ly/YySQH*)
- SSL versus TLS: Difference between communication protocols | AWS (*https://oreil.ly/JLto8*)
- Constraints | Delta Lake (*https://oreil.ly/09ifi*)
- Models in Unity Catalog Example | Databricks (*https://oreil.ly/GPdb0*)
- Data Collaboration Service - AWS Clean Rooms (*https://oreil.ly/rZDux*)
- Data Steward vs Data Owner: 11 Key Differences & Relationship! (*https://oreil.ly/EBgW8*)
- What Is Analytics Engineering? (*https://oreil.ly/OB9Ca*)
- What, Exactly, Is dbt? (*https://oreil.ly/qCgPg*)

CHAPTER 7

The Big Picture: Designing and Implementing a Lakehouse Platform

In the preceding chapters, we discussed the individual components of lakehouse architecture and their design considerations. This chapter will discuss how to stitch all these components together to design and implement a modern, scalable, and secure lakehouse platform.

This chapter will help data architects design an end-to-end platform based on lakehouse architecture. It will also guide data engineers in implementing various data management processes and best practices in a lakehouse. Other data personas, like data analysts, scientists, stewards, and platform administrators, can read this chapter to get a detailed understanding of various lakehouse processes and how they may impact their day-to-day work.

We will first discuss the pre-design activities, like requirements gathering and understanding the existing system and its challenges. These activities involve asking the right questions of the right people. Next, I'll help you to establish the guiding principles that lay the foundation of your lakehouse platform.

I'll then explain the design considerations for key components like data ingestion, processing, storage, consumption, metadata management, governance, security, and operations. We will discuss the interdependencies between these components and the best approaches for implementing them from a lakehouse perspective.

In the last section of this chapter, I'll provide you with a step-by-step design guide that you can refer to during the design phase of your lakehouse project. I'll also provide a list of questions you can ask when interviewing different stakeholders as part of your pre-design activities.

Pre-design Activities

Before starting the design phase of your lakehouse project, there are some pre-design activities that can help you gather essential input to inform the design of your platform. Figure 7-1 shows the pre-design activities that you should perform, all of which involve speaking with different stakeholders.

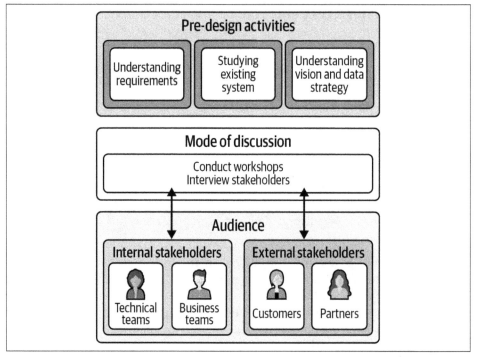

Figure 7-1. Pre-design activities

As shown in Figure 7-1, there are three key activities you should perform before starting the lakehouse platform design:

- Understand the platform requirements and expectations.
- Study the existing systems and their challenges.
- Understand the organization's vision and data strategy to achieve it.

Understanding Platform Requirements

Data platforms help organizations get insights and make predictions from their raw data. These platforms support several BI and analytics workloads that aim to understand what happened and why it happened. If organizations want to predict what *can* happen and how to make it happen, they can leverage AI/ML models.

Some of the common requirements for a data platform are:

- It should support all workloads, including BI, AI/ML, real time, ETL, and data sharing.
- Different data personas should be able to use the platform according to their roles and skills.
- It should be vendor-agnostic for data consumers. Data consumers using other vendor products should be able to consume data.
- It should be future-proof and flexible to support new source systems, changing business requirements, and leverage technology advancements.
- It should be secure, compliant, and cost-effective.
- It should be able to support different use cases, per functional requirements.

Studying Existing System

In addition to understanding the platform requirements, it is crucial to understand where an organization is in its data journey. You don't want to suggest generative AI or large language models (LLMs) to an organization that doesn't have clean, good-quality, or well-governed data.

Most large organizations have an existing data platform. These platforms are typically either:

- A standalone central data storage system where all the data resides in a single on-premises system, modern data warehouses, or data lake
- A combined architecture comprising a data lake and data warehouse implemented using on-premises or cloud technologies

It's important to first understand the challenges the organization is facing while using these platforms. These challenges are often the driver for embarking on a journey to build modern data platforms that are simple, open, and easy to scale.

Some of the platform-related challenges that I've often heard from customers are:

- We cannot scale our on-premises data platform during workload spikes (high usage).
- We are facing severe performance issues when running our BI dashboards.
- Our business users have to wait longer to get query responses when running ad hoc queries.

- We are not able to support workloads like AI/ML or streaming.

- We cannot share data with our partners, as we deal with sensitive customer data.

- There is too much operational cost involved to keep our cloud workloads running.

- The current platform has no access controls or does not comply with the mandatory governance and regulatory policies.

Speak with various stakeholders to understand such challenges, pain points, recurring issues, and limitations. Think through these when you design the new lakehouse platform.

 Some smaller organizations might not have a central data storage (like a data warehouse or a data lake). They would generally run siloed, department-specific analytics workloads. In such scenarios, understand the limitations of these siloed BI workloads and accordingly design a central, holistic platform.

Understanding the Organization's Vision and Data Strategy

Most organizations that aspire to become data-driven have a vision and a well-defined data strategy to achieve this vision. Some common high-level objectives in a data strategy are:

- Breaking multiple data silos and democratizing data for more efficient use and decision making

- Building a strong data foundation for future business needs

- Governing, securing, and sharing data with customers, partners, and consumers

- Monetizing data and AI/ML assets and publishing these in the marketplace

- Consistently delivering accurate, up-to-date, complete, and trustworthy data, insights, and recommendations to consumers

- Becoming a fully compliant and best-in-class organization within their industry

Talk to the data leaders to understand the organization's vision and data strategy, and consider their objectives when designing the new platform.

Conducting Workshops and Interviews

One of the best approaches to learning about existing challenges and platform expectations is interviewing different stakeholders. These stakeholders can be internal (department heads, data leaders, architects, and developers) or external (customers, partners) to the organization. You can also conduct workshops for brainstorming sessions on topics that need collective consensus.

Getting the correct information depends on the stakeholders who attend these meetings, their exposure to existing systems, and their domain knowledge. Be sure to interview the right subject matter experts to make informed design decisions.

 While working as a data architect, speaking with different stakeholders helped me get answers to some of the critical questions that influence design decisions. I've compiled a list of these critical questions that you can refer to when designing your data platform. You can find this list at the end of this chapter.

Carefully consider all the requirements, challenges, and objectives before designing the platform and making the architecture and technology choices for its implementation. The chosen architecture will eventually help you define the design principles and components to build a platform that aligns with the data strategy to achieve the organization's larger vision and business goals.

Choosing the Right Architecture

After carefully studying the platform requirements and understanding the platform expectations, the first step is to evaluate various architectural patterns for implementing your data platform.

Figure 7-2 shows the different architecture options for implementing a data platform.

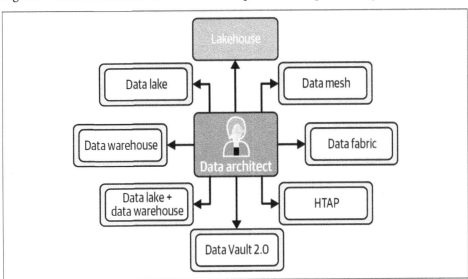

Figure 7-2. Architecture choices for implementing a data platform

Select the right architecture based on your organization's needs and use cases. Table 7-1 provides a primer on these architecture options, many of which we've discussed in earlier chapters.

Table 7-1. Architecture options for implementing data platforms

Architecture	When can you use it?
Data warehouse	Best suited for organizations that want to create a central data storage system and deal with structured data. Their main goal is to generate business insights from multiple siloed systems and applications that store structured data.
Data lake	Works well for organizations that deal with a lot of unstructured data and want to perform various AI/ML workloads. They have limited BI use cases and do not focus on faster BI performance, fine-grained governance, or improved data quality.
Combined architecture: Data lake and data warehouse	Combined architectures are best suited for organizations that want to build data platforms supporting all their use cases—from BI to AI. They have large volumes of structured and unstructured data and need faster BI performance, better governance, improved data quality, and AI/ML capabilities.
Lakehouse	Suits most of the organizations that want to build a data platform. Organizations that do not have a data repository, have implemented a standalone data warehouse or data lake, or have taken the combined approach can all benefit from the simple, open, and unified approach of a lakehouse. You can also use lakehouse architecture to implement organizational-level data management approaches, like data mesh. We will discuss these approaches in more detail in Chapter 9.
Data Vault 2.0	Data Vault 2.0 is primarily known for its modeling approach. However, it also provides industry-standard methodology, architecture, and implementation standards integrating people, processes, and technology for agile system delivery.
Data mesh	Organizations that want to implement a decentralized approach for storing and managing data can embrace the data mesh approach. In data mesh architecture, the domain teams own and share their data (as data products) with other domain teams while adhering to governance rules and regulations.
Data fabric	Data fabric provides a unified abstraction layer for accessing enterprise data across transactional and analytical systems (on-premises or cloud). Data fabric uses multiple modern, intelligent tools, technologies, and platforms (sometimes across clouds) to provide different data personas quick and easy access to required data.
HTAP	Hybrid Transaction/Analytical Processing (HTAP) architecture suits organizations that want to execute their OLTP and OLAP workloads within a single platform. SingleStore (*https://www.singlestore.com*) and Snowflake Unistore (*https://www.snowflake.com/en/data-cloud/workloads/unistore/*) are some examples of platforms with HTAP capabilities.

You can select any one of these approaches or use a combination. For example, you can consider implementing a decentralized data mesh by creating multiple domain-specific lakehouses.

As we covered in Chapter 2, lakehouse architecture has emerged as one of the best approaches for implementing a modern data platform that is simple, open, and supportive of several data and AI use cases. There may be scenarios when other architectural approaches are a better fit for your organization. However, it is outside the scope of this book to dive deep into all the architectures listed in Table 7-1. If you want to explore these architectures further, I suggest referring to *Deciphering Data Architectures* by James Serra (O'Reilly).

As this chapter (and book) focuses on lakehouse architecture for implementing your data platforms, the subsequent sections are written considering the lakehouse architecture approach.

Once you have finalized the lakehouse as your architectural approach, the next step is to establish the guiding principles to design and implement your data platform.

Establishing Guiding Principles

As discussed in Chapter 1, there are guidelines across different functions that help implement an optimized, reliable, well-governed, and secure platform. These guiding principles ensure that everyone follows a consistent design and common implementation standards across all data processes.

Every CSP provides design principles for architecting solutions using their services. One of the best examples is the AWS Well-Architected Framework (*https://oreil.ly/ FXHmn*), built around six pillars. You can establish the unique guiding principles for your data platform along similar lines.

While you may create your own set of guiding principles, there are some fundamental principles you *should* follow for designing and implementing a lakehouse platform. I've grouped these principles across five different categories based on their relevance, as seen in Figure 7-3.

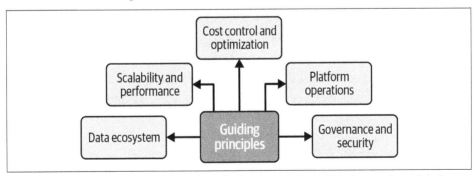

Figure 7-3. Fundamental guiding principles for designing and implementing a lakehouse

Data Ecosystem

When architecting your end-to-end lakehouse ecosystem, consider the following principles:

- Design a simple, open platform for every data persona, business user, non-technical user, and downstream consumer, irrespective of which vendor product they use.

- Avoid using proprietary, purpose-built storage. Store all the data in cloud object storage using open file and table formats. This layer should act as the single source of truth, where all data resides.

- Refrain from using too many tools and products that can complicate the platform's technology landscape and increase the learning curve for platform users.

- Provide unified access to data and AI/ML assets so that users can perform all data engineering, analysis, experiments, reporting, and other activities from a single platform.

- Design a data ecosystem that is simple but future-proof. It should be scalable and flexible to accommodate future business and technology advancements.

- The platform should use modern technologies to support rapid innovations and faster time-to-market product lifecycles.

- Make provisions for different compute engines for different data personas. Data engineers, analysts, scientists, business users, data stewards, and others should feel comfortable and confident (based on their skills) in using the platform.

Scalability and Performance

Scalability and performance are top priorities for any data platform. Adhere to the following principles to enable quick scalability and enhanced performance:

- Use separate storage and compute resources to ensure these can be scaled independently. The platform should be scalable to handle the performance needs as data grows.

- Provision compute engines that can provide data warehouse-like performance on data lakes, so that there is no need to provision a separate cloud warehouse engine to achieve the expected performance.

- Don't try to optimize performance only at the compute layer. Performance also depends on the storage layer. Design your write processes to support optimum read performance. Leverage the features of open table formats like compaction, Z-order, and partitioning to optimize performance while querying data and running BI workloads.

Cost Control and Optimization

Cost is one of the critical parameters observed closely by the management and program sponsors. Adhere to the following principles to help optimize cost without compromising the platform's capabilities:

- Maintain a fine balance between cost and performance based on the use cases and performance requirements.
- For handling complex workloads or spikes in processing activities, your first option should be tuning the code to achieve faster performance rather than scaling your computing capabilities.
- Teams should perform frequent cost analyses to understand their high-cost activities and identify approaches to reducing these costs.

Platform Operations

Modern data platforms need minimum administration and maintenance efforts. Automate data management processes to reduce manual efforts as much as possible. Consider the following guidelines:

- Use highly available services that are deployed across availability zones. Design a platform that can failover to secondary systems for disaster recovery.
- Automate administrative processes such as user creation, cluster creation, granting access, and other DataOps and MLOps processes (covered later in this chapter).
- Track all user activity performed on the platform. You will need these logs for audit and compliance purposes.
- Data observability is important for modern data platforms. Plan to implement and integrate it with data management processes to maintain the data health.
- Use cloud native or managed services wherever possible. Use IaaS with self-managed software only where required and when other alternatives are unavailable.

Governance and Security

Governance and security are day 0 activities. You should have strong guiding principles, as follows, to implement data processes that are well-aligned with governance and security:

- Provide minimum required privileges to users as per their roles and responsibilities. For example, sales department users should only have access to sales data, not to the organization's finance data.

- Protect your data at all stages—whether at rest, in transit, or when it's being accessed by users. Sensitive data should be detected, abstracted, and alerted to respective data owners. Data should move within the private network as much as possible (and not through the public internet).

- Govern all your data and AI assets. Governance policies often ignore AI assets like ML models and feature tables. Ensure that you govern AI assets along with data assets.

- Always have good-quality data that consumers can trust. When you design the platform, keep data quality at the core of every process. Data should be validated, cleansed, and maintained across nearly every zone of the lakehouse storage.

These are only some of the key guiding principles for implementing a standard lakehouse platform. You can add or ignore some of these based on your requirements, tech stack, and use cases. Establishing a list of unique guiding principles at the start of your project is essential and you should ensure that all platform users adhere to them to maintain consistency.

Design Considerations and Implementation Best Practices

As discussed in Chapter 1, the data platform comprises different core components. The selected architectural approach helps define these core components and their interdependencies, define the tech stack, and establish guiding principles to align the platform with the organization's overall data strategy and vision.

In this section, we will explore how lakehouse architecture influences the design and technology selected for these core components.

Architecture Blueprint

Your platform design process starts with creating the architecture blueprint of the platform. As a first step, create a high-level blueprint illustrating the platform's core components, based on the selected architectural pattern.

Figure 7-4 shows the five core components of a data platform. This diagram is the simplest representation of *any* data platform and can be a good starting point for data architects.

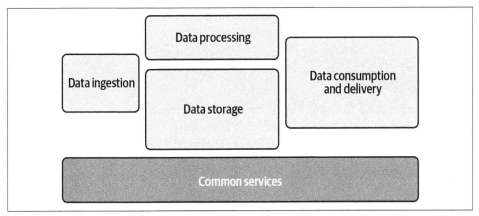

Figure 7-4. Core components of a data platform

Based on the selected architectural pattern—in our case, lakehouse architecture—add the finer technical elements to these core components.

Figure 7-5 represents an architecture blueprint for a data platform that is to be built based on lakehouse architecture.

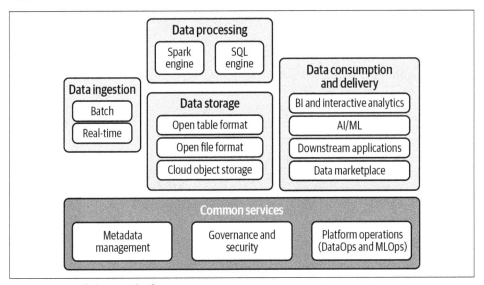

Figure 7-5. Lakehouse platform core components

You can use Figure 7-5 as a reference for designing your lakehouse platform. Most of the lakehouse platforms will have a very similar high-level architecture blueprint.

The next step is to carefully design and implement each component, based on various considerations. Let's discuss the design considerations, technology choices, and implementation best practices across these various components.

Data Ingestion

Data ingestion is the first step to getting data in your lakehouse platform. Figure 7-6 shows the various elements that form the data ingestion process.

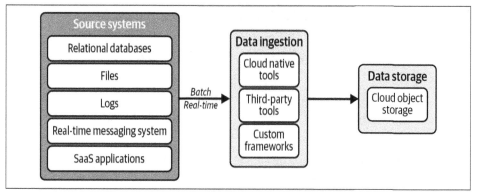

Figure 7-6. Data ingestion process

Data ingestion considerations

While designing the data ingestion process, you should understand the source systems, the nature of the data they store, and the frequency of ingestion. Consider future data sources, too, and make relevant provisions within the platform.

Ingestion frequency. You can ingest data as EoD (end-of-day) batches, microbatches, or in real time. Modern platforms are shifting toward unifying the batch and real-time processes, to avoid writing separate codebases for individual processes. Therefore, I recommend designing a solution that is capable of ingesting data in batch and in real time.

Source system types. The source systems can be RDBMs (structured data), files, logs (unstructured data), or real-time messaging systems like Apache Kafka. Additionally, there can be SaaS applications from where you might need to ingest data into your platform. Make provisions within your lakehouse platform to ingest data from many different source systems.

You can use cloud native ETL tools like AWS Glue or ADF, as they can seamlessly integrate with other cloud services, or you can consider third-party tools due to their out-of-box connectors. Another option is to write custom code and build reusable frameworks that you can easily configure to add new source tables.

Identify incremental data (change data capture). Another important design consideration when implementing a data ingestion process is whether the source system can
identify *incremental data*. Incremental data means the changes in the source system's
data after the last batch was ingested. This process of identifying the incremental
changes is also known as change data capture (CDC).

Some systems might be unable to identify the incremental changes; if so, you can use
third-party tools like Fivetran (*https://www.fivetran.com*) or Airbyte (*https://
airbyte.com*) to determine incremental changes. An alternative option is to write a
custom code to manually identify incremental data by comparing data between two
subsequent batches.

Sensitive data. Check if there is any sensitive data in the source systems. If yes, consider how you want to handle this sensitive data. Sometimes, source systems might
not allow moving sensitive data to the cloud, and you must remove such data before
moving it to the cloud. The alternative option is to tokenize, encrypt, or abstract that
data at the client side before ingesting it into your lakehouse.

Technology choices

There are many tools and technologies available for implementing data ingestion. No
one tool can fit all the use cases. Choose tools and technologies based on your
requirements, cloud platform, and organization's strategic investment. Here is a quick
guide to selecting the right tools and technologies for data ingestion.

Use cloud native tools when you need:

- Low-code or no-code ETL tools with GUI-based development
- Easy integration with other native cloud services like identity management and
  monitoring

Examples of cloud native tools for data ingestion are AWS Glue and ADF.

Use third-party tools when you need:

- Wide variety of out-of-box connectors
- Low-latency streaming, reading source redo logs to identify incremental changes
- A multi-cloud strategy, as these tools can work with multiple cloud platforms

Examples of third-party tools for data ingestion are Fivetran and Airbyte.

Write custom code when you need:

- A framework-based ingestion approach with more control and flexibility
- Additional features such as masking sensitive data, on-the-fly transformations, and schema validations
- Incremental data extraction based on source attributes (watermarking approach), like date columns

An example of custom code is a Spark Structured Streaming framework executed using Databricks or EMR clusters.

Best practices

Here is a list of best practices for implementing a data ingestion process within a lakehouse:

- Give preference to tools that can ingest and store data in open table formats. Save the effort and time required to convert raw files like CSV or JSON into open table formats. Some tools like Glue can also create Apache Iceberg tables in the Glue Data Catalog, reducing the metadata creation efforts.
- When selecting the ingestion tools, study their features and support for the preferred open table format and version. Refer to Chapter 5, where we discussed this in detail.
- Real-time ingestion needs an "always on" compute cluster, which can result in higher costs. If latency is not a concern, try executing these workloads as micro-batches (one to five minutes) to lower the cost.
- Spark Structured Streaming is a good option for real-time ingestion. However, if you need an extremely low-latency solution (sub-seconds), you can consider using Apache Flink.
- Understand the current and future needs and make provisions for cloud native or third-party tools or custom frameworks accordingly. You can also consider provisioning more than one tool for handling specific use cases, like CDC handling or low-latency streaming.

Data Storage

The design of lakehouse storage is similar to data lake storage—both architectures use the cloud object storage for persisting data. However, lakehouse storage is better organized, governed, and cataloged compared to that of data lakes.

Storage zones considerations

In lakehouse architecture, storage is categorized into various zones, or layers. This approach is also known as the medallion architecture. Figure 7-7 shows the important zones and underlying directories within lakehouse storage.

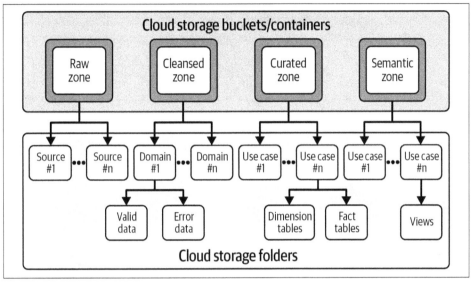

Figure 7-7. Lakehouse storage zones

Raw zone. As the name suggests, data extracted from the source systems is stored as is in the raw (or bronze) zone. For example, if a source system sends data as JSON files, these will be stored as is in the raw zone without any conversion, transformation, or quality validations.

The raw zone is the staging area to persist the source data. Consider these points when planning a raw zone:

- As the raw zone consists of files with raw data, you cannot use this data for analysis or insight generation. As a result, you don't need to create tables on top of these.
- The underlying folders within the cleansed zone should be based on the source system. Create folders for each source system and sub-folders per table.
- The raw files are typically required for reprocessing data or, in the future, for audit and compliance. It is essential to persist these raw files for extended periods.
- Archive these raw files to cold tier post-processing to reduce the storage cost.

Some data architects prefer creating a landing zone before the raw zone in order to decouple the source systems from the lakehouse storage. For example, if you have a Kafka source, the messages are ingested into the landing zone as JSON or Avro files and moved to the raw zone for further processing. Kafka ingestion to the landing zone can happen continuously or as micro-batches. You can later move and process the files in the raw zone based on the lakehouse jobs schedule, thus decoupling the data ingestion and processing activities.

Cleansed zone. The next zone in the hierarchy is the cleansed (also known as the enriched or silver) zone. Data from the raw zone is moved to the cleansed zone after appropriate data quality checks are applied. This zone holds valid as well as invalid data. The valid data is transferred to higher zones for processing, while the data stewards analyze the invalid data and send it back to the source system for correction.

You can create two levels within the cleansed zone:

- The first level can have 1:1 tables per the raw zone with tables persisting the valid data post-data quality validations.
- The second level can consist of the integrated tables, consolidating the first-level tables and combining them across source systems based on domains like customers and products.

Consider the following when designing the cleansed zone:

- Convert data in open table formats when storing it in a cleansed zone.
- Data scientists often use the cleansed zone for exploratory data analysis (EDA) and technical users leverage it for ad hoc querying. Create tables on top of these files for easy discovery and running SQL queries.
- In the cleansed zone, you can create normalized tables using the Entity Relationship (ER) model based on domains like customers and products. Along similar lines, you can create folders per domain containing valid and invalid data files.
- Alternatively, larger organizations can also consider using a Data Vault as the data modeling approach. We'll cover this in more detail later in this chapter.
- If the underlying table format allows, consider assigning primary and foreign keys (for informational purposes, not enforced constraints) for tables in order to identify relationships between various entities.

Curated zone. The curated (also known as the presentation or gold) zone holds the data that is arranged per business processes using industry-specific models. You can create BI reports and dashboards on the curated zone tables.

Design considerations for the curated zone are as follows:

- Consider using the dimensional modeling (star schema) approach for designing curated zone tables. Dimensional modeling is one of the most widely used approaches for improving BI performance.

- Add the proper dependencies between dimensions and facts when loading data.

- Retain all historical data (and older versions of records) in curated zone tables for performing descriptive analytics and insight generation.

Semantic zone. Some organizations might create an additional semantic zone for storing data modeled for business users so that they can understand and query the data easily. This layer is an abstraction of the curated zone and can consist of several materialized views, which are created by joining the data from underlying curated zone tables. These views hold pre-computed aggregations for faster performance.

Consider these points when designing the semantic zone:

- Business and non-technical users leverage semantic zone tables for self-serve analysis. Design these tables considering these data personas.

- Consider tools and technologies for designing and modeling semantic zone tables. For example, Atscale (*https://www.atscale.com*) is a third-party product that provides these capabilities.

- For custom implementation, leverage materialized views (MVs) with pre-computed aggregates based on the expected business queries.

You can create additional zones within the storage hierarchy, which are listed in Table 7-2.

Table 7-2. Additional lakehouse storage zones

Zone name	Zone usage
Archive zone	• Use for storing older data files • You can use cold storage tiers like Amazon S3 Glacier (*https://aws.amazon.com/pm/s3-glacier/*) to minimize the cost
Logs zone	• Use for storing all the system logs • You can apply lifecycle policies to delete these files at regular intervals (like every six months) to reduce the lakehouse storage cost
Ad hoc zone	• Used by platform users to upload their data; these users should have write access only on this zone

Data modeling considerations

There are three approaches for modeling the data within the lakehouse: entity relationship (ER) modeling, Data Vault modeling, and dimensional modeling.

Entity relationship (ER) modeling.   The ER model is popular among OLTP systems and is also used by organizations to implement enterprise data warehouses based on Bill Inmon's approach. You can organize the tables in the ER model as related entities linked by primary and foreign keys. Using standard normalization guidelines, you can use ER modeling to implement the cleansed zone tables in their third normal form (3NF).

 Database normalization is an approach to organizing database tables to avoid data redundancy and maintain data integrity. There are various forms of data normalization, such as 1NF, 2NF, 3NF and so on. 3NF is the most common normalization form that is used in ER modeling for organizing tables.

The ER model is best suited for creating the cleansed zone tables, which can enable faster writes and help users easily understand and query the data.

Data Vault modeling.   The Data Vault modeling approach is best suited for large organizations that have sources with frequent schema changes. The Data Vault model uses hubs, satellites, and links to store the data and accommodate frequent source-side changes. Hubs consist of business and technical keys, satellites consist of attributes that describe the entities, and links provide the relationship between hubs and satellites. Data Vaults also consist of two levels—raw vault and business vault—for creating the cleansed zone.

Data Vault modeling is not easy to implement. Look for certified experts with a good deal of experience implementing Data Vault modeling in a lakehouse. Also, carefully study the need of Data Vault modeling for your use case and explore how the open table format features can be leveraged for implementing Data Vault processes.

Dimensional modeling.   Dimensional modeling is a common practice for implementing data warehouses based on Ralph Kimball's approach. To implement a dimensional model, you must use a star schema approach to organize the tables as dimensions and fact tables. Dimensional modeling is best suited for implementing the curated, or gold, zone of your lakehouse. It helps improve BI performance and supports storing large volumes of historical data.

Dimensional modeling is a widely adopted approach for implementing data marts in traditional systems. You can use the same approach in lakehouses for organizing your higher storage zones.

You can consider all of these approaches for organizing the lakehouse data; however, all are challenging to design and implement. Data modeling is one of the most difficult puzzles to solve when designing a data platform and using lakehouse architecture is no exception. There are multiple challenges that you can face when implementing a real-world lakehouse. We will study these in more detail in Chapter 8.

Best practices

Lakehouse storage plays a significant role in managing data within the lakehouse. To get the most out of your lakehouse, follow these best practices when designing the storage tier:

- Always store data in the cleansed zone (and other higher zones) in open table formats to support updates, deletes and ACID operations within the lakehouse.

- Always encrypt the data files in cloud storage for additional security.

- Avoid providing direct access to data files to internal users; instead, provide all access through cleansed and curated tables by implementing suitable access controls. Also, abstract any sensitive data from non-authorized and non-eligible users.

- Use separate encryption keys for the ad hoc and other additional zones to increase the security of the three key layers—raw, cleansed, and curated. This approach will ensure that the non-technical users (with access to ad hoc zone encryption keys) do not have access to the encryption keys of all other zones.

- If implementing a semantic zone, consider tools that can also federate data from source systems that do not send data into the lakehouse. This will help you to implement a single source of truth for the entire data ecosystem.

Data Processing

You must perform various processing activities when you move data from lower zones (like raw) to higher zones (like cleansed and curated). Figure 7-8 shows the various data processing activities including data validations, cleansing, transformations, enrichment, and aggregation.

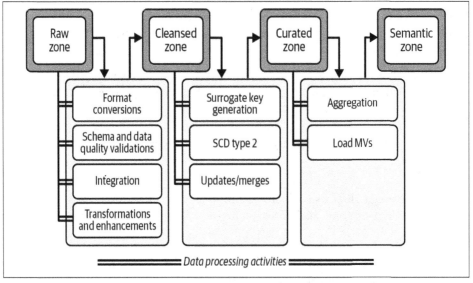

Figure 7-8. Data processing activities

Data processing considerations

Data processing helps to transform raw data into meaningful information, and later to model it per your business processes before serving it to platform users. These data processing activities are discussed in detail below.

Open table format conversion. As discussed in Chapter 3, open table formats provide the required transactional support for implementing warehouse-like capabilities on cloud storage. Convert the raw data into the preferred open table format *before* storing it in the cleansed layer.

Consider these points when storing data in open table formats in your lakehouse storage:

- Explore and leverage tools provided by open table formats for format conversion. For example, Delta Lake provides an API to convert a Parquet table to Delta Lake using PySpark.
- If you already have an existing data lake, you must convert this data when migrating to a lakehouse. For example, suppose the current data lake stores data as Parquet files; then, you can convert the Parquet files to Delta Lake or Iceberg format in the lakehouse.

Schema and data quality validations. When storing files in the cleansed layer, the first data processing task is to validate the schema. If any records are not as per the agreed schema, you can either reject the error records or evolve the schema. Next, perform data quality validations to load only clean and accurate data in the target tables and store the invalid records in the error tables.

Consider the following points when implementing the data quality validations:

- For schema evolution, leverage the schema evolution features provided by the chosen open table formats.
- Validate data based on technical as well as business rules.
- You can add technical validations based on metadata of the attributes like datatype, length, and format. For example, columns defined as "integer" should not have string values.
- You can add business validations based on the actual value or min and max values of data. For example, the average monthly balance for a bank account should always be greater than $1,000 (minimum balance).
- You can also consider using frameworks like Great Expectations (*https://greatex pectations.io*), or other similar open source or commercial tools or products, for implementing a robust data quality framework.

Data integration. Depending on your data modeling approach, you can organize the tables in the cleansed layer as normalized, domain-specific tables (like customers, products, or accounts). The data for these tables should be integrated from all the different source systems. For example, customer details can come from Customer Relationship Management (CRM) systems like Salesforce, Enterprise Resource Planning (ERP) systems like SAP, and other marketing systems.

When integrating data from different source systems, keep the following considerations in mind:

- The integration process depends on your data modeling approach for building the cleansed zone. For normalized tables, you will have to integrate data from different sources. If you follow Data Vault modeling, you can create separate tables (satellite tables) for each source system.
- You might need to implement a *Master Data Management (MDM) system* to persist the master record among the several duplicate records coming from different source systems.

What Is Master Data Management?

MDM helps you retain one master record for domains like customers or products. As part of the MDM process, you deduplicate multiple records across different data sources to maintain a single copy of the records that is consistent and representative of the most accurate information. Identifying the master (also known as golden) record is based on multiple rules and record-matching algorithms.

Modern tools can perform ML-based matching and deduplication to determine the golden copy of the record. MDM ensures that there is always a single source of truth for master data that you can use in further analysis and insight generation.

Please note that MDM is not just another data management process, but can be a separate project for large organizations with multiple source systems handling master data like customers or products.

Data transformations and enrichment. You can enrich your raw data by augmenting it with external data (like exchange rates or weather information) or internal reference data (like country codes). You will have to perform several lookups or joins to add this information to raw data and make it consumable by business users. You will also have to perform several other transformations like aggregations, surrogate key generation, Slowly Changing Dimensions (SCD) operations, updates, or merges to load data in your curated zone tables and refresh MVs in semantic zones.

Key points to remember when implementing data transformation processes are:

- Create surrogate keys for dimension tables to join them with the fact tables. Do not use the business keys from source systems, as they can be the same across sources.

- When creating the surrogate keys for lakehouse tables, use hashing functions (like SHA-2 or MD5) instead of database sequences used in traditional warehouses. Sequences are not well-suited for distributed processing workloads.

- Leverage the features provided by open table formats to execute merge and upsert queries when implementing SCD operations.

Best practices

Data engineers are primarily responsible for implementing data pipelines that perform all of these data processing activities. While doing so, they should follow these best practices:

- Consider tools that offer out-of-the-box features that perform data quality checks, CDC processing, and SCD Type 2 merges. For example, Databricks Delta

Live Tables (DLT) jobs offer all of these features and can considerably reduce implementation efforts.

- For custom implementations, build data processing frameworks, utilities, or reusable components that you can use across other data pipelines. Implement user-defined functions (UDFs) wherever possible and share them with different data personas so that they may leverage them in their day-to-day activities.

- There can be low-latency use cases that need streaming analytics. Based on the latency requirements, build these pipelines using the appropriate technologies like Flink.

Data Consumption and Delivery

In Chapter 5, we discussed the necessary points to consider when selecting the compute engines for BI and AI/ML workloads. For other workloads, like sharing data with downstream applications, users can access the data directly from the lakehouse storage using APIs. You might also consider sharing lakehouse data with your partners and customers. Figure 7-9 shows these various data consumers and the storage zones from which they can access the lakehouse data.

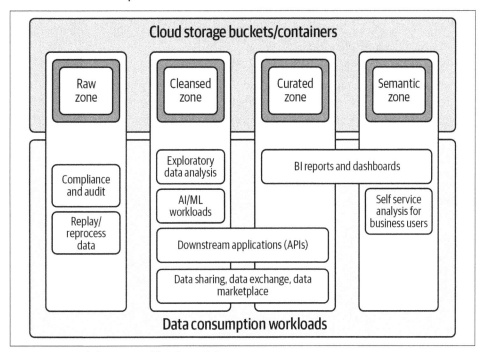

Figure 7-9. Lakehouse workloads and data consumers

Workload considerations

Different workloads and consumers will use data that is present in different lakehouse zones. Consider the following when implementing these workloads:

- As shown in Figure 7-9 and explained in subsequent points, leverage data from the suitable zones for supporting relevant workloads.

- For requirements related to compliance and auditing, you might need access to the raw files sent by source systems. If these raw data files are archived, you can copy them from the archive zone to the raw zone. You can also use the raw data files to reprocess or replay any source files.

- BI and AI/ML workloads are the most common workloads for your lakehouse. You can perform these by accessing the tables in the cleansed, curated, and semantic zones. Leverage available connectors to integrate the data with different BI tools.

- The semantic zone is best suited for supporting the self-service analytics conducted by business users. Complement it with data catalogs with business definitions of data to enable seamless self-service analytics for platform users.

- Several downstream applications will consume data from your lakehouse. Implement APIs for such applications to interact with your platform irrespective of their products or platforms.

- Data sharing enables organizations to implement a marketplace to sell and purchase data and create clean rooms to share data with your partners for secure, collaborative working. Leverage open table format features (like Delta Sharing protocol (*https://delta.io/sharing*)) to implement data sharing use cases.

Best practices

Best practices for implementing various workloads are as follows:

- Do not make copies of data when sharing it with your consumers. Unlike traditional warehouses, you do not need to extract the data in files for sharing with downstream applications.

- Make provisions for consumers to access data in the lakehouse. You can create APIs for downstream applications or leverage Open or Java Database connectors (ODBC/JDBC) for BI tools to query the lakehouse tables.

- Ensure you implement the right access control policies when sharing the data. Implement column-level access controls to manage fine-grained permissions.

- Explore compatible compute engines and native connectors for the selected open table format and encourage your consumers to leverage them for faster access.

- Explore and leverage relevant open table format features, such as Delta Sharing protocol by Delta Lake.

Common Services

Common services support various data management processes in your platform and help users perform their day-to-day activities. Here is a quick overview of the three common services:

- Metadata management enables platform users to easily understand the data by using data catalogs that provide technical metadata and business definitions.
- Governance and security help users comply with rules and regulations, protect their data, and share it securely.
- Platform operations, including DataOps and MLOps, help automate various data and ML management processes. DataOps helps to automate the deployment and orchestration of data pipelines and increases data trust by validating the quality of production data. MLOps helps improve model performance and automate the ML lifecycle, including model building, training, testing, and deployment processes.

While we've discussed the first two points (metadata management in Chapter 4 and governance and security in Chapter 6), we have not yet discussed platform operations. We'll focus on the different platform operation activities in this section. But first, let's quickly recap the metadata management, and governance and security processes.

Metadata management

In Chapter 4, we discussed how data catalogs help in the metadata management of all data and AI assets in a lakehouse. Best practices for metadata management are:

- Leverage lakehouse features to implement a unified data catalog and centrally manage all of your data and AI assets.
- Enable quick search and discovery across tables, views, files, ML models, and feature tables.
- Always provide users with business definitions of the data, as well as technical metadata to better understand data and perform self-service analysis.

Governance and security

In Chapter 6, we discussed various processes for governing and securing data in a lakehouse. Here is a quick summary of these processes:

- Employ governance processes and review them frequently to comply with industry- and region-specific regulations.

- Implement processes to protect your data—whether at rest, in transit, or when it's being accessed.

- Design consistent access controls when sharing data with internal and external consumers and review them frequently to validate any changes in access levels.

- Implement processes to monitor and maintain the quality of data within the lakehouse to ensure consumers' continued trust in data.

- Leverage the right abstraction and masking techniques for handling sensitive data.

Platform operations

You might already know about DevOps, a set of processes for better collaboration between developer and operations teams to manage software lifecycles. DevOps processes focus on the automation of code versioning, testing, integration, and deployment. Along similar lines, there are Data Operations (DataOps) for managing the data lifecycle and ML Operations (MLOps) for managing the lifecycle of ML models, as shown in Figure 7-10.

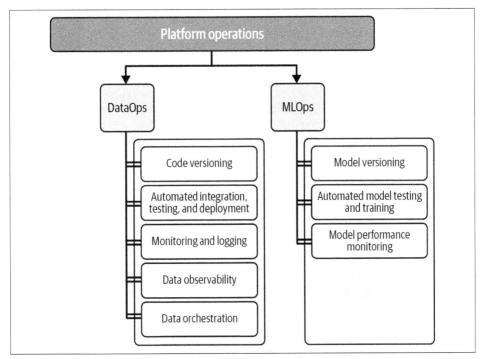

Figure 7-10. Lakehouse platform operations

DataOps. DataOps aims to improve cooperation between data producers and consumers. It focuses on automating the data management processes and reducing manual efforts.

DataOps is a set of processes for:

- Automating the testing, integration, and deployment of data pipelines
- Improving quality of production data by using various data observability processes
- Orchestrating the end-to-end flow of data within the ecosystem

Key benefits of implementing DataOps in your organization are:

- Reduced efforts and time for deploying data pipelines across environments
- Minimized data issues in production, ensuring that final reports show accurate, complete, and up-to-date data
- Increased collaboration between data and business teams

Along with the data pipeline deployment processes, DataOps significantly impacts data observability and data orchestration processes:

Data observability

Modern data platforms often employ cloud monitoring and logging services— like Amazon CloudWatch (*https://aws.amazon.com/cloudwatch*), AWS Cloud-Trail (*https://aws.amazon.com/cloudtrail*), or Azure Monitor (*https://oreil.ly/ pA_2U*)—to monitor infrastructure usage and access. You need similar processes for monitoring and logging production, or live, data. Such data monitoring falls under a category known as *data observability*, which aims to improve the quality of data present in the production environment.

Data observability validates production data based on its quality, accuracy, freshness, and other parameters as it moves through the system. It proactively monitors data quality by detecting anomalies based on historical statistics. Some examples of these anomalies include spikes in daily data volumes, increased occurrences of duplicate records, and significant increase in null values.

Several data observability tools are available that you can consider for your lakehouse. These tools should:

- Provide out-of-the-box validations for detecting data anomalies
- Have the flexibility to write custom validations based on user-provided SQL queries
- Provide insights that can help you take preventive actions to avoid data issues
- Integrate with data catalog tools so that data issues can be highlighted to users while browsing the catalog. For example, Monte Carlo's data observability platform (*https://oreil.ly/wPxYt/*) integrates with Alation and can show data quality issues to users browsing tables within the Alation catalog
- Integrate with ticketing systems like Jira and communication channels like Slack

Data orchestration

Orchestration is the glue that connects the various data management processes. Design the end-to-end flow of these processes using orchestration tools that can schedule jobs per required time intervals, manage dependencies, and serve as a single pane of glass for support engineers to get the status of all processes.

Like data observability tools, there are several orchestration tools available from different product vendors. These tools should:

- Offer flexible scheduling for triggering batches daily, weekly, monthly, annually, or per user-provided custom schedule

- Raise alerts and notify users, groups, or service roles through different channels like email, phone, Slack, and Microsoft Teams
- Integrate easily with ticketing systems like Jira
- Provide management for controlling access for administrators, support staff, and read-only users
- Have simple UI and APIs for supporting standard workflow management features like checking job status, duration, dependencies, and re-triggering

Apache Airflow (*https://airflow.apache.org*) is one of the most widely adopted workflow management tools. You can also consider using the managed offerings of Airflow that are provided by cloud platforms.

MLOps. MLOps is a set of processes for automating different ML workflows like model development, data preparation, model training, model tuning, and deployment across environments. MLOps helps standardize the development and deployment of ML models across various stages of the ML lifecycle.

Some of the key features and benefits of MLOps are:

- Support for model versioning and the ability to roll back to previous versions as and when required
- Automation of various processes like model integration, testing, and deployment to higher environments, thus reducing the overall efforts and time
- Maintaining model performance and quality

Most cloud services, like Amazon SageMaker (*https://aws.amazon.com/pm/sagemaker*), that are used for implementing ML workloads offer built-in support to automate processes across the ML lifecycle. Based on your tech stack, you can explore these services or consider using MLflow (*https://mlflow.org*), a widely adopted open source platform for the ML lifecycle. Databricks also offers a managed offering of MLflow within its ecosystem.

Best practices

As discussed in this section, several activities comprise DataOps and MLOps. Here is a list of best practices that you can follow while implementing these activities:

- Use managed or SaaS offerings instead of self-hosting and managing the DataOps tools to minimize the platform complexity and reduce administration efforts.
- Store the code using version-controlled repositories like Git or AWS CodeCommit (*https://aws.amazon.com/codecommit*) instead of storing the code in cloud

object storage like S3. Most modern tools seamlessly integrate with these repositories and can execute code directly by connecting to them.

- Proactively monitor your production data pipelines and ML models. The data
team should be able to detect and resolve any data issues before the end users
raise any data problems.

- Make provisions for orchestration tools that can support various platforms. For
example, third-party platforms like Databricks provide Databricks Workflows for
orchestrating Databricks jobs. Consider tools like ADF or Airflow if you have
jobs outside the Databricks ecosystem.

- Maintain model registry and model versions; this can help you to easily browse
and roll back to previous models.

- Monitor model performance regularly and take corrective actions when required.

As seen in this section, lakehouse architecture influences the design and implementation of these core components. While implementing the various data management
processes, ensure that you follow the guiding principles established at the project's
start and adhere to best practices for implementing individual data processes.

Design References

This section provides a couple of essential design references, including a step-by-step
design guide and a design questionnaire. You can refer to these when embarking on
your lakehouse design journey.

Step-by-Step Design Guide

You can use this step-by-step guide as a reference for the planning, analysis, and
design phase of your lakehouse project. Figure 7-11 shows the design activities and
their sequence.

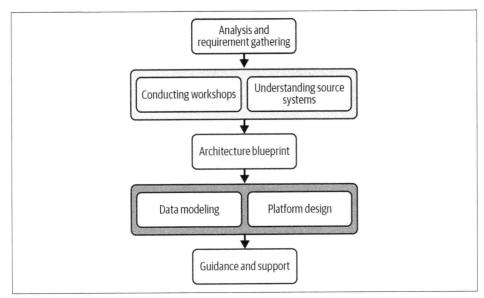

Figure 7-11. Lakehouse design activities

You can perform some of these activities (like conducting workshops and understanding the source systems) in parallel. Also, if you have different people working as data modelers and data architects, then data modeling and platform design can be carried out together. These two activities take considerable time and are ideally carried out by different individuals who are experts in their areas. Table 7-3 provides a detailed description of these lakehouse design activities.

Table 7-3. Lakehouse design activity details

Step	Design activity	Activity description
1	Analysis and requirements gathering	• Study business specifications and requirement documents • Understand expected workloads and use cases for the lakehouse platform • Spend time understanding the domain
2	Conduct workshops and interviews	• Interview relevant stakeholders and conduct workshops to get everyone's views • Understand the existing system and stakeholders' top challenges and issues with it • Understand stakeholder expectations from the new platform
3	Understand source systems	• Go through the source system documents • Profile source system data and perform data analysis to better understand the data • Get connected to data owners and identify the point of contact for each source system
4	Architecture blueprint	• Create high-level architecture with platform components • Create data flow diagrams • Compile list of possible technologies for implementing the platform

Step	Design activity	Activity description

5	Data modeling	• Create conceptual, logical, and physical models based on:
		  − Cleansed zone: normalized ER or Data Vault
		  − Curated zone: dimensional modeling
		  − Create source to target mapping documents

6	Platform design	• Establish guiding principles for design and implementation • Create storage layer design • Perform PoCs and feasibility checks to evaluate tools and technologies • Finalize the tech stack for each component • Conduct review sessions with the right stakeholders to finalize the design
7	Guidance and support	• Conduct design walkthroughs for developers, testers, analysts, and other teams • Provide architecture guidance and technical support during the implementation phase • Perform change request (CR) impact analysis for possible design changes • Support testing, data reconciliation, and data validation activities

Design Questionnaire

Table 7-4 provides a list of questions you should ask when interviewing or conducting workshops with internal and external stakeholders of the organization. The table also explains how the responses can help you make design decisions.

Table 7-4. Design questionnaire

Category	Questions to ask	How responses can influence design decisions
Existing system	• Is there an existing central data storage system used for BI and analytics workloads? • If yes, what architecture does it use— data warehouse, data lake, or combined (data lake + data warehouse)? • Is the existing system on-premises or built on a cloud platform? What is the cloud platform used? • What are the top challenges and limitations of this existing system? • Do you often face any technical restrictions like limited scalability, frequent downtimes, poor data quality, or no option for self-service analytics?	A good understanding of the existing system and its top challenges and limitations helps you design the new system to overcome these challenges. For example, if the existing system does not have provisions for adding a business glossary, it can limit self-service analysis. In this case, you can consider adding data catalogs that can add business context to technical metadata.

Source systems	• What are the different source systems (for example, RDBMS, files, Kafka)?
	• For each source system:
	  − What type of data is sourced—structured, semi-structured, unstructured?
	  − Is it a batch or streaming source?
	  − Can the source send daily incremental changes?
	  − What is the daily volume of data generated by the source system?
		Based on the source systems, you can design your data ingestion process.
		Depending on the existing source and what might be added in the future, you can consider specific tools for ingesting data in your lakehouse. For example, consider using third-party ETL tools that can connect to multiple sources

Category	Questions to ask	How responses can influence design decisions
Tools and technologies	• What tools are used in the existing tech stack? • Do you want to replace any legacy tools used in existing systems? • Are there any internal, home-grown tools that you want to reuse or replace in the new system?	Some larger organizations might use homegrown or legacy tools that lack modern features like scalability and real-time ingestion. They would likely benefit from replacing such tools with modern cloud native offerings. Look for such tools and evaluate new, advanced technologies that can be good alternatives. Some organizations might have an approved list of strategic tools that you will have to continue using in the new platform.
Workloads and use cases	• What are the different types of use cases you plan to implement (for example, BI, ML, streaming)? • Do you have streaming use cases where you want to see real-time reports? Do you want to process these in a few minutes or seconds? • Do you want to offer self-service analytics for business and non-technical users? • Do you want to share data with your partners or external consumers?	When selecting an architecture and designing the platform, you must understand the platform use cases. Explore the current and future use cases and, based on these, evaluate different architectural patterns. Based on the use cases, design a platform and select tools that can support them. For example, semantic layer solutioning products like Atscale provide self-service analytics and delta sharing enables sharing data with external consumers.
Data strategy, vision, objectives	• Are there any organization-approved data platforms or products that you have to use? • Do you have a multi-cloud strategy? • Do you have a governance committee in place? Is there a data governance strategy or guidelines? • Do you plan to build a data marketplace to monetize your data?	Your data platform should align with the overall data strategy and business goals. The data strategy influences a lot of critical design decisions. One example is the decision to use cloud native or third-party tools. If your organization has a multi-cloud strategy, then cloud-agnostic, third-party tools can be a good choice.
Platform users	• How many users are present in the existing system? • How many concurrent users access the reports? • What is the expected YoY growth of users? • What are the various data personas you expect your platform to support?	A good understanding of platform users helps design the data consumption and delivery processes. Based on the platform's data personas, you can recommend the most appropriate compute engines. And knowing the number of concurrent users can help you estimate the required compute capacities.
Platform data	• What is the volume of historical data that you need to migrate to the new lakehouse platform? • What is the expected YoY growth of this data? • What is the volume of daily incremental data processed in the existing system?	Historical data volumes drive the data migration process. For vast volumes of on-premises data, data transfers through the public internet won't help much. You must consider options providing fast, direct connectivity to on-premises systems or physical data transfer using cloud services like AWS Snow family devices.

Category	Questions to ask	How responses can influence design decisions
Data quality	• Do you have a list of business rules for validating data quality? • Do you have a list of frequent data quality issues for the last few months? • Have users complained about continuous degradation of data in the last few months? • Are you measuring the quality of data ingested within your platform? • Have you profiled the data from source systems? Are there any known data issues?	A list of known data quality issues in the existing system can help you implement appropriate validation and cleansing rules in the new lakehouse system. If business rules are not documented, you must run a separate project to compile a list of all required business validations by collaborating with various data owners.
Sensitive data and compliances	• Is there any sensitive data within your ecosystem? • Are there any compliance requirements restricting storing sensitive data in raw or unencrypted form? • Is there a need to perform joins on masked data attributes?	There are multiple approaches to abstracting sensitive data. Based on the requirements, you can finalize the process and suggest external tools, custom frameworks, or anonymizing the data.

Key Takeaways

We have covered a lot in this chapter—from design considerations to implementation best practices. Table 7-5 provides a quick summary of key topics we've discussed.

Table 7-5. Summary of platform components

Platform component	Key points to remember

Data ingestion	• Understand the source systems before designing the ingestion process.
	• Unify batch and real-time processing to maintain a single copy of code.
	• Provision ingestion tools that:
	  – Integrate well with overall ecosystem
	  – Support the selected open table formats
	  – Support structured, semi-structured, and unstructured data
	  – Support batch and real-time workloads
	  – Are configurable and flexible to support future source systems

Data storage	• Implement a zone-based approach to store raw, clean, and curated data. • Design additional zones like semantic, landing, archive, log, and ad hoc based on requirements. • Store data in open data formats in higher zones. • Data modeling plays a significant role to get better BI performance. Get experts who understand the domain and the data to perform data modeling. • Mask sensitive data before storing it, based on compliance requirements.
Data processing	• Build reusable components wherever possible. • Apply data quality checks and only load valid data in higher storage zones. • Leverage open table format features while implementing transformations.

Platform component	Key points to remember
Data consumption and delivery	• Do not make copies of data for sharing with consumers. • Consume data from the appropriate zones of the lakehouse storage. • Leverage connectors, APIs, and data sharing protocols for easy, secure, and controlled data delivery with downstream applications.
Common services	• Metadata management, governance and security, and platform operations play significant roles in overall data management. • DataOps helps to automate data management processes and MLOps helps to automate the ML lifecycle. • Modern platforms need data observability to maintain data health and trust. Implement observability processes to ensure data teams are the first to identify any data issues. • Look for orchestration tools that offer end-to-end workflow management and provide a single pane of glass for support engineers to see the operational health of the lakehouse platform.

In this chapter, we discussed the best practices for implementing an ideal lakehouse platform. However, the reality is always much different than the ideal world. In the next chapter, we will discuss the practical challenges you will face when implementing lakehouse architecture for your organization.

References

- Core Principles of System Design | Cloud Architecture Center (*https://oreil.ly/K0dTl*)
- Design principles for Azure Applications | Microsoft Learn (*https://oreil.ly/HIwwB*)
- Converting from Parquet to Delta Lake (*https://oreil.ly/PoblJ*)
- Data Vault Alliance (*https://oreil.ly/Kno0g*)
- What Is HTAP? (*https://oreil.ly/couEL*)
- HTAP: Hybrid Transactional and Analytical Processing | Snowflake (*https://oreil.ly/Tkx3k*)
- What Is MLOps? | AWS (*https://oreil.ly/3o-Y9*)
- What Is the Medallion Lakehouse Architecture? | Microsoft Learn (*https://oreil.ly/Slj7e*)

CHAPTER 8

Lakehouse in the Real World

We are approaching the end of this book and, so far, we've discussed various components, design considerations, tools and technologies, and best practices for implementing a lakehouse platform. In all these discussions, we've looked at the *ideal* design approaches and optimized solutions for building a lakehouse. However, as we all know, reality is much different than the ideal world. Implementing a lakehouse in the real world comes with several unforeseen challenges. To overcome these challenges, you will have to make some practical decisions and technical adjustments based on your judgment and experience.

In this chapter, I'll discuss what it means to build a lakehouse in the real world—a world where projects get delayed by months (if not years), requirements keep changing, budgets keep reducing, and old platforms never get decommissioned! We will discuss several technical and non-technical challenges across the planning, design, implementation, and support phases of a lakehouse project.

Building a data platform is a long journey that can take several months to years. In the sections that follow, I'll guide you through estimating, planning, and executing your lakehouse project and help you overcome some common, practical challenges. I'll also provide you with a list of project deliverables and reference architectures that can help you kickstart your lakehouse journey.

Delivering a Real-World Lakehouse

As discussed in the previous chapters, an ideal lakehouse has good-quality data, excellent BI performance, solid security standards, and well-governed policies. It acts as the single source of truth, is highly reliable, and is always available to its users.

So, what does a real-world lakehouse look like? Is it any different than the ideal lakehouse I've just described?

Like the utopian world, there is no place like an ideal lakehouse! In reality, you will face several challenges while implementing an ideal lakehouse. Considering these challenges, you will have to take a pragmatic approach to building a more realistic lakehouse by compromising some features and benefits that an ideal lakehouse could provide.

A real-world lakehouse might not have the best performance or zero downtime. It might not leverage the best tools available on the market. However, it can still support the intended workloads and business use cases. The real-world lakehouse use a practical design that is feasible to implement and easy to maintain.

A typical data project has four main phases:

1. Estimation and planning
2. Analysis and design
3. Implementation and testing
4. Support and maintenance

Let's explore the technical, functional, and operational challenges a data team can face when implementing lakehouse architecture across these four phases. I'll mention the ideal and real-world scenarios at the start of each section and discuss possible approaches for implementing a realistic solution.

Estimation and Planning Phase

As part of your lakehouse journey, you will have to collect the business requirements, finalize the tech stack, assemble a team of talented developers, deliver the project on schedule, and productionize and maintain the platform. For all of this, you need meticulous planning to finalize the delivery milestones and hit target dates.

Your lakehouse project planning largely depends on where you are in your current data journey. Figure 8-1 shows the two types of project implementations—brownfield and greenfield—which are standard terms in software development.

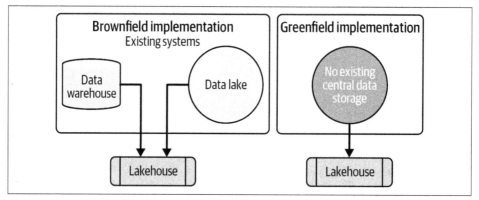

Figure 8-1. Brownfield and greenfield implementations

Estimation

Ideal scenario

Can be delivered as per the initial estimates and timelines

Real-world scenario

Delayed delivery due to challenges specific to brownfield implementations

A brownfield implementation means you already have an existing system and want to build a new platform to replace it. A greenfield implementation means you don't have an existing central data platform and want to build one from scratch.

Most large organizations have existing systems and would fall under the brownfield category. Some new organizations that have recently started their business operations might not have a central data platform and would need a greenfield implementation.

To seek budget approvals and finalize the lakehouse delivery timelines, you must estimate the efforts required to design, implement, and productionize the lakehouse platform. Estimation is the key driver for planning the project and determining the timelines. However, data teams often struggle to correctly estimate lakehouse projects and tend to overlook some key activities.

Here are some of the important points that you should consider while estimating your efforts for a lakehouse project:

- Consider the appropriate amount of effort for data modeling and creating mapping documents by collaborating with data owners and business units. This is one area that often gets underestimated.

- Consider the skills of your data team and estimate the platform build time accordingly. Data engineers who are new to lakehouse technologies will need time to explore the open table formats and features supported by different compute engines.

- Efforts required for building deployment pipelines are often ignored during estimation. Ensure that you consider the efforts to create and automate deployment processes.

- Like under-estimation, over-estimation can also impact the delivery timelines. One of the prime reasons for over-estimation is lack of automation. For example, you should not estimate ingestion efforts based on the number of source tables or files. Nor should you estimate orchestration efforts based on the number of workflows to be created. Instead, look to build reusable, configurable frameworks or leverage third-party tools that you can configure for onboarding new source tables and entities.

- Ensure you have adequate efforts for data governance, security, and monitoring activities.

Planning

Ideal scenario

> The plan created before starting the lakehouse project does not change throughout the project lifecycle.

Real-world scenario

> Multiple revisions to the plan due to practical challenges.

A project plan is created at the start of the project, when the visibility of the entire project is not very clear. In brownfield implementations, there is often a scope creep due to new findings, observations and learnings related to existing code components and their complexities, or selected tech stack limitations. All of these factors eventually result in delay of deliverables, and you will have to adjust your plan accordingly.

For brownfield implementations, you must include several additional activities in your plan. These extra activities can consume considerable effort and time in real-world projects, resulting in pushing the delivery deadlines.

Here are some of the important points to consider while in the planning and estimation phase:

- Upgrading an existing system to a lakehouse includes additional activities like understanding the existing ecosystem, historical data migration, data reconciliation, code reverse engineering, and system decommissioning. Include all of these activities in your plan.

- Add efforts to implement data quality validations, integration, deployment, governance, security, and orchestration. These are often ignored or not planned.

- Run the existing system and the new lakehouse in parallel for a few months and compare the final results. Plan for a few cycles of these parallel executions before decommissioning the old system.

- For greenfield implementations, plan for multiple cycles of functional validation to ensure that the lakehouse platform is capable of supporting the business use cases. On similar lines, plan for multiple rounds of performance test cycles to validate all the non-functional requirements (NFRs) are met.

You can refer to "Delivery References" on page 220 to understand various lakehouse project deliverables. Use it as a starting point for creating your lakehouse delivery plan.

Analysis and Design Phase

As you start the analysis and design phase, you will have to make some tough choices. Several challenges are associated with analyzing existing systems, deciding the data modeling approach, and finalizing the tech stack. These challenges should be addressed during the analysis and design phase of your lakehouse projects.

Analyzing the Existing System

Ideal scenario
> Data consumers of the new lakehouse platform should consume data only from the lakehouse storage (cloud object storage).

Real-world scenario
> Data consumers will have to consume data from the existing data warehouse *and* the new lakehouse storage in initial phases of the project.

An ideal lakehouse should have one storage tier that can act as a single source of truth for supporting BI and AI/ML workloads. However, this might not always be feasible, at least at the start of the lakehouse project. Most larger organizations today have existing central data storage, which can be a data warehouse or a data lake, with large volumes of historical data.

Migrating all this data to the lakehouse can take several days, sometimes even months. During this migration process, you will have to maintain both storage systems.

Analyze your existing system, understand the applications and databases that hold historical data, and plan the migration process and execution of BI workloads on the new lakehouse or the existing system accordingly.

Figure 8-2 depicts how data consumers leverage data from old and new systems during the migration phase.

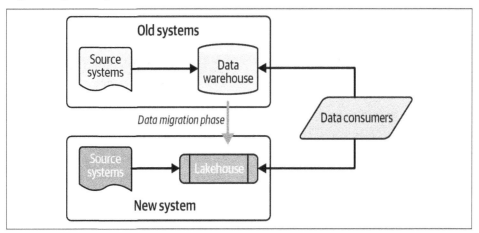

Figure 8-2. Data consumption during migration phase

Some organizations may have heavy investment in cloud data warehouses and will prefer to leverage cloud warehouses along with the lakehouse platform. In such cases, you can consider moving only business-critical BI workloads to the warehouse and continue using the lakehouse platform for most use cases. This additional warehouse layer can cause data duplication but you can restrict it to only mission-critical, performance-intensive workloads.

Data Modeling

Ideal scenario

You don't need expert data modelers to design the lakehouse data models.

Real-world scenario

Selecting and designing the lakehouse model is challenging and requires input from technical and domain experts.

A general misunderstanding is that you don't need experienced data modelers to model lakehouse data since no data warehouse is involved. However, data modeling is as essential for lakehouses as it is for data warehouses. You must model the higher zones of the lakehouse for users to be able to understand and query data quickly. There is a lot of confusion and debate over the best approach to model the different zones in a lakehouse. You can either use an ER model (with normalized tables) or a Data Vault approach for the cleansed zone and dimensional modeling (with denormalized tables) for the curated zone.

I've often seen projects get stuck at this point due to the lack of subject matter experts who can create these data models. Be sure to identify experts in the organization who understand the source systems and also have a good grasp of the domain. Table 8-1 provides a list of challenges related to data modeling and approaches to address them.

Table 8-1. Data modeling challenges and solutions

Challenges	Possible solutions
Limited domain expertise within data teams	Onboard business analysts who have the required domain knowledge and can help the data architect and data modeler in their activities.
Selecting the suitable data model for the cleansed and curated zones	You will have to thoroughly study the source systems, domain, and business to finalize the data model. It is also important to consider the skills of your data teams. ER modeling is much easier than Data Vault modeling; most data modelers have ER modeling experience.
Data Vault expertise is rare, and not many data practitioners have knowledge or experience implementing it	Try to onboard certified individuals with experience in Data Vault modeling.
In smaller data teams, the data architect also plays the role of data modeler; managing both activities becomes challenging	You can keep these two roles separate so that both activities can be performed in parallel.

Challenges	Possible solutions
Frequent changes to requirements and source systems impact the design, models, and mapping documents	Design a system that can accommodate changes. Leverage features like schema evolution for accommodating source schema changes.

Finalizing the Tech Stack

Ideal scenario

You always use the right tool for the right job when implementing lakehouse platform components.

Real-world scenario

Platform and tool selection decisions are also driven by non-technical factors.

One of the critical decisions that data architects will have to make is selecting the right tech stack for the lakehouse platform. Many parameters drive the selection of technology—some might also be non-technical and related to budget approvals, previous investments, or strategic decisions.

The top three most common, debatable, and critical decisions to make when selecting the tech stack are:

- Which cloud platform should you choose?
- Should you use third-party data platforms like Databricks, Snowflake, Dremio, Tabular, or Onehouse?
- Should you continue to use existing tools and products in which organizations have made strategic investments?

Selecting the cloud platform is an important decision. However, unlike other design decisions, it is not a decision that a data architect can make alone. Multiple factors influence the CSP selection, and here are the questions you should ask:

- Has the organization already invested in any of the cloud platforms? Is any cloud platform identified as an organization-wide strategic platform?
- Do you have any on-premises licenses you want to reuse in the cloud? For example, you can use Microsoft hybrid licenses (*https://oreil.ly/V-ddt*) for on-premises licenses on Azure.
- Is there a parent group or company that should participate in this decision? Are there any restrictions on using the same CSP as the parent group?
- Are there any compliance restrictions to storing data within the country? Does the CSP have a data center within your country?

- Are the required cloud services available in your preferred primary and disaster recovery (DR) regions?

Explore the services you plan to use and check their availability (within the primary and DR regions). If you intend to use all cloud native services for implementing your lakehouse, go through all the considerations we discussed in previous chapters for selecting the storage, compute, catalog, and other services. Your input will help your organization's data leaders to make an informed decision. As mentioned earlier, selecting a CSP is not just based on data workloads; it is also based on an organization's overall strategy.

As a data architect, though the CSP selection is not entirely your decision, you can recommend third-party data platforms. If your organization has a multi-cloud strategy, then there will be an inclination toward using third-party platforms that are cloud agnostic. While many organizations use Databricks and Snowflake, lakehouse-specific platforms like Dremio, Tabular, and Onehouse can help implement lakehouse platforms quickly.

A Question I Get from Most Customers: "Should We Use Databricks or Snowflake?"

Databricks and Snowflake are both widely adopted and popular platforms. Some organizations have invested in both products. You can use either of them to implement a lakehouse architecture, as discussed in Chapter 5. If you want to select one of them, you can perform a detailed study based on these points:

- Databricks supports Delta Lake, and Snowflake leverages Apache Iceberg (in preview) to support lakehouse implementations. Make a call based on your preference for the open table format. However, we might soon see interoperability between these formats, opening up many new possibilities—more on this in Chapter 9.

- Both platforms have some unique features that can help in implementation. For example, Databricks offers DLT for declarative ETL, Databricks Workflows for job authoring and orchestration, and Photon engine for enhanced performance.

- Snowflake provides capabilities to write stored procedures using different languages, native Iceberg table support, and micro-partitioning and caching features for enhanced performance. Study these features and determine which can bring you the most benefit.

- Understand your use cases—not just current but future ones. For example, consider AI/ML and generative AI use cases. Check whether the preferred platform can support these.

- One of the major driving factors is whether your organization is already using one of these platforms. Your decision on which platform to use will depend on existing investment and acceptance to make fresh investments in new platforms.

These points are just a primer on these platforms; you can absolutely do a more detailed study. At the same time, also explore the lakehouse-specific platforms like Dremio and Onehouse. There will always be one platform with more desirable features. As discussed in the previous chapters, take a holistic view based on your requirements. Look at the compute, storage, catalog, and overall configuration and management features.

Throughout this book, we've discussed several open source, cloud native, and third-party tools and products. However, we've not provided an exhaustive list of options. I've referred only to the most popular and widely adopted tools and products. There are many other products on the market that you can consider based on your use case and required features. My intention with this book is to discuss how you can design and implement a lakehouse architecture to build a modern, scalable data platform. Comparing different cloud platforms, tools, and products is beyond the scope of this book.

Implementation and Test Phase

During the implementation phase, you will face different challenges regarding the people, processes, and technology aspects of lakehouse architecture. In this section, I'll discuss some of the most common challenges, critical decisions you will have to make, and possible solutions.

Historical Data Migration

Ideal scenario

All historical data is migrated in a single migration cycle.

Real-world scenario

Historical data migration can take weeks to months across multiple migration cycles.

If you already have a central data ecosystem, you will have large volumes of historical data. The volume of this data would depend on how long the existing system has been up and running. Decades-old systems can have petabytes of data, especially if they store unstructured data from social media, IoT devices, or weblogs.

All this historical data needs to be migrated to the new lakehouse platform before you start executing your production workloads. Depending on the existing systems, there are different approaches to performing this migration. The existing system might use on-premises infrastructure, or the same or different cloud platform as the new system. And the architecture used for implementing the existing system can be a data warehouse, data lake, or a combined architecture. Figures 8-3 and 8-4 depict these migration approaches based on existing infrastructure and architecture.

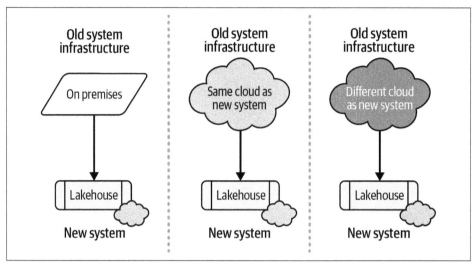

Figure 8-3. Migration based on existing system's infrastructure

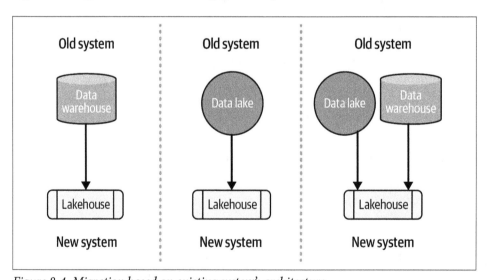

Figure 8-4. Migration based on existing system's architecture

Tables 8-2 and 8-3 provide details of these migration approaches based on existing infrastructure and architecture, respectively.

Table 8-2. Migration approaches based on existing infrastructure

Infrastructure used by existing system	Migration approaches
On-premises system	Consider using physical data transfer devices like AWS Snow devices (*https://aws.amazon.com/ snow/*) for petabyte-scale volumes. For a few 100s of terabytes, consider using dedicated networks or virtual private networks between the cloud and your data center.
Same cloud platform as the new lakehouse platform	If data is on the same cloud platform as the lakehouse, you can leverage the same cloud object storage as your lakehouse storage tier.
Different cloud platform	You can move the data from an existing cloud platform to a new one using ETL tools or cloud migration services. If you have a multi-cloud strategy, you can keep the data in the existing cloud platform and consider implementing a lakehouse across cloud platforms. For example, you can use S3 shortcut (*https://oreil.ly/BA6ud*) to access Amazon S3 data from Microsoft Fabric (*https:// oreil.ly/wfhS9*). More on this in Chapter 9.

Table 8-3. Migration approaches based on existing architecture

Architecture used by existing system	Migration approaches
Data warehouse	Extract the data as Parquet files and convert these into the open table formats of your choice. Leverage the tools provided by open table formats for this conversion (for example, Parquet-to-Delta converter by Delta Lake).
Data lake	Explore options to convert these into the open table format of your choice. Leverage the tools provided by open table formats for this conversion.
Combined architecture	In such cases, the historical data migration depends on which storage tier has the complete history. Often, the data warehouse might only hold a portion of the historical data; you will have to convert the data lake files in the selected open table format when migrating to the new lakehouse.

Based on the approach you choose, you will have to perform multiple migration cycles to move the data to the new lakehouse. You will also have to reconcile data after each cycle, debug the mismatches, fix the issues, and re-run the migration process. You will have to perform multiple migration cycles until all the data is reconciled and validated.

Data Reconciliation and Testing

Ideal scenario

You want to reconcile complete historical data post-migration to lakehouse.

Real-world scenario

You will have to perform reconciliation based on sample datasets or aggregated values.

The data reconciliation process involves comparing data from the existing system to data in the new lakehouse system. To prove the new platform's success, you will have to reconcile the data (historical and daily) between the old and new platforms and prove that there are no differences.

After migrating the historical data in the new lakehouse, you should ideally compare every record and attribute to ensure there are no data issues post-migration. However, data reconciliation becomes complex for large volumes of data and comparing every record might not be feasible. If the data model of the existing system and the new lakehouse differs, it is extremely challenging to compare the data in these two systems since the models and tables are entirely different.

In such cases, you can follow these approaches to reconcile the lakehouse data:

- Compare based on summarization or aggregation for specific categories. Some examples are:
  - Validate the total sum of account balances at the end of each month.
  - Check the number of active customers at the end of a specific day.
  - Count the number of unique values for attributes with a string or varchar datatype.
- Do a functional validation of sample records with the help of data analysts. For example, check the number of transactions and balances post-transactions for high-net-worth individuals (HNI).
- In most cases, final reports from existing and new systems would have the same format. You can compare these reports to find any anomalies.
- Automate the data reconciliation process. Build internal accelerators that you can use across projects for such comparisons. Leverage open source Python packages like DataComPy (*https://oreil.ly/y3QiQ*) that can help to perform comparisons using the Spark framework.

Reverse Engineering

Ideal scenario
Up-to-date design and mapping documents of existing systems are available.

Real-world scenario
You will have to perform reverse engineering to derive business logic from existing code.

Reverse engineering of code means analyzing the given code and understanding its functionality and business purpose. In the case of brownfield lakehouse implementations, chances are high that the design and mapping documents are either out-of-date or, in the worst case, nonexistent. In such cases, you will have to reverse engineer the code to understand the existing functionality for implementing the new data pipelines in your lakehouse.

Analyzing legacy code written using different programming languages or frameworks is challenging. If your developers do not have the skills to understand existing code, you will either have to get experts to perform this activity or upskill your team.

Consider automating the reverse engineering process by developing internal accelerators or using third-party tools. You can also look for options to convert existing code to new lakehouse-compatible code. For example, convert existing Cloudera Spark scripts to Databricks Spark scripts, or convert an Oracle PL/SQL script to Snowflake stored procedures.

Data Quality and Handling Sensitive Data

Ideal scenario
> Business validations and sensitive attributes are well documented by business teams and shared with data teams.

Real-world scenario
> Business data quality expectations are not well documented, and a list of sensitive attributes might not be readily available.

Ensuring the quality and security of data are common challenges for most organizations. Yet, in most cases, data architects get pushback if they propose using third-party tools to implement these processes. Some organizations are more inclined to use cloud native services or implement custom frameworks to validate data quality and implement data security. The apparent reason for this is to reduce the overall cost. However, it is difficult for data engineers to compile a list of business validations or identify sensitive attributes as this varies from domain to domain. Most of the time, you will need the business team's help to create this list.

One of the best approaches to mitigate these challenges is to use third-party tools that provide out-of-the-box features specific to your domain. Table 8-4 lists various challenges in implementing a custom framework to validate data quality and implement data security, and how third-party tools can help to address them.

Table 8-4. Custom frameworks versus third-party tools

Custom framework challenges	Benefits of third-party tools
In most cases, there are no documented business rules to validate the data. Data engineers have to implement business validations based on their limited domain knowledge.	Third-party tools have built-in validations, based on the domain, for validating the data.
Writing custom code for validating data quality is a tedious job and can consume a considerable amount of effort and time.	You only have to configure the attributes to use the built-in rules, reducing effort and time spent writing custom code.
You have to compile a list of sensitive attributes by collaborating with business and data owners, and write custom code to abstract them.	Third-party security platforms have built-in features to identify and anonymize sensitive attributes without manual interventions.

If you still plan to create custom code (due to budget or other constraints), you can consider using open source frameworks like Great Expectations (*https://greatexpectations.io*), Deequ, (*https://oreil.ly/O7A7y*) or Soda (*https://oreil.ly/0z8Ce*) for performing these validations. Some of these frameworks provide built-in validation rules to check data completeness, accuracy, and freshness.

Support and Maintenance Phase

The support activities for a lakehouse project are similar to any other data project. There are practical challenges, though, concerning disaster recovery (DR) setup, auditing and tracking, and decommissioning of the old system. We'll discuss all of these challenges in this section.

Auditing and Tracking

Ideal scenario
 You will always get clean, error-free data from source systems.

Real-world scenario
 Source systems can send erroneous or incomplete data.

There can be situations when the source systems send you erroneous files, or you accidentally rerun a job processed earlier. In such cases, you can easily use the time travel features provided by the open table formats to restore the older table versions. However, in production systems, there will be multiple jobs and processes loading a single table. To track which job has loaded which records in lakehouse tables, you can add audit attributes like batch_id, source_id, job_id, and update_timestamp to your lakehouse tables. These audit attributes can help you track each record in these tables and get information like:

- Which source system sent a specific record
- Which user loaded the record (service user or manually entered)
- When was the record created or updated
- Which batch or job loaded the record

Based on these audit attributes, you can back out the erroneous data and reload the correct data files. Consider adding these audit attributes in higher zone tables of the lakehouse.

Disaster Recovery Strategy

Ideal scenario

> You should be able to switch to a secondary site within minimum recovery time.

Real-world scenario

> You will have to design a disaster recovery strategy considering cost optimizations that can result in increased recovery time.

Building for failures is one of the critical design considerations for distributed systems. There can be situations when specific cloud services or the entire cloud region might be down. In such cases, you should have a secondary lakehouse system in another cloud region as part of your Business Continuity Plan (BCP). This process of failing to the secondary system to continue with business activities is known as disaster recovery (DR).

Creating an appropriate DR strategy is necessary for any production system in order to reduce the impact of infrastructure downtime. Implementing a DR system is a common practice for data platforms. Two key parameters for designing your DR strategy are recovery time objective (RTO) and recovery point objective (RPO):

Recovery time objective (RTO)

> RTO is the maximum time for which your data platform can be unavailable. It is also the maximum allowed time for your secondary system to be up and running, and supporting the *business-as-usual (BAU) processes*. If you have an RTO of 30 minutes, this means your secondary site should be ready within 30 minutes of your platform becoming unavailable.

Recovery point objective (RPO)

> RPO is the maximum amount of time for data loss. Though it is related to data, it is also measured in time and is impacted by when the last backup was taken. If you had taken a backup 30 minutes before the disaster, you would lose 30 minutes' worth of data. If you have an RPO of 15 minutes, you should take backups every 15 minutes or less.

> BAU processes are the activities or operations required to execute your business on a day-to-day basis. In the context of DR, you should ensure that on failure of the primary cluster, the secondary cluster is able to support the business teams to perform their daily, routine activities required for business continuity.

If you want to keep RTO and RPO to a few minutes, you will need a secondary system that is always up and running with the latest data so that failover can quickly happen. Figure 8-5 shows a high-level view of the primary and secondary systems that are part of DR strategy.

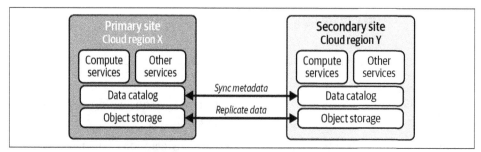

Figure 8-5. Primary and secondary sites for DR implementation

There are two different approaches for designing your DR strategy: active-active and active-passive:

Active-active approach

In this approach, you always have the primary and secondary (DR) sites up and running. When the primary goes down, when the disaster hits, it will failover to the secondary (DR) site. Since the secondary site is always active, no significant data or time is lost between the primary system going down and the secondary system taking over. This approach can satisfy the lowest RTO and RPO service level agreements (SLAs), but it is expensive.

Active-passive approach

In this approach, the secondary site is not always up and running. It is made available only when there is a disaster. This arrangement needs a higher RPO and RTO but can significantly reduce costs.

Select the approach you want to implement for your lakehouse platform based on your requirements. Consider the following when implementing your DR strategy:

- Back up your primary storage to secondary storage on a regular basis. Leverage the services provided by the cloud object storage. For example, Azure ADLS offers Geo-zone-redundant storage (*https://oreil.ly/aDqPY*) (GZRS) for replicating data to secondary regions.

- Before finalizing cloud services, check whether they are available in the secondary region.

- There is always a trade-off between RTO, RPO, and cost. Look for different approaches to balance these by considering a passive secondary site.

- Consider a lighter "always-up" secondary cluster with reduced compute resources that can scale up as needed when disaster strikes.

- Plan quarterly cycles to switch between primary and secondary sites, to validate your DR strategy and its activities.

In a real-world project, your DR strategy must balance cost and system downtime. Determine if you really need an active-active strategy, as it can add to overall operations cost. An active-passive approach is good enough in most of the use cases where you are not supporting real-time analytics.

Decommissioning the Old System

Ideal scenario

You want to decommission the old system as soon as the new lakehouse is live.

Real-world scenario

You will have to execute multiple parallel executions of old and new systems and reconcile data before decommissioning the old system.

The success of your new lakehouse system is based on:

- Data reconciliation between the old and new systems
- Correct reports and dashboards generated by the new lakehouse system
- Adoption of the new lakehouse system by platform users for their day-to-day work
- Minimal usage of the old system for any BAU activities

To validate the data in the new lakehouse system, perform multiple parallel executions of the old and new systems and reconcile the data between these two systems. Perform parallel runs for daily, weekly, and monthly workloads for at least a couple of cycles before making the new lakehouse system your primary system to support all BAU workloads. You can decommission the old system once you move all workloads to the new lakehouse system.

Some of the practical challenges for decommissioning the old system are as follows:

- You will have to wait until you complete all planned parallel executions before decommissioning the old system. These parallel executions can take several weeks to months.
- Data might not get fully reconciled after completing all planned parallel runs. You will have to see if the partially compared data is good enough to prove the success of the new lakehouse system or if you need more cycles of parallel execution and reconciliation.
- Since costs are incurred from both the old and new platforms, there will always be business pressure to decommission the old system quickly. You will have to make adjustments, prioritize activities, and align engineers to focus on decommissioning the old system.

Delivery References

You can refer to this section when planning the different phases of your lakehouse project. The project deliverables section summarizes key deliverables across the project's design, implementation, and support phases. The reference architectures section covers implementations based on cloud native and third-party platforms.

You can use these as starting points and make further changes per your requirements and use cases.

Project Deliverables

Table 8-5 lists project deliverables for implementing a lakehouse platform. You can consider these while planning your lakehouse delivery schedule.

Table 8-5. List of project deliverables

Category	Deliverables
Documents	• Project plan • Architecture blueprint • Design documents covering various data management, governance, security, and operations processes • Data model diagrams for cleansed, curated, and semantic zones • Source-to-target mapping documents for lakehouse tables • DR strategy document covering the failover approach • Testing and data reconciliation strategy to validate data
Frameworks	• Data ingestion frameworks that are configurable and flexible to quickly onboard new entities • Data processing and data load frameworks supporting schema and data quality validations, transformations, and data loads in tables across different zones • Orchestration frameworks for creating workflows, adding dependencies, and scheduling workflows
Utilities/ accelerators	• Utilities and user-defined functions (UDFs) for repeatable operations • Data reconciliation utilities for validating historical data post-migration • Utilities to perform daily data validation during parallel executions • Miscellaneous utilities for supporting BAU activities like checking job status, job durations, and daily operational dashboard population
Setup and configurations	• Set up and configure data catalogs, metadata ingestion, and access control policies • Set up data encryption and key management services for data security • Configure data lifecycle policies for data archival and housekeeping • Set up and configure the secondary site/cluster for DR and data replication between primary and secondary regions • Set up continuous integration/continuous delivery (CI/CD) processes for automated deployment, integration, and testing • Set up data observability process for anomaly detection of production data • Set up sensitive data identification and anonymization processes

Category	Deliverables
Workshops, interviews, and sessions	• Workshops with technical, business, and other stakeholders for analysis, design, and data modeling activities • Interviews with source system owners to understand data domains • Design sessions by the data architect to explain architecture, design principles, and implementation approaches • Sessions to educate platform users on how to use the new lakehouse platform

Some caveats for Table 8-5 are as follows:

- These deliverables are specific to the core data platform activities. Based on your use case, you will have to plan deliverables to onboard new sources, create ETL jobs and scripts, and implement the required reports, ML models, APIs, and queries.

- If you use third-party tools for any activities, you don't need to build frameworks. You will only have to perform the required configurations.

- Infrastructure administration deliverables are not listed here as the focus is only on data activities.

- If you don't have an existing system, you can ignore the activities related to historical data migration and its reconciliation.

Reference Architectures

As we've discussed, architecture blueprints are the first step in your design phase. You can refer to this section when creating the architecture blueprint for your lakehouse. Remember, the technology stack will depend on your preferred CSP, use case, and any strategic investments in existing tools.

I've provided two reference architectures based on:

- Cloud native services (AWS)
- Third-party platforms (Databricks)

Please use these only for reference and make appropriate changes based on the design considerations discussed in earlier chapters. You can create similar architectures for other cloud or third-party platforms.

Cloud native implementation

Cloud native implementations make use of the services available within the cloud platform. This approach helps to easily integrate these services and minimizes the overall platform cost. Figure 8-6 depicts a lakehouse architecture blueprint based on the AWS cloud platform and Table 8-6 provides a quick summary of the AWS native services for implementing a lakehouse platform.

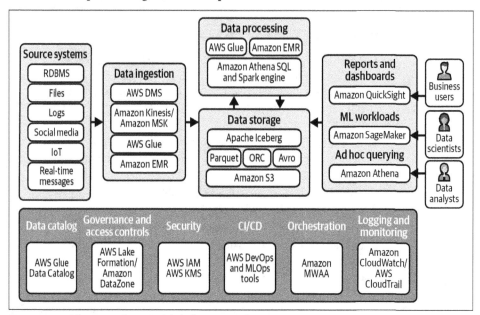

Figure 8-6. Blueprint for AWS lakehouse implementation

Table 8-6. AWS services for lakehouse implementation

Processes	AWS services and their purpose
Data ingestion	• AWS DMS (*https://aws.amazon.com/dms*) can help to migrate historical data from existing systems. It can also help to perform incremental data ingestion daily. • You can use Amazon Kinesis (*https://aws.amazon.com/kinesis*) or Amazon MSK (*https://aws.amazon.com/msk*) for ingesting streaming data into the lakehouse. • AWS Glue (*https://aws.amazon.com/glue*) and Amazon EMR (*https://aws.amazon.com/emr*) provide Spark-based data ingestion capabilities.
Data storage	• Amazon S3 (*https://aws.amazon.com/s3*) is the cloud object storage for storing your lakehouse data. • You can use Iceberg as an open table format for storing files in Parquet, Avro, or ORC. You can also consider other table formats like Hudi or Delta Lake.
Data processing	• You can use AWS Glue and/or Amazon EMR for data processing and transformations. • You can also consider using Amazon Athena's (*https://aws.amazon.com/athena*) SQL and Spark engines for lightweight processing.

Processes	AWS services and their purpose
Data consumption and delivery	• You can leverage Amazon SageMaker (*https://aws.amazon.com/sagemaker*) for ML workloads, Amazon Athena's SQL engine for ad hoc queries, and Amazon QuickSight (*https://aws.amazon.com/quicksight*) for building your reports and dashboards.
Common services	• AWS Glue Data Catalog stores technical metadata. You can complement it with Amazon DataZone (*https://aws.amazon.com/datazone*) to add business context. AWS Lake Formation (*https://aws.amazon.com/lake-formation*) helps control access for users and roles. • For security, you can use AWS IAM (*https://aws.amazon.com/iam*) for user authentication and AWS KMS (*https://aws.amazon.com/kms*) to encrypt data stored in S3. • You can explore various AWS services for DataOps and MLOps, like AWS CodeCommit (*https://aws.amazon.com/codecommit*), AWS CodeBuild (*https://aws.amazon.com/codebuild*), and AWS CodeDeploy (*https://aws.amazon.com/codedeploy*). You can use the Amazon MWAA (*https://oreil.ly/UaZOC*) (based on Apache Airflow) for orchestration. Amazon CloudWatch (*https://aws.amazon.com/cloudwatch*) and AWS CloudTrail (*https://aws.amazon.com/cloudtrail*) can provide the required monitoring capabilities.

Similarly, you can design your platform using Azure or GCP native services. Please note that these implementations are not cloud agnostic, and you cannot easily migrate the workloads to other cloud platforms.

Third-party platform implementation

Third-party platforms like Databricks can help you to implement a cloud-agnostic data platform. You can leverage its internal services for your lakehouse architecture. However, in most cases, you will have to use the underlying cloud services to implement identity management, data encryption, CI/CD processes, and monitoring processes. You can also consider using third-party products for reporting and data observability. Figure 8-7 depicts a lakehouse architecture blueprint based on Databricks platform and Table 8-7 provides a quick summary of the Databricks features for implementing a lakehouse platform.

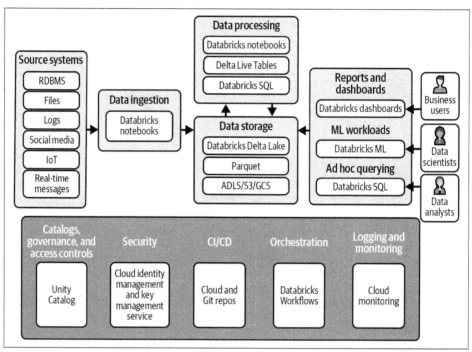

Figure 8-7. Blueprint for Databricks lakehouse implementation

Table 8-7. Databricks features for lakehouse implementation

Processes	Databricks features and their purpose
Data ingestion	• You can create a custom Spark framework using Databricks notebooks to ingest data from various sources.
Data storage	• You can use cloud object storage provided by AWS, Azure, or GCP to store your lakehouse data. • Databricks supports Delta-Parquet for storing data in open formats.
Data processing	• Consider using Delta Live Tables for processing, as it provides features for creating delta tables, performing incremental processing, and adding data quality constraints. • You can also use notebooks to run Spark code or use Databricks SQL to execute queries for transforming data.
Data consumption and delivery	• You can leverage Databricks ML for ML workloads and Databricks SQL engine for ad hoc queries. • You can use the internal reports and visualization features for creating simple reports and dashboards. For advanced features, consider visualization platforms like Power BI and Tableau.
Common services	• Unity Catalog can store technical metadata and help manage access to various tables. • Using the cloud platform's key management features, you can encrypt the data at rest. You can do user management using the cloud identity services. • Databricks supports code repositories like Git. You can also use cloud services for CI/CD processes. • You can use Databricks Workflows to orchestrate the internal Databricks jobs. For monitoring/logging, you can leverage the underlying cloud services.

Along similar lines, you can design your lakehouse platform using other third-party platforms like Snowflake, Dremio, and Onehouse (with appropriate changes as required).

Key Takeaways

A real-world lakehouse is not significantly different from an ideal lakehouse. However, it is based on specific workarounds and trade-offs to optimize cost, adhere to schedules, and support required workloads. Table 8-8 summarizes the features of the ideal versus the real-world lakehouse.

Table 8-8. Ideal versus real-world lakehouse

Ideal lakehouse	Real-world lakehouse
It has only a single storage tier that can act as the ultimate source of truth.	Most organizations have an existing warehouse with large volumes of data that can take a few months to migrate to the new lakehouse. Until all the historical data is migrated, you might need to consume data from multiple storages.
It uses the right tools for the right job.	Organizations might have significant investments in some of the existing tools that you will have to use in the new system.
Complete historical data is migrated to the new lakehouse within a few execution cycles, which takes only a few days.	Large volumes of historical data need multiple execution cycles executed over several weeks or months.
It has fully reconciled historical data post-migration from existing systems.	Due to the large volumes of historical data, you might be unable to reconcile every record and column.
In the case of DR, it can switch to the secondary cluster/site immediately to avoid data loss and adhere to system downtime SLAs.	You might not implement a fully automated failover to optimize cost, which can lead to considerable downtime exceeding the business's expected SLAs.
Old systems can be decommissioned as soon as the new lakehouse goes live.	Decommissioning the old system can take time, as data in the new lakehouse needs several validation cycles.

In this chapter, we focused on building a real-world lakehouse. In the next and last chapter of this book, we'll look at what the lakehouses of the future might look like and how new technologies can change the way lakehouses are built in the future.

References

- Establishing RPO and RTO Targets for Cloud Applications | AWS Cloud Operations & Migrations Blog (*https://oreil.ly/Mw4v-*)
- Disaster recovery | Microsoft Learn (*https://oreil.ly/DWVgT*)
- Choosing an Open Table Format for your Transactional Data Lake on AWS (*https://oreil.ly/wMBB_*)
- Converting from Parquet to Delta Lake (*https://oreil.ly/qDgvW*)

- soda-core/docs/overview-main.md GitHub (*https://oreil.ly/C4m_6*)
- DataComPy for comparing dataframes (*https://oreil.ly/XOSc9*)
- OneLake shortcuts | Microsoft Fabric (*https://oreil.ly/llyQ2*)
- PyDeequ | PyPI (*https://oreil.ly/erz3f*)

CHAPTER 9
Lakehouse of the Future

Congratulations! You've reached the last chapter of this book. I hope you now understand lakehouse architecture, its core concepts, and the different technology options available for implementing a lakehouse.

In the previous chapter, we discussed how to build a lakehouse in the real-world. In this chapter, I will discuss some of the alternative, unconventional, and futuristic approaches to building a lakehouse. I've handpicked a few technologies, products, and design approaches that I think will shape the future of lakehouse design and its adoption by the data community. While some have already become mainstream, some are still in experimental mode.

In this chapter, we will explore:

- Different approaches like data mesh, HTAP, and Zero ETL, in combination with lakehouse architecture, to implement data platforms
- Interoperability features and upcoming file and table formats
- Managed platforms that can simplify lakehouse implementations in public and private clouds
- Use of AI in a lakehouse

As the data world changes rapidly, some of these design patterns and methodologies might become the standard approach for implementing data platforms, while others might not attract many takers. In either case, I felt it a good idea to conclude this book by exploring the endless future possibilities that technological advancements can offer.

Warehouse to Lakehouse: What's Next?

Like modern technologies, modern architectures also evolve with time. In the initial chapters of this book, we discussed how lakehouses have evolved from data warehouses and data lakes. However, lakehouse is certainly not the last architectural pattern. In the future, new approaches will leverage lakehouse capabilities and combine them with other architectural designs to build innovative data platforms. Large organizations have already started adopting the data mesh approach using lakehouse architecture. Let's discuss data mesh and other possible approaches (such as HTAP and Zero ETL) for implementing a lakehouse.

Data Mesh

Traditional data and analytics platforms used a centralized approach to storing and managing data. Then, in her book *Data Mesh* (O'Reilly), author Zhamak Dehghani introduced a decentralized approach to organizing data known as *data mesh*. In a data mesh approach, the ownership and accountability of data belongs to the domain teams. They are responsible for maintaining and sharing their data with other domain teams. Figure 9-1 shows this decentralized approach to data management.

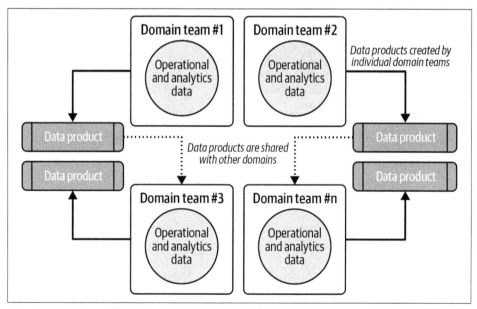

Figure 9-1. Decentralized data management in data mesh

The four main pillars of a data mesh are:

- Decentralized data ownership should be with the domain teams that produce data.
- Data should be treated like a product and shared with other domains.
- There should be a shared infrastructure (data platform) that domain teams should leverage (self-serve) to build their data products.
- There should be central governance policies that every domain follows and implements for their data products.

Organizations embarking on a data mesh journey can consider lakehouse architecture when building their data products. Some of the key benefits that the lakehouse provides to data mesh are:

- Ability to store structured, semi-structured, and unstructured data for creating the final data products
- Support for all types of workloads—from BI to AI
- Flexibility for different domain teams to use compute engines of their choice
- Ability to share data products across domain teams
- Federated governance across data and AI assets by using unified data catalogs

Combining data mesh with lakehouse architecture has already become a popular approach and is being adopted by larger organizations.

HTAP

Conventionally, we have been building separate systems to support transactional (OLTP) and analytical (OLAP) workloads. An additional ETL process is required to move the data from the OLTP systems to the OLAP systems to support various BI and analytics use cases. This extra step of performing ETL adds to operational costs and causes processing delays.

In the past, organizations have tried different approaches to reduce these costs and delays, in order to enable users to access the latest analytics data as soon as possible. One of the popular approaches is hybrid transactional/analytical processing (HTAP).

HTAP combines OLTP and OLAP in a single system. Figure 9-2 shows a data platform implemented using an HTAP approach that unifies the transactional and analytics workloads.

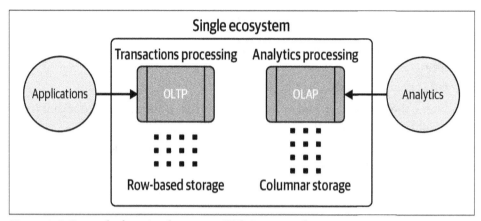

Figure 9-2. Data platform implementing HTAP approach

Key benefits of the HTAP approach are as follows:

- It enables you to implement a single ecosystem that supports transactions and analytics workloads.
- It removes the ETL process for moving data between OLTP and OLAP systems.
- It helps to perform streaming analytics because data is available in real time for analysis.
- It helps implement a simple architecture that is easy to manage and maintain.

Considering these benefits, various vendors have launched products that offer HTAP capabilities. For example, Snowflake introduced a feature called Unistore (*https:// oreil.ly/fLJ1o*) based on hybrid tables. When users insert data in a hybrid table, Snowflake stores it as a row store, creates another copy, and stores that copy using a columnar approach. The row store is used for OLTP use cases and the columnar data is used for OLAP use cases. SingleStore (*https://www.singlestore.com*) is another platform that also provides HTAP capabilities for implementing data platforms.

You may be wondering: How can the HTAP approach impact lakehouse implementations?

In this book, we have discussed how lakehouse architecture unifies analytics workloads. HTAP supports the unification of transactional and analytics workloads. In the future, we might see organizations implementing lakehouse architecture using Snowflake Iceberg tables (as discussed in Chapter 5) and complementing these with hybrid tables for joining transactional data—all within a single platform. We might also see hybrid tables using open table formats like Iceberg to store a columnar copy of data. This is speculation, of course, and there might be several limitations to build such a feature. But with the HTAP and lakehouse combination, there can be several possibilities and opportunities for innovation.

Zero ETL

While HTAP is an excellent approach to unifying transactional and analytics systems, there can be specific design constraints when you need to decouple or isolate these systems. In such cases, you can consider a *Zero ETL* approach. Zero ETL is a term that refers to removing or minimizing the efforts required to build ETL pipelines for moving data from OLTP to OLAP platforms.

Figures 9-3 and 9-4 show the two options—data replication and data federation—with the Zero ETL approach.

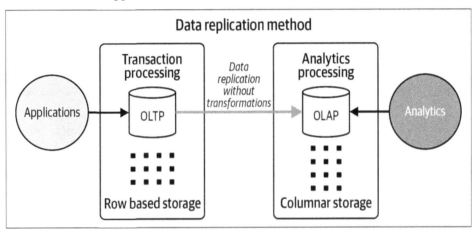

Figure 9-3. Data replication option in Zero ETL

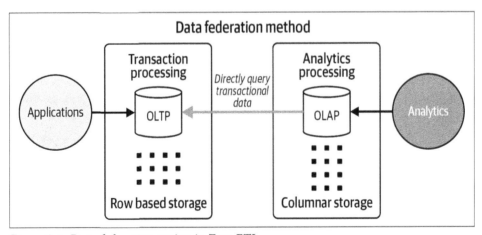

Figure 9-4. Data federation option in Zero ETL

As shown in Figures 9-3 and 9-4, you can either replicate data from transactional systems to analytical systems (without transformations) in real time or federate (directly query) the transactional systems from the analytics platform. Leading CSPs now offer services and features supporting Zero ETL. For example, Azure provides Synapse Link (*https://oreil.ly/lW51r*) to integrate Azure SQL DB and Synapse Analytics. AWS offers Aurora Zero-ETL (*https://oreil.ly/4Zc1b*) integration with Redshift.

Data practitioners have started adopting the Zero ETL approach while implementing a lakehouse. This approach can help query data directly from source systems on the lakehouse platforms. For example, Databricks Unity Catalog supports running federated queries to query source data. Microsoft Fabric shortcuts can help you access S3 data. We will discuss Fabric in more detail later in this chapter.

Both the HTAP and Zero ETL approaches can become excellent alternatives to building complex data pipelines to move data between transactional and lakehouse systems. With their capabilities, you can unify not only your analytics (data and AI/ML) workloads but also your transactional workloads. These approaches can also simplify the technical landscape for organizations implementing the data mesh, where each domain is responsible for maintaining and managing both transactional and analytical data.

Interoperability and New Formats

In Chapter 3, we explored the unique features offered by different open table formats. We also discussed key considerations for selecting the right format based on your requirements, ecosystem, and other factors. However, we did not discuss the possibility of exchanging data across the three open table formats using interoperability features. Let's explore how you can implement and leverage interoperability between these table formats.

Choosing one of these formats is a tough decision you'll have to make at the start of the project. You might not have complete clarity of the project at this stage and may end up selecting a table format that is ultimately not the best fit for your requirements. You also have to invest a lot of time and effort in studying features, reviewing performances, and performing assessments to finalize a format. And there is always the limitation of losing some of the excellent features that other formats offer.

To address these challenges, you can consider solutions that provide interoperability between various formats.

Figure 9-5 shows the open table formats and their metadata layers.

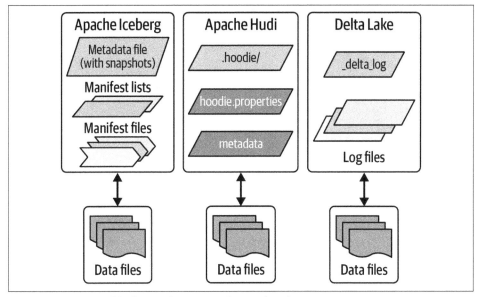

Figure 9-5. Open table format layouts and metadata layers

As shown in Figure 9-5, all these formats differ at the metadata level. They do, how‐ ever, store data in standard, consistent formats like Parquet. You can operate across the table formats by converting the metadata layer. Currently, there are two tools available to perform this conversion:

- Universal Format (UniForm) by Delta Lake
- Apache XTable (formerly known as OneTable)

Universal Format (UniForm)

Delta Lake's Universal Format (UniForm) enables compute engines to read delta tables as Iceberg tables. UniForm converts the metadata of delta tables into Iceberg-compatible metadata so that engines supporting Iceberg can understand and read it. The underlying data file remains as is and is not duplicated. UniForm is available in Delta Lake 3.0 onward. Figure 9-6 shows the Delta Lake metadata conversion process into Iceberg-compatible metadata.

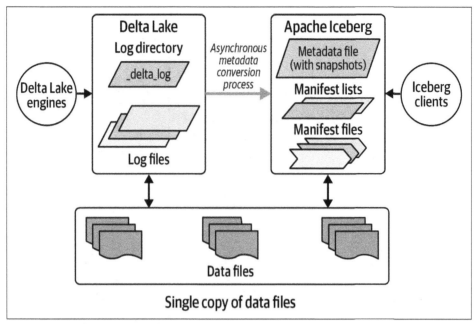

Figure 9-6. Delta Lake-to-Iceberg metadata conversion process using UniForm

You can enable UniForm support for your tables, considering any future workloads or downstream applications needing Iceberg compatibility. However, while consuming data such as Iceberg tables, you must study the current limitations (*https://oreil.ly/NJJbF*) of UniForm.

 UniForm is unidirectional, meaning you can only read the delta tables as Iceberg tables, not vice versa. UniForm also supports Hudi tables. At the time of writing this book, this feature is in preview (*https://oreil.ly/6g-lk*).

Apache XTable

Apache XTable (*https://xtable.apache.org*) is another initiative (formerly known as OneTable (*https://oreil.ly/vJClp*), created by Onehouse.ai) to provide interoperability between the open table formats. The main difference between XTable and UniForm is that XTable provides omnidirectional interoperability between Iceberg, Hudi, and Delta Lake formats. You can use XTable to convert metadata between the three open table formats. Figure 9-7 shows the metadata conversion process.

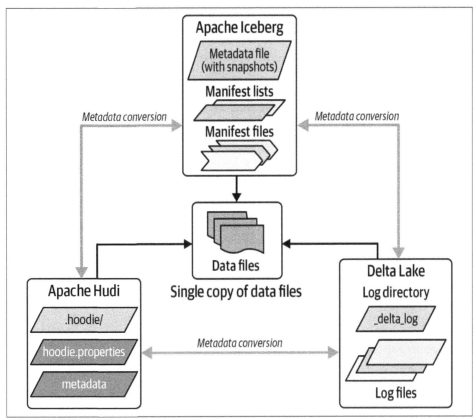

Figure 9-7. Omnidirectional metadata conversion process using XTable

As shown in Figure 9-7, XTable identifies one format as primary and creates metadata for the other formats, which are considered secondary. Like UniForm, XTable converts only metadata, so you don't need to duplicate the data.

XTable is currently in the incubating stage as part of Apache Software Foundation (ASF) and provides a neutral space for vendors to collaborate and work toward implementing truly open lakehouse architectures. In the future, you will not be confined to just one table format and will be able to design a lakehouse by leveraging different table formats that suit your use cases. This also allows you to use your preferred platform (like Databricks or Azure Synapse) that may have native Delta support but can still integrate with Iceberg and Hudi clients using interoperability features.

Upcoming File and Table Formats

In Chapter 3, we also discussed the open file formats like Parquet, ORC, and Avro. While these formats have been used since the Hadoop days, there are ongoing initiatives to create new formats. One such initiative is the Puffin format, introduced by the Iceberg community.

Before we discuss Puffin, let's recap how data skipping works in the Iceberg-Parquet format. Each Parquet data file holds the column-level stats for its data in its footer. The compute engine reads this footer from each file when accessing data and can skip the rows for faster processing. Open table formats like Iceberg hold these column-level stats in the manifest file, skipping the unwanted data files and reading only the required files, which optimizes query performance.

Iceberg created Puffin to store information that cannot be stored in Iceberg's manifest files—information like stats and indexes of underlying data files.

Puffin can help improve the query performance of Iceberg-managed tables. The stats and indexes that Puffin collects can help users quickly perform calculations (such as estimating the number of distinct values). Puffin is in its early stages and it will be worth tracking its progress to see how you can use it along with Iceberg to implement lakehouses in the future.

Modern technologies have enabled organizations to easily implement use cases that were once extremely challenging. One such use case is streaming analytics, which is becoming mainstream and part of every organization's wish list. Performing analytics on streaming data is complex, and it becomes more challenging if you need extremely low-latency streaming analytics.

Many organizations have been using Apache Flink to address low-latency streaming use cases. As discussed in Chapter 5, Flink can offer sub-second latency and enable unified batch and streaming use cases. Flink's creators, Ververica, created Apache Paimon to help implement a *streamhouse*, a term to describe streaming analytics in a lakehouse. Paimon is an open table format still in its incubation phase as part of the ASF.

Some of the key features of Paimon are:

- It supports high-speed data ingestion, change data tracking, and real-time analytics.
- It has strong integration with Apache Flink.
- It supports unified batch and stream processing.

Hudi also supports streaming use cases and is a top choice for implementing them in a lakehouse. You can explore and evaluate Paimon as an alternative to Hudi. If you plan to implement streaming use cases, it's worth keeping an eye on this space and exploring the advancements and optimizations in storage and compute options for streaming use cases.

As data communities and product vendors create new file and table formats to address specific challenges, initiatives like UniForm and XTable can help implement a simple, open lakehouse architecture. Explore these initiatives and consider them when designing your lakehouse to make it future-ready and independent of any one format.

Managed Platforms for Public and Private Clouds

In the preceding chapters, we discussed the different components of a lakehouse platform and the technology options to implement them. If you recall the key considerations, there were multiple points related to integrating these components with open table formats, checking version compatibility, and the underlying cloud ecosystem dependency.

When implementing a lakehouse architecture using cloud native, vanilla services, you must first provision the infrastructure and perform multiple configurations to ensure a secure, performant, and cost-optimized system. This requires a considerable amount of administration and management efforts. You can minimize these efforts by setting up the data infrastructure using managed lakehouse platforms offered by different product vendors. Figure 9-8 shows managed lakehouse platform components.

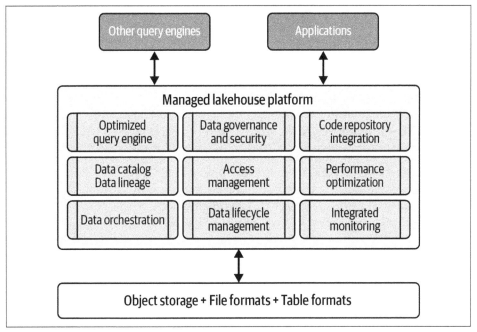

Figure 9-8. Managed lakehouse platform components

Some of the standard characteristics of a managed lakehouse platform are:

- They abstract the complexity involved in cloud infrastructure resource provisioning. You only need to focus on the development of your code.

- They provide flexibility in choosing open table formats or might have specialized offerings based on a specific table format.

- They provide a performant compute engine (or runtime environments), catalogs, data security, data lifecycle, and other features that can help you to implement a lakehouse faster and easier.

- They are generally cloud-agnostic and can work on AWS, Azure, and GCP infrastructure.

- They simplify your lakehouse implementation process.

Considering these benefits, managed platforms might become the default approach for organizations implementing lakehouses. In this section, let's explore some of the modern managed lakehouse platforms.

Microsoft Fabric and Other Platforms

Throughout this book, we've discussed various lakehouse scenarios by citing examples across managed platforms like Databricks and Snowflake. Considering the increasing demand for a unified analytics platform, Microsoft launched Microsoft Fabric in 2023 as an all-in-one SaaS analytics solution. For organizations that have embraced Azure as their cloud platform, Fabric is becoming a prime contender for implementing lakehouse platforms.

Fabric supports several use cases, including data engineering, data warehousing, data science, real-time analytics, and BI—all from a central platform. These workloads are known as *experiences* in Fabric. Figure 9-9 shows a simple representation of the Fabric architecture.

All experiences can store and retrieve data from the central data lake, known as One-Lake. OneLake is similar to lakehouse storage—you can store all your data in Delta-Parquet format using the ADLS service. Data engineers can write Spark code to create delta tables using the Synapse Data Engineering experience, and data analysts can write SQL code to query these delta tables using the Synapse Data Warehouse experience.

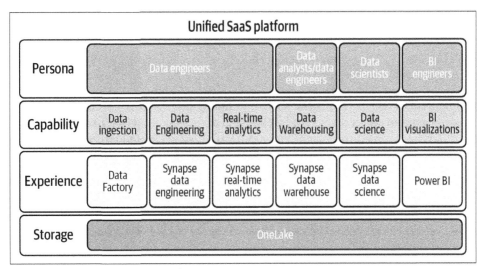

Figure 9-9. Microsoft Fabric architecture

Key features and benefits of the Fabric platform are:

- It is easy to use. As a SaaS solution, it abstracts the complexity of infrastructure and lets developers focus on writing code to solve business problems.
- It enables you to unify all your workloads in a single place, without moving outside the Fabric platform.
- As it offers a single storage based on Delta-Parquet, you get all the benefits of lakehouse architecture.
- You can create individual or department-specific workspaces. Workspaces are like containers that you can use to collaborate with others and govern access based on user roles.
- It offers a feature known as shortcuts. These shortcuts can reference data stored in other locations, such as other workspaces or external sources like S3.

Fabric stores all data in OneLake so that all data personas can access it based on their skills and preferences of compute engines. Fabric can be a good alternative to creating a custom lakehouse by self-provisioning cloud resources for organizations that prefer a simple, SaaS-based platform.

Some key differentiators (at the time of writing) between Databricks, Snowflake, and Fabric are:

- Fabric is a SaaS offering based on the Azure cloud platform. You cannot run it on other cloud platforms, and it only works with Delta Lake.

- Snowflake is cloud-agnostic but only supports Iceberg as native tables for implementing an open lakehouse.

- Databricks is also cloud-agnostic and offers an excellent Spark runtime but only supports Delta-Parquet formats.

While Databricks and Snowflake have been in this space for the last few years, Fabric is a new entrant. With the rise of lakehouse architecture, there are also other specialized lakehouse platforms like Dremio (*https://www.dremio.com*) and Onehouse (*https://www.onehouse.ai*) that you can consider to simplify your implementation.

As mentioned in earlier chapters, choosing between one of these managed platforms depends on your use cases, preferred and approved technology stack, overall ecosystem, and needed open table format features. Considering the ever-changing technology landscape that adds to data infrastructure complexity, I predict data practitioners and organizations will be more inclined to implement lakehouses using managed platforms in the future.

Managed Lakehouse for Private Cloud Platform

So far, we have primarily focused on building a lakehouse using public cloud platforms like AWS, Azure, and GCP. The object storage service these CSPs offer is one of the fundamental building blocks of lakehouse architecture. However, some organizations might have constraints or internal compliances that restrict them from moving to a public cloud. In such cases, they would need to look for solutions to implement a lakehouse within their private cloud setup. This is where they can consider a platform like MinIO.

MinIO (*https://min.io*) is a unified storage solution for implementing a data lake or a lakehouse architecture. It is an object store (similar to S3) that can run on any public cloud or on-premises infrastructure. It is open source and can be considered an alternative to S3.

Key features of MinIO are:

- It offers high performance for reading and writing operations in its object store.
- It has all the key features of cloud object stores, like object locking, versioning, tiering, encryption, lifecycle management, and replication.
- It supports all major Kubernetes distributions on public and private clouds.
- It supports public and private clouds as well as edge devices.

Storage tiering means using different tiers for storing your data. There are generally hot and cold tiers provided by the cloud object storage services. You can readily access the data stored in a hot tier, but if you want to access data from a cold tier there is generally a wait time of a few minutes to hours. The key benefit of tiering is its cost efficiency—you pay less for cold tiers compared to hot tiers. You can keep your archival data in cold tiers like S3 Glacier Deep Archive to reduce storage costs.

Figure 9-10 shows a simple lakehouse architecture using MinIO.

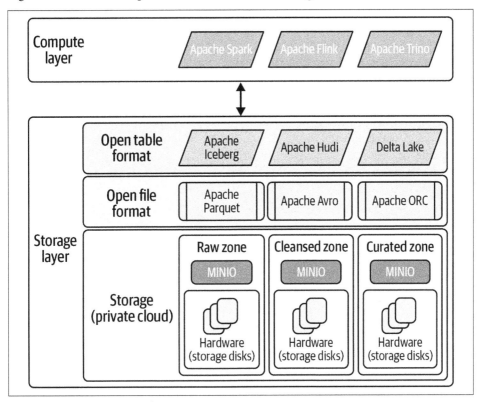

Figure 9-10. Lakehouse architecture using MinIO

Key benefits of implementing a lakehouse using MinIO are as follows:

- It supports all three open table formats—Iceberg, Hudi, and Delta Lake—for implementing a lakehouse architecture.
- It supports all major S3-compatible query engines, including open source (Spark, Presto/Trino, Flink), cloud native (Amazon Redshift, Google BigQuery), and third-party (Snowflake, Dremio).

- It enables the implementation of a decoupled compute and storage setup, which gives you the flexibility to scale lakehouse storage independently and use any compute engine of your choice.

With MinIO, you can implement a lakehouse platform that you can easily migrate to other cloud platforms. It is also a good alternative for performing lakehouse PoCs like open table format evaluation, query engine compatibility checks, and performance benchmarking without spending much on cloud services.

AI in a Lakehouse

Nearly every modern, data-driven organization today wants to leverage AI to improve their decision making. Nearly every product vendor wants to integrate AI into their products to enable users to leverage data effectively. And nearly every data practitioner wants to learn about AI and understand how it can impact their role. AI is everywhere.

As the capabilities of generative AI and large language models (LLMs) mature, these technologies will empower your lakehouse platform users to quickly and easily discover data, ask questions, and get answers. These AI capabilities will make your lakehouse platform ready for the future.

 Leveraging AI features in the lakehouse differs from supporting AI use cases. In previous chapters, we discussed how a lakehouse can support your data and AI use cases. This section discusses how to leverage various AI features to make your lakehouse platform most efficient for its users.

Seemingly every data persona can benefit from AI features within a lakehouse:

- Technical users can benefit from AI assistants because they can help generate boilerplate code, Spark notebooks, and SQL queries based on user prompts.
- Non-technical users can ask questions (in natural language) and get answers quickly.
- Analysts can benefit from the predictive query optimizations supported by AI.
- AI can help to identify and anonymize sensitive data present within the data platform.
- Business leaders can easily discover data across various assets and also learn how to ask different types of questions to gain more insights.

If you are building a lakehouse platform, consider leveraging the following AI features (either by using out-of-the-box product features or building custom capabilities) to make it future-ready:

AI assistants
Most modern products now offer an AI assistant with intelligent capabilities that can be leveraged for data discovery and data analysis. Assistants can take inputs from users in plain English and provide results by scanning the entire ecosystem.

Data quality within catalogs
Integration between data observability and cataloging tools can enable users to identify any data quality issues from the catalog itself. AI-based catalogs can highlight possible anomalies, sensitivity, and trends while the user is browsing the data during data discovery.

Metadata-based queries
You should be able to auto-generate queries based on the metadata of tables stored in catalogs. AI can help to suggest domain- and industry-specific queries by scanning the underlying metadata attributes for data analysis. For example, for an ed-tech customer, based on the tables related to students and admissions, you should be prompted with queries like:

- How many students enrolled for a newly launched course in the last quarter?
- Which courses have a 100% admission rate?

Natural language processing (NLP) queries
This is probably one of the most common AI use cases. You should offer features for your users to use natural language (English) to ask queries. Your platform should be capable of converting these plain queries into context-aware SQL queries and displaying the results as well as the actual queries that users can further tweak as required. In the future, as deep learning capabilities mature, you should be able to use native language to ask questions.

Sensitive data identification
Your platform should be able to identify sensitive data based on the attribute names and the domain. Employ AI/ML techniques that can analyze the metadata, models, feature tables, and internal documents to identify attributes that can hold sensitive data.

Automated documentation
Leverage AI to generate automated documents for your code, metadata, ML models, and any other assets wherever it makes sense. There are various efforts in this direction by different product vendors. For example, Databricks Unity Catalog has the ability to suggest AI-generated comments (powered by LLMs) for describing tables or columns.

As part of your lakehouse platform, be sure to offer AI capabilities that can help users more efficiently perform their day-to-day activities. While lakehouses can bring simplicity to the data architecture, proper use of AI can certainly make the lives of all data personas much easier.

Key Takeaways

There will be endless possibilities for implementing a lakehouse in the future. New formats, innovative approaches, and intelligent products can simplify the lakehouse implementation and help its users do their jobs efficiently. Table 9-1 summarizes the various topics discussed in this chapter.

Table 9-1. Summary of future options and alternatives for lakehouse implementations

Future options and alternatives	Quick summary
New architectural patterns and approaches	You can combine lakehouse architecture with different design approaches like data mesh, HTAP, or Zero ETL. You can use various tools, products, or platforms to implement these patterns and support your use cases. As technologies advance and architectural patterns mature, we will see a lot of innovative implementations of lakehouses in future.
New formats and interoperability	New file and table formats will be created in the future. Puffin and Paimon are just two examples. You should look for interoperability features to ensure your platform can support accessing data from any of the formats and help implement a true open lakehouse. Explore UniForm and Apache XTable for your lakehouse implementations.
Managed lakehouse platforms	Managed lakehouse platforms might get more adoption in the future. The modern data world needs simple solutions and managed lakehouse platforms like Databricks, Snowflake, and Microsoft Fabric address this need. For private clouds and on-premises implementations, you can explore solutions like MinIO.
AI in lakehouse	In the modern data world, AI is everywhere. Lakehouse is no exception. Employ various AI features to make your platform capable of performing tasks quickly and to enable users to easily discover data, ask questions, and find answers.

Book Conclusion

Lakehouse is not the first architectural pattern and it certainly will not be the last one. There will always be a need for new architectures and approaches for two major reasons:

1. Traditional approaches might not work in the future data world as data volume, variety, and velocity increase; the number of data producers rises; and AI goes mainstream.

2. There will be major advancements in technology, increases in organizations' data maturity, reduction in the cost of IT infrastructure, and easier access to a skilled workforce.

Be ready to adopt new technologies and embrace new architectural patterns. Explore new combinations and methods for implementing data platforms. The key design principles will always revolve around performance optimizations, cost reductions, operational excellence, and implementing robust security and governance processes. However, the most important factor should be how simple, easy, and adoptable the platform is. Lakehouse ticks all these boxes.

As a data practitioner, your primary focus should be on making data available for everyone—technical or non-technical users, internal or external consumers, machines or humans. With lakehouse architecture, all of this is possible—not just with data; but AI as well. Data and AI are the pillars of modern, data-driven organizations. Remember the opening sentence of the first chapter of this book: All data practitioners, irrespective of their job profiles, perform two common and foundational activities—asking questions and finding answers. Democratizing data using an open lakehouse architecture can help them do just this!

References

- Lakehouse in Data Mesh (*https://oreil.ly/VSmXy*)
- What Is Microsoft Fabric | Microsoft Fabric, Microsoft Learn (*https://oreil.ly/PczP4*)
- Puffin spec | Apache Iceberg (*https://oreil.ly/LRrhm*)
- Puffins and Icebergs: Additional Stats for Apache Iceberg Tables | Dremio (*https://oreil.ly/5WOvo*)
- Apache Paimon: The Streaming Lakehouse (*https://oreil.ly/ZagE_*)
- Universal Format (UniForm) | Delta Lake Documentation (*https://oreil.ly/APuIZ*)
- Announcing Onetable (*https://oreil.ly/oBx4z*)
- The Definitive Guide to Lakehouse Architecture with Iceberg and MinIO (*https://oreil.ly/Nh_Eh*)
- Product experiences: Discover Microsoft Fabric (*https://oreil.ly/6Xt8d*)
- HTAP: Hybrid Transactional and Analytical Processing | Snowflake (*https://oreil.ly/_WtFF*)
- MinIO for Modern Datalakes (*https://oreil.ly/8wqbL*)
- What Is Lakehouse Federation | Azure Databricks, Microsoft Learn (*https://oreil.ly/RbVA8*)
- OneLake Shortcuts | Microsoft Fabric (*https://oreil.ly/7WcDL*)
- Pushing HTAP Databases Forward with SingleStoreDB (*https://oreil.ly/j0_f9*)

- Federated Queries (Lakehouse Federation) | Azure Databricks (*https://oreil.ly/D_3ct*)

- Add AI-Generated Comments to a Table | Databricks on AWS (*https://oreil.ly/4T2QW*)

- Streamhouse Unveiled (*https://oreil.ly/63U8H*)

- Introducing Predictive Optimization: Faster Queries, Cheaper Storage, No Sweat | Databricks Blog (*https://oreil.ly/gNukh*)

Index

A

access controls
  better access control in data warehouses, 36
  consistent, in unified data catalog, 104
  difficulty of, in combined architecture for data platforms, 46
  fine-grained, using AWS Glue Data Catalog, 107
  fine-grained, using Iceberg tables in BigLake, 111
  limited, in data lakes, 40
  for metadata, 98
access management, 157-158
  coarse-grained versus fine-grained, 157
  three Rs—restrict, review, and revoke, 157
accounts (cloud), cross-account access, 118
accuracy (of data), 151
ACID properties
  compliance with, 35
  Hudi support for, 80
  Iceberg support for, 77
  in lakehouse architecture, 14
  no support in data lakes, 40
  support by Linux Foundation's Delta Lake, 83
  support by table formats in lakehouse storage, 84
  support for in data warehouses, 34
active-active approach to DR strategy design, 218
active-passive approach to DR strategy design, 218
ad hoc/interactive analysis, 11
ADF (Azure Data Factory), 128, 178, 179

ADLS (Azure Data Lake Storage), 7, 17, 43, 108
  ADLS Gen 2, 7
  Geo-zone-redundant storage (GZRS) for replicating data to secondary regions, 218
  use of Synapse serverless SQL pools with, 129
administration and management, comparisons for different architectures, 52-53
adoption
  benefits of lakehouse architecture and, 27
  components playing significant role in, 11
  data architecture and platform adoption, 3
  of data lakes due to support for all data formats, 39
  of table formats in lakehouse storage, 86
aggregation of data, 9
agility, expectation for modern data platforms, 48
Ahana, 125, 133
AI (artificial intelligence), 245
  AI in a lakehouse, 242-244
  compliance and regulations for AI assets, 150
  data platform support for AI workloads, 11
  lineage across AI assets, 152
  support for AI use cases in lakehouse, 22
  unified governance across AI assets in lakehouse architecture, 148
AI/ML workloads
  compute engines for, 140
  implementing with lakehouse, 25
  no support in data warehouses, 37

support by combined architecture for data platforms, 45

support by data lakes, 39

Airbyte, 179

Amazon Athena, 106

about, 127

evaluating, 134

limitations of, 87

using for data exploration, 108

Amazon DataZone, 107

Amazon EMR, 19, 106, 124, 126

evaluating, 134

option for data ingestion and processing in Delta Lake-based lakehouse, 137

Amazon QuickSight, 127

Amazon Redshift, 43

cloud data warehouse, use in combined architecture for data platforms, 44

Amazon Redshift Spectrum, 127

Amazon SageMaker, 127

building, supporting, and training ML models, 140

Amazon Simple Storage Service (S3), 7, 17, 43

cloud data lake, use in combined architecture for data platforms, 44

encrypting data in, 159

Amazon Web Services (see AWS)

analysis and design phase for lakehouse platform, 207-211

analyzing the existing system, 207

data modeling, 208

finalizing the tech stack, 209

analysis, ad hoc/iterative, 11

analytics engineers, 165

analytics on streaming data, 236

analytics services

AWS Glue, Amazon EMR, and Amazon Athena, evaluating, 134

AWS, for Iceberg, Hudi, and Delta Lake, 127

Azure Synapse Analytics, 128

interactive analytics with Amazon Athena, 127

offered by cloud service providers, 117

analytics workloads

columnar format best suited for data retrieval, 72

department-specific in organizations not having central data storage, 170

HTAP supporting unification with transactional workloads, 230

unification with transactional workloads, 232

analytics, real-time, Fabric support for, 238

anonymizing sensitive data, 160

Apache Avro (see Avro)

Apache Flink (see Flink)

Apache Hive (see Hive)

Apache Hudi (see Hudi)

Apache Iceberg (see Iceberg)

Apache ORC (see ORC)

Apache Paimon, 236

Apache Parquet (see Parquet)

Apache Spark services, managed, 19 (see also Spark)

Apache XTable (see XTable)

APIs, 11

architecture blueprint for lakehouse platform, 176

architecture, choosing for data platform, 171-173

artificial intelligence (see AI; AI/ML workloads)

Athena (see Amazon Athena)

Athena Spark notebooks, 127

Athena SQL, 135

write support need in, considering Iceberg for, 87

atomicity (ACID), 35

atomicity, consistency, isolation, durability (see ACID properties)

attributes, 96

audit, 216

classifying, 100

auditing, 147, 156, 216

end-to-end auditing of data in lakehouse, 156

availability, cloud object storage, 63

Avro, 18, 64, 68, 92

comparison to Parquet and ORC, 69-72

file layout, 68

key features compared to TXT, CSV, and JSON, 69

AWS (Amazon Web Services)

Amazon QuickSight, creating interactive reports and dashboards in, 139

Aurora Zero-ETL integration with Redshift, 232

excellent performance for BI workloads
with lakehouse, 20
lackluster performance of in data lakes, 40
lakehouse architecture support for, 16
preferred compute engine for BI engineers,
137
BI engineers, 164
BI workloads
best-in-class performance for by data warehouses, 34
compute engines for, 139
enhanced performance with lakehouse
architecture, 118
executing in Databricks, 132
Fabric support for, 238
on Hadoop in data lakes, 39
implementing using a lakehouse, 25
siloed, challenges of, 170
support by combined architecture for data
platforms, 45
BigLake (GCP), 111, 130
BigQuery, 111
about, 130
bit packing, 66
bottom-up approach to data warehouse creation, 36
bronze zone (see raw zone)
brownfield and greenfield implementations,
204
business analysts, 163
Business Continuity Plan (BCP), 217
business metadata, 96
business outcomes
comparisons of data warehouses, data lakes,
and lakehouse architecture, 54-55
business roles (governance committee members), 161
business sponsors, 161
business validations (of data), 8
business-as-usual (BAU) processes, 217
bzip2, 64

C

California Consumer Privacy Act (CCPA), 150
capabilities and limitations
comparisons of data warehouses, data lakes,
and lakehouse architecture, 49-50
cataloging tools, 73
catalogs (see data catalogs)

change data capture (CDC), 179
tools offering CDC processing, 188
classification of data, 100, 110, 157
clean data (in data warehouses), 33
clean room, 155
cleansed zone, 182
cloning support in Delta Lake, 84
cloud
advantages for combined architecture for
data platforms, 45
cloud data warehouses and cloud data lakes,
43
benefits of, 43
combining, 44
limitations of, 43
cloud native ETL tools, 178
cloud native lakehouse implementation,
222-223
cloud native services versus managed open
source for lakehouse implementation,
138
cloud native tools for data ingestion, 179
compliance of platforms and services with
regulations, 150
data warehouses storing all versions of data,
27
data warehouses, leveraging along with
lakehouse platform, 208
deciding which cloud platform to choose,
209
key benefits of using for modern data platforms, 41
managed platforms for public and private
clouds, 237-242
managed services based on Spark or Presto/
Trino supporting open table formats,
125
object storage (see cloud object storage)
services used for implementing ML workloads, 195
storage buckets/containers and underlying
directories in lakehouse storage, 181
storage offerings supporting lakehouse
architecture, 17
technologies in data lakes, 39
using cloud native or managed services
wherever possible, 175
cloud object storage, 20, 62-63
accessing directly in lakehouse, 28

backup services provided by, 218
benefits of using to implement a lakehouse, 18
cloud, proprietary storage formats on, 13
compute performance of queries on data stored in, 119
general storage, services for, 7
storage characteristics, 62
use in lakehouse, 15
cloud service providers (CSPs)
consulting documentation for limitations of table formats, 87
design principles for architecting solutions using their services, 173
managed and serverless offerings for big data workloads, 42
metadata management services across, 114
offerings for modern data platforms, 42
spot instances/machines using spare compute capacity provided by CSPs, 42
cloud-first approach, data platforms built on, 41
Cloudera, 39, 64
clustering, 61, 119
support by table formats in lakehouse storage, 85
code
converting existing code to lakehouse-compatible code, 215
reverse engineering, 214
Collibra, 114
column-level statistics, 61
columnar storage
in ORC file format, 67
statistics stored in file footer, 68
in Parquet files, 66
row storage versus, 60
combined approach to implementing modern data platforms, 44
benefits of, 45
combined architecture, data lake and data warehouse, 169, 172
comparison to other modern data platforms
administration and management, 53
business outcomes, 54
capabilities and limitations, 50
implementation activities, 51
limitations of, 45
commercial engines, 19

commercial product support for table formats in lakehouse storage, 90
commit timeline (Hudi), 80
commodity hardware in data lakes, 39
common services, 11, 191-196, 201
best practices for implementing, 195
data governance and security, 11
data operations, 12
DataOps, 193
metadata management, 11
MLOps, 195
community support, table formats in lakehouse storage, 87-88
comparisons
data warehouse, data lake, and lakehouse architectures, 48-55
administration and management, 52
business outcomes, 54
capabilities and limitations, 49
implementation activities, 51
summary of, 56
file formats, 69-72
summary of, 92
Git repositories for Iceberg, Hudi, and Delta Lake table formats, 87-88
key differentiators between Databricks, Snowflake, and Fabric, 239
managed open source versus cloud native versus third-party products for lakehouse implementation, 138
table formats, Iceberg, Hudi, and Delta Lake, 91-93
completeness (of data), 151
compliance and regulations, 150
different compliances, 150
compression
comparison of Parquet, ORC, and Avro file formats, 70
Parquet file format, 66
compression ratios (good) in file formats, 64
compute and storage, tightly coupled in data warehouses, 36
compute engines
choosing for lakehouse platform, design considerations, 133-140
data consumption workloads, 139-140
ecosystem support, 136
evaluating compute options in AWS, 134

batch ingestion, 6
design considerations, 178
identifying incremental data, 179
implementation best practices in lakehouse
        platform, 180
ingestion frequency, 178
near real-time, 6
sensitive data, 179
source system types and, 178
technology choices for implementing, 179
data integration, 9, 187
Data Lake
    Linux Foundation, 93
data lakehouses, 13
    (see also lakehouse architecture)
data lakes, 13, 37-41, 172
    ACID compliance and, 35
    architecture of, 38
    benefits and challenges of, 39
    characteristics of, 39
    comparison to data warehouses and lake-
        house architecture, 48-55
    converting data to open table formats when
        migrating to lakehouse, 186
    data swamps and, 24
    features in lakehouse architecture, 14
    limitations and challenges of, 40
data layer
    in Hudi, 79
    in Iceberg, 75
        file formats supported, 77
    in Linux Foundation's Delta Lake, 83
data lineage, 101, 152
    challenges in siloed metadata, 102
    end-to-end, with unified data catalog, 104
    understanding data flow, 153
    using in identifying unused objects, 154
    using in tracking sensitive data, 154
    using to perform impact analysis, 153
data marts, 36, 185
data mesh, 172
    decentralized data management in, 228
    key benefits provided by lakehouse to, 229
    main pillars of, 229
data migration (see historical data migration)
data modeling, 208
    challenges and solutions, 208
data modeling in lakehouse, 184-185
    data vault modeling, 184

dimensional modeling, 184
entity relationship (ER) modeling, 184
data movement through intranet/VPN/secure
    channels, 160
data observability, 12, 194
data operations, 12
data orchestration, 194, 196
data owners, 155, 162
    versus data stewards, 155
data platforms
    architecture options for implementing, 172
    common requirements for, 169
    core components of, 176
    studying existing system, 169
data processing, 8, 185-189, 200
    activities involved in, 185
    data curation and serving, 10
    data integration, 187
    data transformations and enrichment, 188
    data validation and cleansing, 8
    implementation best practices, 188
    open table format conversion, 186
    schema and data quality validations, 187
data products, 10
data protection laws and regulations, 118
data quality, 151, 215
    in combined architecture, 51
    keeping at core of data processes, best prac-
        tices for, 152
    measuring, 151
    reduced quality in data lakes, 40
    tools offering out-of-the-box features per-
        forming quality checks, 188
    using custom frameworks versus third-
        party tools, 215
    validations of, 85, 187
data reconciliation and testing, 213
    approaches to reconcile lakehouse data, 214
data scans
    comparison of Parquet, ORC, and Avro file
        formats, 71
    reducing and retrieving results quickly, 61
    retrieval time and amount of data scanned,
        61
data science
    data lakes' support for use cases, 39
    Fabric support for, 238
    lakehouse architecture support for, 16
    open table formats and, 140

data scientists, 1, 164
  preferred compute engines, 137
data security, 11, 145
  access management, 157-158
  benefits of, 147
  benefits of unified governance and security
    processes in lakehouse, 165
  critical points to remember, 166
  data protection, 158-160
    best practices for implementing, 159
    data at rest, 159
    data in transit, 159
    lakehouse data protection technologies,
      158
  defined, 146
  guiding principles to implement processes
    well-aligned with, 175
  handling sensitive data, 160-161
  Immuta and Privacera for fine-grained
    access controls, 158
  implementing for lakehouse platform, 215
  processing included in, 147
  sharing data, 155
  unified governance and security in lake-
    house architecture, 148
data sharing in lakehouses, 23, 154
  benefits of well-governed processes, 154
  sharing features of table formats, 91
data skipping or row skipping, 61, 236
data sovereignty, 118
data stewards, 155, 162
  versus data owners, 155
data storage (see storage)
data strategy, aligning with, 4
data swamps
  avoiding with lakehouse architecture, 24
  risk of data lakes becoming, 41
data transformations, 8
  about, 9
  data aggregation, 9
  data enhancement, 9
  data integration, 9
  ETL and ELT, 10
  key points to remember when implement-
    ing, 188
  not possible on partition columns in table
    formats earlier than Iceberg, 77
  SQL-based ELT operations for, 25
data types

changing between data lakes and warehouses, eliminating with lakehouse, 22
different, support in lakehouse architecture,
  21
data validation, 8
  in lakehouse architecture, 24
  missing in data lakes, 40
Data Vault 2.0, 172
data vault modeling, 184
data warehouses, 7, 13, 32-37, 172
  architecture of, 33
  benefits and advantages of, 34
  characteristics of platform built on, 33
  cloud, leveraging along with lakehouse plat-
    form, 208
  cloud, processing different types of data, 13
  comparison to data lakes and lakehouse
    architecture, 48-55
  creating, bottom-up and top-down
    approaches to, 36
  features in lakehouse architecture, 14
  features of, how lakehouse obtains them, 15
  implementing data platform using, steps in
    process, 33
  limitations and challenges of, 36
  warehouse-like performance on data lake,
    20
database normalization, 184
databases, 7
  lake, Synapse Spark pools managing, 108
  limitations for data storage, 32
  Synapse SQL databases, management of,
    108
Databricks, 16, 105
  benefits of, 139
  blueprint for Databricks lakehouse imple-
    mentation, 223
  customer question about using Databricks
    versus Snowflake, 210
  Delta Lake, 19
  Delta Live Tables (DLT) jobs, 188
  features for lakehouse implementation, 224
  implementation of data catalogs, key points
    in, 115
  importing metadata from, support by
    Microsoft Purview, 110
  key differentiators between Databricks,
    Snowflake, and Fabric, 239
  managed offering of MLflow, 195

DLT (Delta Live Tables), 132
downstream applications
    data integration for consumption by, 9
    data products shared with, 10
    interactions with data platform, 11
Dremio, 16, 75, 133, 210
    benefits of, 139
    Reflections feature to enhance BI perfor-
        mance, 120
duplication of data
    in combined architecture for data platforms,
        46
durability
    ACID property, 35
    cloud object storage, 62

E

ecosystem support
    for compute engines, 136
    for table formats in lakehouse storage, 87
ELT (extract, load, and transform), 10
    lakehouse providing unified platform for
        ETL/ELT workloads, 25
EMR (see Amazon EMR)
encoding techniques
    for data on open file formats handling big
        data, 66
encryption
    encrypting data at rest (in cloud storage),
        159
    encrypting data in transit, 159
encryption keys access logs, 156
enhancement of data, 9
enriched or silver zone (see cleansed zone)
enrichment of data (see data enrichment)
enterprise cataloging tools, 114
entity relationship (ER) modeling, 35, 184
estimation phase for lakehouse platform, 205
    important points to consider, 205, 206
ETL (extract, transform, and load), 10, 16
    cloud native ETL tools, 178
    ETL process in data warehouses, 33
    ETL/ELT workloads, lakehouse providing
        unified platform for, 25
    support by combined architecture for data
        platforms, 45
    using Spark in lakehouse for ETL work-
        loads, 124
    Zero ETL, 231

EU (European Union), General Data Protection
    Regulation (GDPR), 150
external source systems, 5

F

Fabric (Microsoft), 129, 238
    key differentiators between Databricks,
        Snowflake, and Fabric, 239
    key features and benefits of, 239
    shortcuts aiding access to S3 data, 232
features supported by table formats in lake-
    house storage, 89
Federal Risk and Authorization Management
    Program (FedRAMP), 150
federated catalogs, 113
file compaction, 119
file formats
    comparisons between, 92
    key points about, 93
    open formats used in cloud storage, 18
    open formats used in lakehouse storage, 15
    in storage layer of lakehouse, 63-72
        ORC, 67
        purpose-built formats to handle big data,
            64
        similarities, differences, and use cases,
            69-72
    support by Hive, 74
    support by Iceberg, 75, 78
    support by table formats in lakehouse stor-
        age, 85
    supported file formats and selection of table
        format, 88
    upcoming, 235
file metadata, 96
file pruning, 61
Fivetran, 179
flexibility
    expectations for in modern data platforms,
        47
Flink, 120
    addressing low-latency streaming use cases,
        236
    features as data engineering tool, 124
    offered by Amazon EMR, 126
    running with Dataproc in GCP, 130
freshness (of data), 151
future options and alternatives for lakehouse
    implementations, 227-244

file formats supported, table format selection and, 88
Health Insurance Portability and Accountability Act (HIPAA), 150
historical data in data warehouses, 34
historical data migration, 211-213
  data reconciliation post-migration to lakehouse, 213
  migration based on existing architecture, 213
  migration based on existing infrastructure, 212
Hive, 16, 72-75
  limitation of, 40
  limitations as lakehouse table format, 74
  no ability to perform updates in data lakes, 40
  ORC file format in, 68
  table directory structure, 73
  use with HDFS in data lakes to support BI, 39
Hive catalog (HCatalog), 98, 105
Hive Metastore (HMS), 73, 98
  Glue Data Catalog as alternative to, 107
  using to implement data catalog, 105
HiveServer2 (HS2), 72
HMS (see Hive metastore)
hoodie.properties file (Hudi), 79
Hortonworks, 39, 64
Hortonworks Data Platform (HDP), 68
  file formats supported, table format selection and, 88
HTAP (hybrid transactional/analytical processing), 13, 172, 229-231
  data platform implementing, 229
  how it affects lakehouse implementations, 230
  key benefits of HTAP approach, 230
Hudi, 18, 93
  checking compatibility with Presto and Trino, 125
  comparison with other table formats for popularity on Git repositories, 87
  considering for AWS-based implementations, 87
  features that help implement lakehouse platforms, 80
  Paimon as alternative to, 236
  pre-commit Validators, 152

table layout, 78
using with AWS services to implement data catalog, 106
hybrid transactional/analytical processing (see HTAP)

I

IaaS, PaaS, and SaaS in cloud-first approach, 41
IBM Netezza, 34
Iceberg, 18, 75-78, 92
  checking compatibility with Presto and Trino, 125
  comparison with other table formats for popularity on Git repositories, 87
  considering if write support needed in Athena SQL, 87
  creating native Iceberg tables in Snowflake, 132
  Delta Lake-to-Iceberg metadata conversion process, 234
  features and benefits, 77
  Puffin format, 236
  support by BigQuery, 130
  table layout, 77
  use in GCP BigLake, 111
  using with Athena for lakehouse in AWS ecosystem, 127
Iceberg-Parquet format, data skipping in, 236
Immuta, 158
immutable storage in data lakes, 39
implementation activities
  comparisons of data warehouses, data lakes, and lakehouse architecture, 51-52
implementation and test phase for lakehouse platform, 211-216
  data quality and handling sensitive data, 215
  data reconciliation and testing post-migration to lakehouse, 213
  historical data migration, 211-213
    migration based on existing architecture, 213
    migration based on existing infrastructure, 212
  reverse engineering, 214
in-memory databases, 8
incremental data processing, support by table formats in lakehouse storage, 85
incremental data, identifying, 179
incremental queries, 80

M

maintenance, challenges in siloed metadata, 102

managed services from CSPs for modern data platforms, 42

Management Studio, 108

manifest lists (Iceberg), 77

MapR, 39

MapReduce, query engine based on in data lakes, 40

master data management (MDM), 187

Merge On Read (MOR) tables, 81

merge support by Linux Foundation's Delta Lake, 83

metadata, 95-97
  adding tags to for data classification, 100
  automated creation of with Glue crawlers, 107
  business, 96
  converting between open table formats using XTable, 234
  Hive Metastore (HMS) repository, 73
  lakehouse data governance polices around, guidance provided for, 149
  metadata layer in Hudi, 79
  metadata layer in Iceberg, 75
    elements of, 77
  metadata layer in Linux Foundation's Delta Lake, 82
  mismatches in combined architecture for data platforms, 46
  open table format metadata layers, 233
  technical, 96

metadata management, 11, 97, 146, 149
  best practices, 149
  central, provided by unified governance, 148
  in GCP, creating data catalog for, 110
  metastores and data catalogs, 98
  services across providers, 114
  siloed, challenges of, 102
  using Databricks Unity Catalog, 113
  using Hive metastore (HMS), 105
  using Synapse Analytics, 108

metastores
  provided by BigLake, 111
  siloed, 102
  working with data catalogs, 98-99

Microsoft Fabric (see Fabric)

Microsoft Purview, 109
  catalog capabilities, 110

Microsoft services, using to implement a data catalog

migration of historical data, 211-213

MinIO, 240
  benefits of, 241
  key features and benefits of, 240
  lakehouse architecture using, 241

ML (machine learning)
  Amazon SageMaker implementing ML models for use on lakehouse platform, 127
  Azure Machine Learning service, 129
  data platform support for ML workloads, 11
  Databricks ML, 140
  implementing workloads with lakehouse, 25
  lakehouse architecture support for, 16
  measuring quality of models, 152
  models complying with regulations, 150, 151
  reading data directly from lakehouse, 22
  support for unstructured data and ML use cases in lakehouse, 22

ML engineers, 164

MLflow, 195

MLflow-Delta Lake integrations, 140

MLOps, 195
  best practices for implementing, 195

modeling data, 35

modern data platforms, 41-48
  benefits of using cloud for, 41
  built using cloud technologies, comparisons of, 48
  expectations of, 46
  implementations of, 31
  standalone approach to implementation, 43

monitoring, 156

multi-cloud strategy, 112, 210

N

near real-time data ingestion, 6, 178

near real-time source systems, 6

non-volatile data (in data warehouses), 34

normalization of data, 184

NoSQL databases, storing all versions of data, 27

O

object storage, 7
  cloud, 45
  MinIO, 240
observability (see data observability)
OLAP (online analytical processing), 7, 13, 229
  moving data from OLTP platform to, using Zero ETL, 231
OLTP (online transaction processing), 8, 13, 229
  moving data to OLAP platforms using Zero ETL, 231
Onehouse, 16, 210
OneLake, 238
open architecture (lakehouse), 21
open file formats, 15, 18
  (see also file formats)
  binary conversion or encoding of data in, 66
open source
  compute engine options, 141
  managed open source versus cloud native offerings for lakehouse implementation, 138
open source catalogs, 114
open source compute engines, 123
  tools for data consumption, 124
    Presto and Trino, 124
  tools for data engineering, 123
    Flink, 124
    Spark, 123
open table formats, 15, 18
  Apache Iceberg, Apache Hudi, and Delta Lake, 75
  comparisons between, 92
  conversion of raw data into, 186
  converting metadata between using XTable, 234
  features to unify data engineering, data analysis, and data science workloads, 140
  Hive, 40
  and metadata layers, 233
  new format, Paimon, 236
  Presto/Trino support for, 125
  Spark support for, 124
  support by Azure HDInsight, 128
  support by compute engines for latest version, 135
  support by Dataproc 1.5.x Spark clusters, 130

support for, considering in selecting lakehouse compute engine, 135
  Synapse analytics support for, 129
  techniques to address BI performance challenges, 119
  use with Athena for compute, 127
  using for time travel through data, 26
open technologies
  expectations for use in modern data platforms, 47
open-source engines, 19
optimize and Z-order features in Delta Lake, 83
Optimized Row Columnar (see ORC)
Oracle Exadata, 34
ORC, 18, 64, 92
  benefits of use with big data, 67
  file layout, 67
  indexes, levels of, 68
  key features compared to TXT, CSV, and JSON, 68
orchestration, 194
orchestration tools, 196
organization's vision and data strategy, 170
ownership of data, 155

P

PaaS (platform as a service), 41
Paimon, 236
Parquet, 18, 64, 92
  benefits for big data workloads, 65
  comparison to ORC and Avro, 69-72
  file layout, 66
  key features compared to TXT, CSV, and JSON, 66
partitioning, 119
  hidden partitioning in Iceberg, 77
  support by table formats in lakehouse storage, 85
partitions, 61
  evolution of, in Iceberg, 78
  on tables in Hive, 74
Payment Card Industry Data Security Standard (PCI DSS), 150
performance
  benchmarking, for table formats in lakehouse storage, 90
  enhanced BI performance with lakehouse architecture, 118

scalability
    cloud object storage, 63
    cloud storage, 17
    of a data lake, 13
    expectations for in modern data platforms,
        47
    guiding principles enabling quick scalabil-
        ity, 174
    in lakehouses, 24
    on-demand, in the cloud, 41, 45
scaling
    independent compute and storage scaling,
        118
    separate storage and compute scaling in
        lakehouse, 20
SCD (Slowly Changing Dimensions), 83
    SCD Type 2 merges, 188
schema evolution
    Iceberg support for, 77
    support by table formats in lakehouse stor-
        age, 84
schema on read (data lakes), 39
schemas
    analyzing impact of source schema changes,
        153
    enforcement and evolution in lakehouse, 24
    example of technical metadata, 96
    in Hive tables, storage in HMS, 73
    of records in Parquet file format, 66
    schema enforcement and evolution, support
        by Linux Foundation's Delta Lake, 83
    validation of, 8, 187
search
    unified, with unified data catalog, 104
    using data catalogs, 100
secondary site for DR implementation, 217
security, 3
    (see also data security)
    cloud object storage, 63
semantic zone, 183
semi-structured data, 6
    in data lakes, 38
sensitive data, 160-161
    anonymizing, 160
    handling in lakehouse platform, 215
    identifying, 160
    ingestion of, handling, 179
    masking for use for ML model training, 151
    tracking using data lineage, 154

serverless
    services offered by CSPs, 42
services, common (see common services)
serving data, 10
sharing data in lakehouses, 23, 154
    sharing features of table formats, 91
simplified architecture (lakehouse), 21
single source of truth (in data warehouses), 36
SingleStore platform, 230
skipping unwanted data for queries, 61
Slowly Changing Dimensions (SCD), 83, 188
Snappy, 64
Snapshot, 77
Snapshot queries, 80
Snowflake, 16, 75
    about, 132
    benefits of, 139
    customer question about using Databricks
        versus Snowflake, 210
    external tables feature, 133
    key differentiators between Databricks,
        Snowflake, and Fabric, 239
    with native Iceberg tables, 132
    Unistore feature with HTAP capabilities,
        230
    use of various levels of caching to improve
        BI query performance, 120
Soda, 216
source systems, 5
    batch, near real-time, and streaming sys-
        tems, 5
    integrating data from different source sys-
        tems, 187
    internal and external, 5
    structured, semi-structured, and unstruc-
        tured data, 6
    types of, 178
Spark, 120
    about, 123
    data catalog API to access metadata in
        HMS, 105
    Databricks and, 131
    Delta Lake's deep integration with, 84
    HDInsight Spark framework, 128
    latest Azure Synapse Runtime for Spark not
        supporting latest Delta Lake version, 136
    managed services, Delta Lake and, 19
    offered by Amazon EMR, 126
    Parquet file format used with, 66

running with Dataproc in GCP, 130
running workloads on Databricks Photon engine, 132
Spark-based notebook service for data engineers, 138
Synapse Spark pools, 108
use for AI/ML workloads, 140
use with Amazon Athena, 127
use with Azure Spark Analytics, 129
using to execute PySpark code to ingest data from source system, 121
using with BigQuery to create Iceberg BigLake table, 130
using with HDInsight to create lakehouse using Iceberg, 135
splitable file formats, 64
    Parquet, ORC, and Avro, 70
SQL
    Athena acting as single service for executing SQL code, 127
    Databricks SQL, 113
    management of Synapse SQL databases, 108
    preferred for data analysis, 124
    querying engine in data lakes, 40
    retrieving older data based on timestamp, 27
    retrieving older data based on version, 26
    SQL-based compute engines, 121
    SQL-based ELT operations for transformations, 25
    Synapse compute engine based on dedicated SQL pools, 129
    Synapse serverless SQL pools, 108, 129
SQL engines
    open source, Presto and Trino, 124
    providing SQL engine for data analysts, 138
SQL Server Management Studio (SSMS), 110
SQL Warehouse (Databricks), 132
SQL/BI on Hadoop, 118
SSL (Secure Sockets Layer), 159
stakeholders
    interviewing to learn about challenges and platform expectations, 170
standalone cloud data lakes
    comparison to other modern data platforms
        administration and management, 53
        business outcomes, 54
        capabilities and limitations, 49
        implementation activities, 51

standalone cloud data warehouses
    comparison to other modern data platforms
        administration and management, 52
        business outcomes, 54
        capabilities and limitations, 49
        implementation activities, 51
standalone implementation of modern data platforms, 43
    benefits of, 43
    limitations of, 43
star schemas, 35, 184
Starburst, 125, 133
statistics maintained by open table formats, 119
step-by-step design guide for lakehouse platform, 196-198
storage, 7, 200
    backing up primary to secondary storage, 218
    cloud storage supporting lakehouse architecture, 17
    decoupled lakehouse architecture with separate storage and compute scaling, 20, 118
    lakehouse storage, 180-185
        best practices for implementing, 185
        storage zones, 181-183
    purpose-built, 7
    single storage tier in lakehouse, benefits of, 22
    single storage tier with no dedicated warehouse in lakehouses, 20
    tight coupling with compute in data warehouses, 36
    two-tier storage in combined approach to modern data platforms, 44
        data duplication in, 46
storage layer (lakehouse), 14, 17, 59-93
    cloud storage, 17
    components, 62-86
        cloud object storage, 62-63
        file formats, 63-72
        table formats, 72-86
    key concepts, 59-61
        row versus columnar storage, 60
        storage-based performance optimization, 61
    open file formats, 18
    open table formats, 18
storage tiering, 241
storage zones (lakehouse), 8, 121, 181-183

Z

Z-order, 83, 119
Zero ETL, 231

About the Author

Gaurav Thalpati is an independent consultant with over two decades of experience building data and analytics platforms. He has worked on various data projects and played different roles, including ETL/BI developer, data engineer, data analyst, and data architect. Based in Pune, India, Gaurav is passionate about sharing his knowledge with other data practitioners and guiding them in designing and implementing scalable and cost-effective data platforms.

Colophon

The animal on the cover of *Practical Lakehouse Architecture* is a cinnamon-banded kingfisher (*Todiramphus australasia*), a tropical bird found exclusively in Indonesia and East Timor, specifically the Lesser Sundas range of islands north of Australia.

This vibrantly colored kingfisher has a blue-green back that contrasts with its sand-colored underpart and cinnamon-striped eyebrow. A wide black line runs through the bird's eye and its head is topped with a dark cap. Juveniles are duller in coloration and have a white-tipped bill.

The cinnamon-banded kingfisher is an insectivore, its diet consisting primarily of grasshoppers, crickets, beetles, and even small lizards. It will perch on a branch, waiting for prey, then swoop down to catch it in mid-air.

These kingfishers are territorial birds and live in pairs. Unlike other nest-crafting birds, they will excavate a nesting hole in a termite mound or a soft bank.

The IUCN status of the cinnamon-banded kingfisher is Near Threatened, indicating that the species is close to qualifying for a threatened category due to its decreasing population trend and habitat loss threats. Many of the animals on O'Reilly covers are endangered; all of them are important to the world.

The cover illustration is by Karen Montgomery, based on an antique line engraving from *English Cyclopedia*. The series design is by Edie Freedman, Ellie Volckhausen, and Karen Montgomery. The cover fonts are Gilroy Semibold and Guardian Sans. The text font is Adobe Minion Pro; the heading font is Adobe Myriad Condensed; and the code font is Dalton Maag's Ubuntu Mono.

O'REILLY®

Learn from experts.
Become one yourself.

Books | Live online courses
Instant answers | Virtual events
Videos | Interactive learning

Get started at oreilly.com.

Printed in the USA
CPSIA information can be obtained
at www.ICGtesting.com
JSHW051338041024
71098JS00005B/165